A Contagion of War

"War is a contagion, whether it be declared or undeclared.
It can engulf states and peoples remote from the original scene of hostilities."

FRANKLIN DELANO ROOSEVELT, OCTOBER 5, 1937

Time-Life Books, Alexandria, Virginia

This volume of The Vietnam Experience attempts to march intimately into battle, portraying what the war was like for the Americans, South Vietnamese, and other allies as well as the Vietcong and North Vietnamese who fought it. Only in passing does this volume deal with major questions of policy and decision-making or with the hundreds of thousands in uniform who served in the rear areas. Of necessity, this book presents only a sampling of the countless battles, pacification efforts, and other activities from the arrival of the first U.S. fighting forces in the spring of 1965 until the end of 1967. Many of these are first-hand accounts. There are many more of them to tell than there is paper to put them on.

Cover: Men of the 1st Squadron, 9th Cavalry, 1st Cavalry Division (Airmobile), leap from a chopper near Chu Lai during Operation Oregon in 1967.

Contents

Americans in Vietnam

"It now sounds incredibly naive, but enlisting in the marines was my alternative to joining the Peace Corps, which I couldn't have done without a college degree. Like many others, I thought I was going there to help an oppressed people in their struggle."

Marine Private First Class John Dojka

On March 8, 1965, men of the 9th Marines splashed ashore at Red Beach 2, northwest of Da Nang. Meanwhile other marine units in the region prepared for possible deployment as reinforcements. In March, men of the 2d Battalion, 3d Marines, participated in a training exercise in Thailand named Jungle Drum III. On April 4, while returning from Thailand to the Philippines aboard ships of Navy Task Group 76.6, the task group commander received orders to steam to an area eighty kilometers east of Da Nang, one day's voyage away. But the ordinary enlisted men, who lived aboard the ships and slept in berthing spaces upon bunks stacked eight high, did not learn why they had changed course.

After arriving in position on April 5, the troop-laden ships loitered off the coast for six days. The men below decks grew anxious. Rumor said it was just another exercise; rumor said it was the real thing. Constant drills, endless inspections, the bad food of the ships' messes, seasickness, and the threat of combat caused anger to mix with anxiety. When at last on April 9 officers passed the order to land the next morning, the tense marines at first felt relieved. Warned to expect a "hot" beach and ordered to prepare for combat, the men grew anxious again. American forces already held the beach, but the enlisted marines who rocked in the holds geared up to defend themselves if necessary.

Richard Ogden, then a nineteen-year-old private, remembered the 2d Battalion's last night at sea. As he wrote later, some of the men were quiet, others exuberant. As they sharpened and resharpened bayonets or stripped and reassembled rifles, they bragged about the feats they'd perform the next day. No one appeared afraid of what might happen. But for Ogden "The thought of killing someone terrified the hell out of me."

On the morning of April 10 the sea was calm as the ships of the task group anchored in Da Nang Harbor. Married to the hulls of their mother ships, utility landing craft (LCUs) loaded equipment, and personnel landing craft (LCPs) loaded troops. Then they broke away and churned toward shore. When the LCP carrying Private Ogden and other men of Hotel Company, 2/3 Marines, reached shallow water, its heavy gate slammed down on the white sand of Red Beach and the marines scrambled out. Fearful yet excited, they scanned the horizon, watching for any sign of an enemy. "I see something!" came a marine's muffled shout. Without taking his eyes from the horizon shimmering in the heat, Ogden snapped open the breech of his M79 grenade launcher, felt a round in the chamber, and snapped the breech shut. Then he squinted at the blurred shape of a man struggling toward him. The next moment a staccato thwacking, thudding sound erupted. Another, then another human shape, each burdened by equipment, swam into view. Ogden picked a target. But then an order came up the line: "Hold your fire!" The thwacking sound increased in intensity; more shapes advanced. Again the order came: "Hold your fire!"

Abruptly the source of all the thwacking and thudding, a brand-new, turbo-powered UH-1E marine helicopter, leaped into sight. Unaccustomed to the chopping sound made by the new aircraft's engine, some of the marines had mistaken it for hostile machine-gun fire. And as the indistinct shapes of men came nearer, what had looked like weapons on their shoulders

---

Nearing a hot LZ *thirty kilometers outside Da Nang in April 1965, marine Lance Corporal James C. Farley fires on VC positions with his M60 machine gun.*

and in their hands took on the appearance of television cameras and microphones. Ogden was able to make out the logos of ABC and NBC and the staring eye of CBS. A marine shouted, this time in a tone of startled disbelief: "It's the press corps!"

"A reporter with a very dark tan, clad in a Hawaiian shirt, shorts, and sandals, came over and struck a mike up to my mouth," Ogden recalled. "A cameraman went down on his knees and moved in close. 'How do you like the Vietnam War so far, son?' the reporter asked me." When Ogden recovered from his surprise, he asked the reporter where the war was. "There's fighting going on everywhere," the reporter answered, "but it's at night. The farmers till the rice fields during the day and pick up weapons at night. Nothing ever happens during the day around here." But the days weren't safe for very long.

At bayonet point

Eighteen-year-old marine Private First Class John Dojka landed with Company C, 1/9 Marines, at Da Nang in June 1965. Dojka enlisted one year before, immediately after graduation from high school. "I was afraid that if I went directly to college the war would be over before I could get there," he remembers. "It now sounds incredibly naive, but enlisting in the marines was my alternative to joining the Peace Corps, which I couldn't have done without a college degree. Like many others, I thought I was going there to help an oppressed people in their struggle."

New to the country and the people, Dojka was fascinated by the peasants' way of life. As he patrolled Da Nang area hamlets—or "villes," as the marines learned to call them—he tried to make friends. But before long he recognized that some Vietnamese did not welcome Americans and did not want American help. Once during a patrol a marine from Dojka's platoon spotted a male VC suspect. When the marine beckoned to him, the man fled into a nearby house. The marine ran after him, entered the house, and cornered the suspect behind a family altar. Then, in order to dislodge the suspect without shooting him, the marine fixed his bayonet on his rifle and probed behind the altar. The suspect lunged, grabbed the two-edged blade with both hands, and tried to wrest the weapon away, badly cutting his hands. The marine who captured the man had to call for help to subdue him. Finally, the suspect was led away for questioning, his bandaged hands tied securely behind his back.

"The suspect's courage left a deep impression on me, and I began to realize just how desperate these people were," Dojka says, "and what kind of opposition we were up against." He heard but was unable to confirm that the VC suspect was turned over to the South Vietnamese and shot to death.

"Following this incident," Dojka recalls, "my initial idealism began to slip."

During the first few months lessons in the facts of life for an effective infantryman were learned the hard way. During another patrol, Dojka's platoon halted for a rest break at a water hole. Two marines put down their weapons and sauntered into a nearby hamlet. Suddenly a Vietnamese man dressed in black pajamas stepped from a doorway and aimed a pistol. He fired several shots, hitting one marine in the stomach and the other in the head, then disappeared.

For patrol after patrol, casualties occurred that way, in ones and twos. There was never any dramatic confrontation with the VC, just a slow, steady attrition from booby traps and sniper fire. Months of tension took its toll. "I think that I went into a state of mild, self-protecting shock," Dojka said. "The primary objective was no longer to help the Vietnamese but rather to get out of the country in one piece."

Back in the United States more American soldiers readied for deployment to Vietnam. On June 16, 1965, Secretary of Defense Robert S. McNamara announced that the army would form an airmobile division at Fort Benning, Georgia. Preparations began at once. On July 1 the 1st Cavalry Division (Airmobile) was activated to carry out a new concept in warfare: heliborne infantry assault. Organized in 1921, when horses were still used, the new 1st Cavalry replaced its flesh and blood mounts with machines, and the helicopter became the horse of the Vietnam War. By combining the rapid mobility provided by helicopters with the firepower and maneuverability of an infantry division, the 1st Cavalry could deliver troops and artillery anywhere a helicopter could land or hover.

The day the 1st Cav was formally activated, the secretary of defense ordered it to achieve a condition of readiness by July 28. It was a large task. Many units faced reorganization; new personnel had to be trained. Night and day preparations went forward, including classes in jungle warfare, rappelling from helicopters, aerial weapons firing, sniping, and helicopter door gunnery.

Staff Sergeant Manuel "Joe" Encarnacao, a Utica, New York, native and a veteran of the Korean War, conducted classes in shooting "suppressive fire" from the open doors of assault helicopters. Encarnacao thought of his instruction as "life insurance for troops going into a fight in helicopters." Corporal Larry Boots, a former adviser who saw fighting in Vietnam in 1964, said "That isn't noise those boys are making. Not to me. It's music." Other preparations were more ordinary. The men were ordered to dye towels, handkerchiefs, and underclothes army green. For weeks after the division left, the Laundro-

mats of the Fort Benning area lent a greenish tint to wash loads.

On the evening of July 28 President Johnson announced that he was ordering the 1st Cav to Vietnam. After feverish weeks of preparations, the men were ready. Unit commanders granted them a few days leave before departure in August, a few days to spend with their families and settle their affairs. Lieutenant Colonel Kenneth D. Mertel, commander of the "jumping Mustangs," the 1st Battalion of the 8th Cavalry Regiment, spent a weekend flying by commercial jet to Philadelphia, Seattle, and Los Angeles saying good-bye to family members. Sergeant Encarnacao said good-bye to his wife

Patricia and their five children, all under age ten. Patricia Encarnacao would remain near the post, among the other military wives and children, while her husband went to his second war.

A murmur of dissent

The men of the 1st Cav were ready to go to Vietnam—but not all were willing. When Private Winstel R. Belton received his orders, he refused to obey them. Instead he staged a hunger strike to protest American involvement in Vietnam. A former

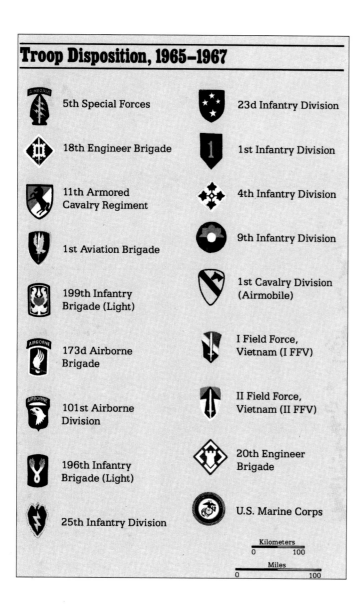

Troop Disposition, 1965–1967

5th Special Forces

18th Engineer Brigade

11th Armored Cavalry Regiment

1st Aviation Brigade

199th Infantry Brigade (Light)

173d Airborne Brigade

101st Airborne Division

196th Infantry Brigade (Light)

25th Infantry Division

23d Infantry Division

1st Infantry Division

4th Infantry Division

9th Infantry Division

1st Cavalry Division (Airmobile)

I Field Force, Vietnam (I FFV)

II Field Force, Vietnam (II FFV)

20th Engineer Brigade

U.S. Marine Corps

Kilometers
0   100

Miles
0   100

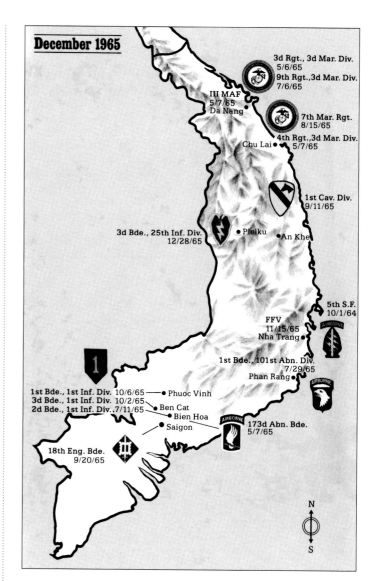

December 1965

3d Rgt., 3d Mar. Div. 5/6/65
9th Rgt.,3d Mar. Div. 7/6/65
III MAF 5/7/65 Da Nang
7th Mar. Rgt. 8/15/65
4th Rgt.,3d Mar. Div. 5/7/65
Chu Lai
1st Cav. Div. 9/11/65
3d Bde., 25th Inf. Div. 12/28/65
Pleiku
An Khe
5th S.F. 10/1/64
FFV 11/15/65 Nha Trang
1st Bde./101st Abn. Div. 7/29/65
Phan Rang
1st Bde., 1st Inf. Div. 10/6/65 — Phuoc Vinh
3d Bde., 1st Inf. Div. 10/2/65 — Ben Cat
2d Bde., 1st Inf. Div. 7/11/65 — Bien Hoa
Saigon
173d Abn. Bde. 5/7/65
18th Eng. Bde. 9/20/65
N
S

---

football player and a graduate of Arizona State College with a degree in fine arts education, Belton, a black man, had been a civil rights worker before he put on an army uniform. After he was drafted in May 1964, the war in Vietnam heated up, and leaders of the burgeoning civil rights movement began to question the American course in Vietnam. On March 21, 1965, in Selma, Alabama, the Reverend Dr. Martin Luther King, Jr., made a speech to demonstrators setting out on a march to Montgomery, the state capital. Dr. King said, "I don't know if I can approve of black boys being drafted and sent to a war 10,000 miles away, for the interests of the white man's world." Belton shared Dr. King's doubts about whether blacks should serve in Vietnam. The army jailed Belton and scheduled a court-martial on October 5 at Fort Sam Houston, Texas.

The soldiers of the 1st Cavalry continued their preparations. Charles Black, a reporter for the Columbus (Georgia) *Enquirer,* said "the effect on the soldiers of Belton's action was

nil." The men were too busy. There was a war on. They were going to it.

Going over

The 1st Cavalry Division was deployed in three stages. On August 2, 1965, the division's Advance Liaison Detachment left by air for Vietnam and arrived there two days later. Between August 14 and August 20, 1,040 officers and men of the division's advance party left Fort Benning. Moving with 152 tons of equipment, including nine UH-1B helicopters, the advance party arrived in Vietnam between August 19 and August 27. These two advance forces met at An Khe, fifty-seven kilometers inland from the coastal city of Qui Nhon, in what was designated II Corps—the second Corps Tactical Zone (II CTZ).

The deployment of the 1st Cav's main body recalled scenes

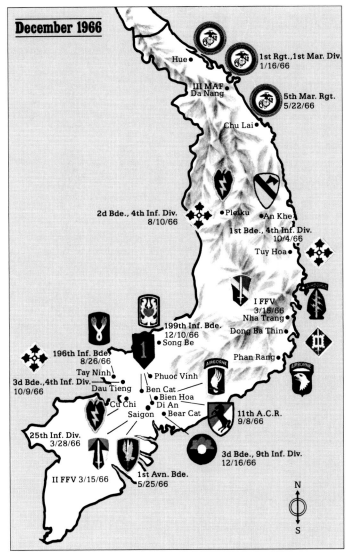

December 1966

Hue •
III MAF
Da Nang
Chu Lai •
1st Rgt.,1st Mar. Div.
1/16/66
5th Mar. Rgt.
5/22/66

2d Bde., 4th Inf. Div.
8/10/66
• Pleiku • An Khe
1st Bde., 4th Inf. Div.
10/4/66
Tuy Hoa •

I FFV
3/15/66
Nha Trang •
199th Inf. Bde.
12/10/66
• Song Be
Dong Ba Thin •
Phan Rang •

196th Inf. Bde.
8/26/66
Tay Ninh •
3d Bde.,4th Inf. Div.
10/9/66
Dau Tieng •
• Phuoc Vinh
• Ben Cat
• Bien Hoa
Cu Chi • • Di An
Saigon • • Bear Cat
11th A.C.R.
9/8/66
25th Inf. Div.
3/28/66
3d Bde., 9th Inf. Div.
12/16/66
II FFV 3/15/66
1st Avn. Bde.
5/25/66

N / S

December 1967

Dong Ha •
Quang Tri •
Khe Sanh •
Hue •
26th Mar. Rgt. 4/26/67
III MAF
Da Nang
23d Inf. Div.
9/25/67
Chu Lai •
Dak To •
Bong Son •
• Pleiku

Nha Trang •
Dong Ba Thin •
3d Bde., 101st Abn. Div.
11/18/67
Phan Rang •

Tay Ninh •
2d Bde., 101st Avn. Div.
11/18/67
• Phuoc Vinh
• Lai Khe
Cu Chi • • Bien Hoa
Long Binh •
Saigon • • Bear Cat
Tan An • • Phu My
Dong Tam •
20th Eng. Bde.
8/3/67

N / S

of troop movements during World War II. In mid-August some 13,500 troops departed Fort Benning and moved by train and bus to Atlantic and Gulf Coast ports, where six troop carriers, four small aircraft carriers, and seven cargo ships stood by to load the men and their equipment. On the sixteenth of August the troopships *Buckner* and *Darby* pulled away from Charleston, South Carolina. Within the next four days, the *Geiger, Rose, Patch,* and *Upshur* followed from Charleston and Savannah, Georgia. After loading some 500 of the division's rotary and fixed-wing aircraft, the *Boxer, Kula Gulf, Croaton,* and *Card* sailed from Mobile, Alabama, and Jacksonville, Florida.

The *Boxer* moved from west to east, sailing into the Mediterranean Sea and through the Suez Canal. It arrived at Qui Nhon on September 9. Other ships made the western passage out of the Gulf of Mexico and through the Panama Canal to California, Hawaii, Guam, and the Philippines. The

sea passage imposed a boring routine of restless sleep, calisthenics, queasy spells at the rail, and card games. But two events stood out. Four black soldiers aboard the *Buckner* attempted to stage a hunger strike to protest assignment to Vietnam. While at sea one of the men was court-martialed and sentenced to six months imprisonment. All were later held at a stockade thrown up hastily at An Khe. The other event was less serious. Aboard the *Boxer*, a task force of navy infiltrators penetrated an army perimeter guard and stamped a light brand saying "USN" on the left flank of Maggie, the white mule mascot of the 1st Cav.

After the men were ashore, giant CH-47 Chinook helicopters lifted them from Qui Nhon Harbor to their base camp at An Khe. General cargo and vehicles traveled up on Highway 19. Within ninety days of formal activation the 1st Cavalry Division had completed organization and training and been transported more than 12,000 miles.

Digging in

What the 1st Cav found at An Khe was a small nest of tents surrounded by dense jungle. Machetes were issued and the men were ordered to "start cutting." September and October could be months of intense heat in that part of South Vietnam, and the men sweated heavily as they hacked out the jungle to clear lines of fire. Gnarled vines and thick hedgerows snagged arms and tripped feet as the men worked. Ants and malaria-carrying mosquitoes plagued them; rats infested living areas. Occasional sniper fire and light probing attacks by the Vietcong harassed them. But scorpions, spiders, and snakes were less prevalent than had been expected, and the local tigers stayed back in the bush.

Brothers in the Nam

by Wallace Terry

Milton Lee Olive, III, left Chicago just before his eighteenth birthday to join the army. In Company B, 2d Battalion, 503d Infantry, 173d Airborne, he was called Preacher, because he dropped biblical quotations with the ease of a prophet. On October 22, 1965, near Phu Cuong—sixteen days before he would turn nineteen—Private Olive fell over a grenade to save the lives of four comrades, two blacks, an Hispanic, and a white officer from Texas.

On April 21, 1966, Lyndon Baines Johnson, tears streaming from his eyes, presented the Medal of Honor posthumously to Olive's father, a warehouse worker. The senior Olive expressed his hope that his son's sacrifice would help unite "Klansmen, the Negroes, the Hebrews, and the Catholics" with a "resolve to study war no more."

At first, blacks went to Vietnam—like their white counterparts—as professionals, anxious to perform their duty, gain quick promotions, and, along the way, defeat the Communist menace. Black "boys" like Olive wanted to grow up and grow out of the ghetto. War, so tradition had it, was the ultimate test of manhood. They would return forever men in a world that long considered their fathers boys at any age. It would not be so easy. Olive had written home: "We all do a man's job and wear a man's clothes and call ourselves men. But some of us are still little boys."

From 1965 to 1967, the armed forces were probably the most integrated institutions in American society. For the first time blacks were fully integrated in combat and fruitfully employed in positions of leadership. Coming from an 11 percent segment of the American population, blacks died in Vietnam at a disproportionately greater rate in those years. In 1965 and 1966, blacks made up 23 percent of Americans killed in action. Where blacks were a third of the crack 1st Brigade of the 101st Airborne Division and half of its reconnaissance commanders, the front lines became known as "Soulville." In 1967, blacks composed 20 percent of the combat forces, 25 percent of the elite troops, and up to 45 percent of the airborne rifle platoons. Some 20 percent of army fatalities were black, 11 percent of marine. Said Daniel "Chappie" James, Jr., a black air force fighter pilot stationed at Ubon, Thailand, in 1967: "I've fought in three wars and three more wouldn't be too many to defend my country. I love America, and as she has weaknesses or ills, I'll hold her hand."

While blacks have fought in all of America's wars, the blacks were segregated from whites in all armed services until President Harry S Truman decreed a phasing out of the Jim Crow forces in 1948. All-black units fought for the last time in Korea.

In Vietnam, Uncle Sam was an equal opportunity employer. Black farm boys yearning for adventure and black city youth yearning to escape learned long before 1965 that the armed forces were more than an employer of last resort. In the army there was a greater measure of integration than could be found anywhere in civilian society. Despite the high casualties, there was little to support the charges of some black leaders that black soldiers were being used unwillingly as cannon fodder. Because past discrimination deprived them of full opportunity, fewer blacks than whites possessed the preparation and training for entrance into more highly skilled occupations, such as electronics, and thus ended up carrying guns or pushing brooms.

In 1966, blacks were flunking the armed forces pre-induction mental test at a far higher rate than whites, 67.5 percent to 18.8 percent. And the first-term army re-enlistment rate for blacks was three times that of whites, meaning more blacks would make their way into the middle enlistment ranks and would return to Vietnam for second and third terms. But many wanted to fight for the sake of fighting, to get the extra pay hazardous duty provided ($55 a month extra for airborne), or found life in the service—even under fire—fairer than the America they left behind and certainly more exciting and challenging than the boredom, defeat, and substandard life of the ghetto slum. Said Chief Warrant Officer Roberto Lugo, a helicopter pilot near Saigon: "I just couldn't take the prejudice in Texas, so I asked to be shipped over here. I fly because I make more money and I stay clean." Captain David J. Travis added: "Obviously I would prefer to be in Alabama conducting a search and destroy operation, but I realize that an attempt is being made here to give this country self-determination just as I would like to have it for all Negroes."

Black fighting men were everywhere. Major Beauregard Brown, III, supervised logistics at MACV. First Lieutenant Dorothy Harris treated Vietnamese beyond the Cu Chi perimeter. Air force Major James T. Boddie, Jr., flew more than 150 F-4 Phantom missions over the North and South. Lieutenant Colonel James F. Hamlet served in the elite 1st Air Cavalry Division. "There was a time when I knew personally every Negro lieutenant colonel," he recalled then. "Thank God, I don't anymore." Medic Lawrence Joel left a broken home in Winston-Salem, North Carolina, to go ar-

After troops widened the perimeter and cleared helipads, they established field fortifications and erected more tents and buildings. But some of the necessary construction had already been completed more than a decade before. On the grounds of the base area Americans discovered rotting log bunkers and sand-filled concrete emplacements installed and abandoned years before by the French. In some the Americans found French records and diaries, including a document detailing a day in the life of the French Groupement Mobile 100, an elite unit once based at An Khe. Some months subsequent to the date of the document, in the summer of 1954, the unit was ambushed by the Vietminh on Highway 19 and annihilated. None of the Americans could have imagined that a decade later, after American forces were withdrawn, An Khe would again be

---

my because "as a Negro, you couldn't make it really big in the world." In November of 1965, near Bien Hoa, his platoon drifted into a crossfire. Shot in both legs, Joel dragged himself from body to body, giving bloody mouth to mouth resuscitation to the wounded. Brought to the White House to celebrate winning the Medal of Honor, Joel said: "Most of the men who have been to Vietnam feel this war is right."

Racial differences were not lost on the Communists. The Vietcong initially tried to exploit the prejudices of their countrymen by slandering the black soldier. Villagers were terrorized by wild tales of black rape, cannibalism, and vampirism. The blood thefts ostensibly took place when black medics inoculated the villagers. To offset the lies, the U.S. command in 1966 distributed materials showing blacks in friendly association with Vietnamese, medics caring for injured Vietnamese, or soldiers playing with Vietnamese children. Many Vietnamese were unconvinced. Said Ronald Richardson: "A bunch of kids stared at me so hard I asked about it. This boy said his parents told him dark people have tails. It hurt me. So I pulled down my pants and showed them I didn't have a tail."

In 1967, the NLF changed its propaganda approach, embracing the black soldier as a fellow victim of U.S. imperialism. Cadres ordered the villagers to treat blacks as equals. In thousands of hand-size leaflets scattered across the land, blacks were urged to surrender and were promised special treatment if they defected. One leaflet read, in part: "Your real enemies are those who call you 'niggers'. ... The Vietnamese people and the Afro-Americans must rise against their common enemies, the U.S. aggressors and racist authorities, Johnson, Rusk, McNamara, and Westmoreland." Despite this effort, the VC, like any Communist fighter, was expected to kill any American soldier. Yet several blacks claimed to have heard or experienced incidents in which individual blacks on patrol or at listening or observation posts were spared because they were black.

At home, newspapers, magazines, and television networks heralded the spirit of brotherhood they discovered in the foxhole. Near Bien Hoa, Specialist 5 Cleophas Mims, a black medic in the 1st Infantry Division, dragged a wounded tank commander to the back deck of his tank, covering his body with his own as a rubber tree cut apart by Communist fire crashed down upon them. The commander was white. Blacks saving whites, whites saving blacks.

Brotherhood at the front lines was one thing. But back at the bases, the signs of future trouble were more obvious. Beneath the integrated surface of the war, the old prejudices still festered. Confederate flags flew from barracks and trucks. On the walls of bars and latrines were scrawled such graffiti as "niggers eat shit" and "I'd prefer a gook to a nigger." After he appeared as the subject of *Time* magazine's 1967 cover story hailing racial progress on the Vietnam battlefields, Clide Brown, a long-range reconnaissance patrol leader, found a cross burning outside his tent.

By the end of 1967, black soldiers still found themselves doing more than their share of the dirty work. Promotions, awards, and coveted rear area assignments were too often slow in coming their way, however well they fought or however high the proportion of their front line casualties. Although blacks made up 12.6 percent of the army enlisted ranks, they were 3.3 percent of the officer corps. In the air force, 10.2 percent of enlisted, 1.8 percent of the officers; in the marines, 11.5 percent of the enlisted, 0.9 percent of the officers; in the navy, 5 percent of the enlisted, 0.4 percent of the officers. And at the end of 1967, there were only 2 black generals among 1,346 generals and admirals, one in the army and one in the air force, Brigadier General Frederic Davison, as commander of the 199th Light Infantry Brigade, became the first black general to lead Americans into battle. The marines had no black full colonels, and only 2 battalion commanders among 380 were black.

One night in early 1967, after a beer too many, a white comrade told Velman Phillips, "I don't like niggers, but you're okay." One week later, the white soldier was shot through the jaw during Operation Cedar Falls. Phillips breathed life into him, and he lasted seven days. Phillips lamented: "That boy from Texas died in ignorance. He never learned good race relations. But that night he was an American, fighting, trying to do the same job we all have to do. He gave his life for me." About the same time, a white mother, Virginia M. Robinson, wrote in the Durham, North Carolina, hometown paper that when her son was shot at Chu Lai his black sergeant carried him to safety. "Neither that sergeant nor his fellow people didn't owe my son a thing, but he saved his life anyway. My son says he would like to kick himself now for ever being in the Ku Klux."

But as the war wore on, the spirit of foxhole brotherhood faded and dark clouds began to gather over the Great Society at home, dimming bright hopes for the racial harmony and progress shared by Lyndon Johnson and the father of a fallen black hero one spring day in the White House Rose Garden.

Wallace Terry covered the Vietnam War for Time magazine from 1967 to 1969. He produced the documentary recording of black soldiers in the war, "Guess Who's Coming Home," and a book, Bloods: An Oral History of the War by Black Veterans.

abandoned as the North Vietnamese Army (NVA) rolled past on its way south to capture Saigon.

In fact, the men of the 1st Cav had reason to believe theirs would be a brief stay. As they dug in at An Khe they learned that the 4th Regiment of the 3d Marine Division had engaged and defeated a Vietcong regiment in Operation Starlite. As the men of the 1st Cav broke jungle and sandbagged bunkers, there was no reason for them to suspect that they were beginning a new phase of what would become their country's longest war.

The faces of war

As summer turned to fall, An Khe was quiet and the men settled in. On September 29 the division ventured its first battalion-sized helicopter assault mission into the Vinh Thanh Valley. No enemy soldiers were found, but 22 Americans were wounded when they stepped on punji-sticks—sharpened bamboo stakes dipped in poison and concealed in the ground. Three weeks later, the division encountered its first full-scale trial by fire during Operation Silver Bayonet, a mission to assist defense of key ARVN and U.S. installations in the vicinity of Pleiku. By November 20, more than 1,500 enemy troops had been killed, many during savage fighting in the Ia Drang Valley—the first large-scale battle between Americans and North Vietnamese soldiers—and more than 300 of "The Flying Horsemen" who arrived from Fort Benning only weeks before had fallen dead in battle.

Back in the United States at the housing development near Fort Benning where Patricia Encarnacao waited for her husband to return, the war touched home. Olive-drab army sedans driven

Four 1st Cavalry Division members *carry the body of a comrade killed in November 1965, during fighting in the Ia Drang Valley. American casualties in the battle of the Ia Drang were the highest to that point in the war.*

The 1st Cavalry Division *could deliver troops anywhere a helicopter could hover. Here 1st Cav troops climb rope ladders hung from a CH-47A Chinook during an operation near Pleiku on January 20, 1966.*

by solemn officers bearing telegrams prowled among the tract houses. The suspense of wondering where each car might stop was shared by every family. "You never think they're wounded," Pat Encarnacao said. "You always think they're dead." Joe Encarnacao knew his wife's attitude and determined to protect her from worry. When he was shot through the shoulder by a Vietcong machine-gun bullet two days after Christmas, Encarnacao insisted through clenched teeth that no telegram was to be delivered. Instead, after treatment he wrote a newsy letter from his hospital bed. At the end of it he mentioned casually that he'd been hurt but was all right.

At Fort Sam Houston, Texas, Winstel Belton had been convicted of malingering to avoid combat. But in return for a guilty plea, and an expression of willingness to perform his remaining eight months of duty in Vietnam, Belton was released. Reassigned to the 1st Infantry Division in South Vietnam's III Corps, Belton ultimately distinguished himself in combat by recovering the radio used by his captain after it was dropped during an ambush. The officer, Captain R. E. Spriggs, recommended that Belton be promoted. Later Captain Spriggs wrote a letter to his battalion commander and had Belton's sentence remitted.

At An Khe one Monday night, mistaking her for a Vietcong, a soldier shot and killed Maggie the Mule, the 1st Cav mascot.

In the spring of 1966, after months of staring in the face of war, marine Privates Richard Ogden and John Dojka returned home safely.

Greetings

On July 28, 1965, when President Johnson announced to the nation that he was ordering the 1st Cavalry Division to Vietnam, he said "We will stand in Vietnam." At the same time the president requested that Congress authorize a 340,000-man increase in all U.S. armed forces personnel. When Johnson spoke, Americans stationed in South Vietnam numbered 81,400. Six months later American forces totaled 250,000, and within two years that figure nearly doubled. For the month of December 1965 the draft call—mostly for the army—reached 40,200, and the army expanded training bases all over the country. At six army basic training centers—Fort Ord in California; New Jersey's Fort Dix; Fort Jackson, South Carolina; Fort Polk, Louisiana; Georgia's Fort Gordon; and Fort Leonard Wood in Missouri—thousands of volunteers and an increasing number of draftees were transformed into soldiers.

They came from almost everywhere—from big city streets and small town squares and isolated farms and from almost everywhere in between—from Minnesota mines and Massachusetts factories; from Mississippi docks and Montana ranches. But they didn't often come from the more expensive addresses in the fashionable parts of major cities or their affluent suburbs: During the war's duration 76 percent of the men (officers and enlisted) sent to Vietnam were from lower middle- or working-class backgrounds; as much as 25 percent came from families with incomes below the poverty level.

Before the draft reforms of 1968 distributed the selective service burden more equally, a man who knew where he was in the social structure knew his chances. If a man didn't go to college, the draft was at his front door, so he went into the military. If he went to college but dropped out, the draft grabbed him quickly: 60 percent of college dropouts wound up in uniform. If he graduated from college but was not then deferred, he might be drafted. Some who were eligible for the draft gained additional exemption by going on to graduate or professional school. Many of those who were to be drafted decided to enlist or "volunteer," often in hopes of avoiding Vietnam. But if a man didn't want to go to Vietnam often he could avoid going. He could starve himself or take drugs and flunk the draft physical. He could join the National Guard. He could hire a lawyer. One California "draft attorney" stated flatly "Any kid with money can absolutely stay out of the army—with 100 percent certainty." A local prosecutor agreed: "If you got the dough, you don't have to go." But most Americans believed military service was a duty, and if assigned to Vietnam, they went.

Who they were

From 1965 to 1967 Brigadier General S. L. A. Marshall, a veteran and a chronicler of combat during World War II and the Korean War, made several trips to South Vietnam. General Marshall thought that the soldiers he saw in Vietnam made up the best forces America ever fielded, anywhere, anytime: "My overall estimate was that the morale of the troops and the level of discipline of the army were higher than I had ever known them in any of our wars." General William C. Westmoreland, commander of U.S. forces in Vietnam from 1964 to 1968, shared this view. "Having fought in three wars, I am convinced the United States never fielded a more professional force."

The American serviceman in Vietnam from 1965 to 1967 was sounder mentally and physically than any that came before him. Some 75 percent of all enlisted men were high school graduates, compared to 48 percent in 1952. A limited, selective draft allowed the military to adhere to strict physical requirements; most soldiers were very good physical specimens and well-motivated individuals.

NINE RULES
for personnel of U.S. Military Assistance Command, Vietnam

The Vietnamese have paid a heavy price in suffering for their long fight against the Communists. We military men are in Vietnam now because their government has asked us to help its soldiers and people in winning their struggle. The Vietcong will attempt to turn the Vietnamese people against you. You can defeat them at every turn by the strength, understanding, and generosity you display with the people. Here are nine simple rules:

Distribution — 1 to each member of the United States Armed Forces in Vietnam.

NINE RULES

1 Remember we are guests here: We make no demands and seek no special treatment.

2 Join with the people! Understand their life, use phrases from their language and honor their customs and laws.

3 Treat women with politeness and respect.

4 Make personal friends among the soldiers and common people.

5 Always give the Vietnamese the right of way.

6 Be alert to security and ready to react with your military skill.

7 Don't attract attention by loud, rude or unusual behavior.

8 Avoid separating yourself from the people by a display of wealth or privilege.

9 Above all else you are members of the U.S. Military Forces on a difficult mission, responsible for all your official and personal actions. Reflect honor upon yourself and the United States of America.

MACV issued a card listing *"Nine Rules of Conduct"* to each American soldier entering Vietnam.

Postings

Twenty-one-year-old William Beck of Harrisburg, Pennsylvania, was drafted into the army on December 1, 1964. Eight months later on August 18, 1965, Private First Class Beck, twenty-two years old and an M60 machine gunner, shipped out of Charleston, South Carolina, aboard the World War II troopship the *Maurice Rose* with the other 3,500 men of the 1st Cav's 3d Brigade, destination South Vietnam.

Twenty-six days out, the captain of the *Maurice Rose* learned that a typhoon was churning from the west through the South China Sea toward the ship. Its winds blew at more than 70 miles per hour, and it drove seas of greenish white spume as high as small mountains. The captain steered south to avoid the storm but the storm turned south too, as if determined to collide with the *Rose*. The captain changed course again and navigated around the typhoon. But for twenty-four hours the *Rose* pitched and heaved through heavy seas and high winds. Her crewmen swarmed over the decks to secure equipment and batten hatches. "They locked us downstairs and tied the hatch doors back with bull rope because they didn't want anybody up there," Beck said. "The ship was really rockin' and rollin' that day." The morning after the storm, sunshine sparkled on smooth seas and a few days later, on September 18, the Rose docked at Qui Nhon. Beck's unit, Company A, 1st Battalion, 7th Cavalry Regiment, choppered up to An Khe, sixty-four kilometers away.

Robert Boarts arrived at the III Corps port of Vung Tau aboard the *Salton* on December 10, 1966, along with another 4,000 soldiers of the 199th Infantry Brigade (Light). That night the men on the *Salton* saw *To Hell and Back,* a World War II film starring Audie Murphy. "I guess they showed it to us, well, sort of to pump us up," Boarts recalled. The next morning he rode in a "deuce and a half"—a two-and-one-half ton truck—to his new home at Long Binh. Units of the 25th Infantry Division and the 101st Airborne Division provided security along the 130-kilometer route. Three days later Boarts went out on his first mission, a helicopter assault west of Long Binh. That first day he encountered death. A man's body was "practically blowed apart" by a land mine. "I hated to see it," Boarts said, "but I was glad it was him instead of me."

As more American troops were sent to Vietnam, the fastest, cheapest way to get them there was by air. Soldiers who arrived in Vietnam by chartered jet all remember the same things. The pilot's announcement over the public address system that their flight was approaching the shores of Vietnam. The rapid, steep, roller-coaster descent to the runway to avoid possible sniper fire. The forced smiles of stewardesses who watched them make their way up the aisles. And at the airplane door, the blast of heat. "Walking into it was like slamming into a wall," one man remembered. Then, carried on the hot air, there was the smell— a smell of sweat and excrement, of rotting fish and cooking fires. Some men remember thinking of it as the smell of death.

In early November 1967, Sergeant Charles Baran got off his flight in Bien Hoa. Assigned to the intelligence section of the 9th Division's 2d Brigade, Baran found his new world "much hotter and dirtier than I could possibly imagine." Five minutes later he climbed aboard the bus that would take his unit to their processing point. Baran noticed screens made of thick steel rods over the windows. "The only screens I'd seen were to keep bugs out." Half-seriously, trying to start a conversation, Baran commented to the driver something about the flies still being able to get in the bus. The driver was not in a joking mood. "He looked at me, shook his head, and said 'Those ain't for flies, man, they're so the gooks can't throw grenades inside. Welcome to Vietnam, kid.'"

Guard duty

Since men first made war, soldiers have stood guard while armies marched or slept. In Vietnam guard duty meant inspecting Vietnamese workers in the morning as they came on the base at Nha Trang to clean barracks. It meant making sure sappers didn't sneak on the runway at Bien Hoa to sabotage a 4-million-dollar supersonic jet fighter some dark night. Or it meant hearing movement outside friendly lines near the demilitarized zone (DMZ) and being deafened a moment later by the blasts of claymore mines exploding in the wire. But often guard duty meant squatting in a hole in the ground half the night out in the middle of nowhere, staring into the blackness, hearing the sounds, watching the shadows.

Private Rick Loffler, MOS 81B20 (draftsman) arrived in Vietnam on November 30, 1966, assigned to the army's 39th Signal Battalion, based at Vung Tau. During the day Loffler might letter signs or paint captain's bars on a "steel pot" (a helmet). But at night, like all the clerks, cooks, and other enlisted men on base, Loffler stood guard. His letters home to his family in Little Neck, New York, capture the feeling of what it was like for one soldier to stand guard in Vietnam.

"One gets to know what night is really like at 3:00 A.M. If in town on guard duty the only noise you hear is a far away

In the middle of a downpour *a soldier wrapped in a poncho catches some sleep atop a sandbagged bunker while a buddy keeps watch, June 1967.*

droning of electrical generators, and an occasional dog bark. Once in a while a two-wheeled cart drawn by some sort of cow comes creaking along, heaped with pineapple or vegetables for the next day's market. Otherwise all you smell is a musty worn out stink, all you see is shadow."

During guard duty at the base the sights and sounds of the night make for a slow, noisy light show, as if to keep the troops awake. Driven out in trucks to bunkers—sandbagged shelters with broken cots inside—a team of three men eat chow at dusk and start the night. "Two stay awake at all times," Loffler wrote his family. "We eat and sit, and sit, and sit. Then the cannon starts.

"About two hundred feet away are 105MM and 155MM artillery emplacements. Their duty is to shell possible enemy zones many miles away. Here are the noises of the ritual of firing one round: Whhirrrrrrr—Kllick. Sssskkkklllaaank! WWhhiirrrkkllaaank. That was the charge and the shell being loaded into the breech. More whirring follows; azimuth and elevation controls are set. Then a guy gives a short yell, and then an instant's silence. Then a BAM-BOOM-TTHHAAT-sound combination that bounces the ground, the cot, and you. Maybe a half hour of this is followed by an hour and a half of silence. Then BBAAMM, BAMM—for another half hour. This goes on all night. Flares can be seen nearby, fired off when somebody sees sumthin out dare [sic]. There's the constant drone of electrical generators, the whine of choppers slipping past with their landing lights blinking red. Mice and rats squeak, and the night goes on."

One night in 1967, as he wrote later, Corporal W. D. Ehrhart was asleep in a bunker on the perimeter of a marine base near Hoi An, while his partner Gerry Gaffney, who was new to the war, stood guard. Gaffney saw something, didn't know what it was, and nudged Ehrhart.

"Hey, Ehrhart, wake up," Gaffney said. "What the hell is that?"

Ehrhart rubbed the sleep out of his eighteen-year-old eyes and pushed himself up to the bunker's lip. "What?" he asked.

"That red thing," Gaffney said, pointing toward the east.

The thing was gone, and the night was quiet. But several miles away in the sky, near the ocean, Ehrhart could see the white lights of an airplane lumbering in the darkness. He was awake now. "Keep watchin'," he said.

The plane continued to circle in a slow orbit, then suddenly a bright red streak erupted silently at an angle from the lights, and a solid bar of electric red color reached down to the ground below. Seconds later, a dull sawing sound like the buzz of a dentist's drill floated through the humid air. The red streak and the low buzzing synchronized for moments while the plane flew a slow, banking arc through the distant blackness. Then the red streak slowly fell away from the circling lights and was swallowed in the earth, leaving the thick buzzing sound sawing, then seconds later silence again.

"That's Puff the Magic Dragon," Ehrhart said to Gaffney, "the gunship. Air force AC-47 with three machine guns." Ehrhart went on to explain that each machine gun worked like a Gatling gun, its six barrels electrically rotated, and that "Puff" fired 6,000 rounds per minute. Fixed in position on one side of the AC-47, guns were aimed by tilting the plane at an angle to the ground.

"That's 18,000 rounds per minute, my man," Ehrhart said, "300 rounds a second. Chops anything and everything like mincemeat. I've seen places where Puff's left his calling card. Unbelievable. Looks like a freshly plowed field ready for planting."

"What are they shooting at?" Gaffney asked.

"God knows. Whatever's down there," Ehrhart said. "I saw a body once," Ehrhart went on, "got chopped up by Puff. You wouldn't have known it was ever a human being. Just a pile of pulp stuck to little pieces of cement and straw that used to be the guy's hooch—or her hooch, absolutely no way to tell the difference. It was so gross, it wasn't even sickening. It was just there, like litter or something." Ehrhart said he'd stand guard and told Gaffney to get some sleep. He pulled his flak jacket down around his shoulders, checked the magazine in his weapon, and watched the circling lights spinning in the night.

Early in March 1967, Randy Clark, aged eighteen years, five months, arrived in Phu Bai to serve as a radio operator with the 1st Field Artillery Group, 3d Marines, 3d Marine Division. Soon after he settled in he got his first assignment—Operation Cumberland, seventy-nine days of patrols among the approaches to the A Shau Valley. When he returned to Phu Bai Clark said, "I was years older and twice as wise."

After fighting the NVA for eleven weeks, Clark found himself linked up in a bunker with three new men who had missed the A Shau Valley action "and were still very green in my book." About midnight Clark saw the officer of the guard checking posts—or trying to catch someone asleep on guard. "This officer, a marine lieutenant, also missed the A Shau Valley. Green as grass!"

No one in other bunkers challenged the man, so Clark woke up his comrades. He whispered to them to keep quiet and told them to "observe." When the lieutenant approached, Clark gave the command to "Halt!" The man responded by saying he was the officer of the guard and continued to approach. Clark ordered him to halt, swung the M60 machine gun around, jacked a round in the chamber, and watched him freeze—twelve feet from the muzzle of the machine gun. "In a very low, but audible voice, I gave him my half of the password for the day—blue. He began stuttering and gave a half-hearted laugh and said he forgot to look the password up!"

Clark ordered the lieutenant to unbuckle his cartridge belt and drop it to the ground, take ten paces to the rear, place his ID or dog tags in his right hand, lay face down in the dirt, and spread eagle. The officer complied. "For all he knew I was hopped up on marijuana (I wasn't), and trigger happy to boot." At this point Clark's three comrades were pulling on his shirt tail and telling him "That's an officer, man—you're nuts!" But Clark had trouble hearing what they were saying because he was listening to the lieutenant's curses and his threats to have Clark court-martialed. "But I was right, the lieutenant was wrong, and I, PFC Clark, was *in charge!*"

Clark walked over to the prone man and placed his .45 caliber automatic pistol behind his right ear, stepped on his wrist, and removed the ID card. "Then I asked him his name, rank, service number, and date of birth. Right out of the Marine Corps manual." Even though the lieutenant answered, it was too dark for Clark to verify what he said. "Finally I told him he had been positively identified as a friendly (ignoring his hostility) and told him to get up. He then reached up and tore my dog tags off my neck and disappeared through the bushes talking about my impending court-martial!"

The next morning Clark was "standing tall" in front of the colonel, charged with a host of offenses. Clark called his three comrades as witnesses to show that the lieutenant didn't know the password, "a minor point that the lieutenant failed to mention in his haste to even the score with me." With tongue in cheek the colonel dismissed the charges and sent Clark on his way. "I would have given six months' combat pay to have heard what the colonel told the lieutenant," Clark said.

Humpin'

If an infantryman wasn't on guard duty, and he wasn't busy with one of the countless tasks his superiors gave him, he was probably out on patrol—across swamps, through jungles, up valleys, over mountains—looking for enemy troops, setting ambushes, avoiding mines, and trying to stay alive. Brooding over maps back in headquarters, the operations planners spoke of allocating "combat infantrymen" for what they called "search and destroy missions," "reconnaissance sweeps," and "clearing actions." The soldier spoke of himself as a "grunt" and called what he did "humpin'." For the man who had to walk the miles plotted on the planners' maps,

patrols were always the same two things—too long and too far.

Corporal John Clancy did a lot of humping in I Corps west of Hue and in the A Shau Valley in 1967 with the 196th Infantry Brigade (Light). The patrols he walked usually lasted four days, and during that time he had to carry anything and everything he needed to live and fight. He wore a steel helmet on his head, securing a camouflaged canvas cover on its outside with an elastic strap, and drew on a sleeveless flak jacket made of bulletproof nylon. Over his shoulders Clancy wore a patrol harness—a set of heavy-duty green canvas suspenders. From this he suspended a pistol belt to which he attached his basic fighting load: two ammunition pouches, two fragmentation grenades, a smoke grenade, a "K-bar," or fighting knife, and two plastic canteens. Next he slung two bandoliers of 100 M60 machine-gun rounds from his shoulders in a heavy, metal "X." On top of this Clancy shouldered a rucksack stuffed with a poncho that served as a raincoat by day and half a tent shelter by night, four days' worth of C-rations, personal effects ranging from toothbrush to Tabasco sauce, and plenty of extra ammunition, including twenty M16 magazines, M79 rounds for the grenadier, and a claymore mine. Inside the top flap of the rucksack Clancy tied an entrenching tool—a collapsible shovel he used to dig foxholes or fill sandbags. In all Clancy was burdened by roughly seventy pounds of weight not his own. Rigged with a release strap that permitted him to drop the "ruck" instantly, sometimes he almost welcomed the enemy contact that let him drop his house off his back. In his right hand he carried an M16 automatic rifle.

In the morning when the call went out to Clancy's platoon to "Saddle up!" the men drew on their rucks, adjusted their loads, and picked up their weapons. A point man started out ahead, a squad went out on both the left and the right flanks, and a rear guard picked up behind. Men in the main squad aligned themselves in five-meter intervals. With the call to "Move out!" Clancy and his fellow grunts started to walk. They spent the next ten hours humping and listening, waiting and watching, wondering and worrying what might happen.

"Patrolling seemed like a never-ending routine," Clancy remembers. Starting and stopping, climbing and sweating, his helmet dug into his skull and his ruck's straps ripped into his shoulders. Leeches dropped from trees, elephant grass slashed arms, heat sapped muscles, there was never enough water, and there was always reason to be afraid. "Most patrols were boring," Clancy says. "Some led to fights, about three in ten, but they were small ones. Really large fights happened less than 10 percent of the time." Some patrols were ordered to exploit intelligence about enemy activity and to flush out the enemy if possible, but many had no specific goal, Clancy recalls, "just 'make contact,' find ammunition, find food, find Charlie. They never told the little guy what we were doing. We were always confused, always mixed up, always asking, 'Where are we going? What are we doing now?' "

Hanoi Hannah

When he wasn't out for the night on patrol or setting an ambush, Specialist Four Michael Clodfelter might spend his evening listening to Hanoi Hannah, the North Vietnamese version of Japan's Tokyo Rose in World War II. Hanoi Hannah's dulcet voice and perfect American speech poured from radios throughout II Corps, where Clodfelter's unit, the 2d Battalion, 502d Infantry, operated. Between spinning the latest discs, Hanoi Hannah harangued her listeners about "U.S. atrocities" and "the Wall Street connection" to "the imperialist American government."

Sometimes her theme would be capitalist exploitation of the working class. "She'd point out that the proletarian sons of American society were forced to carry the guns while the sons of the bourgeoisie carried the briefcases," Clodfelter said. "Hannah had a point."

The sweet-tongued broadcaster didn't succeed at making Clodfelter feel sympathy for those other "proletarian sons," the Vietcong and soldiers of the North Vietnamese Army. But she did make him angry about the antics of antiwar demonstrators—"those soldiers for peace who brandished flowers instead of firearms," as Clodfelter put it. Though the stateside demonstrators may not have attacked the U.S. serviceman directly, their attack against the war as contemptible and dishonorable made those who fought it feel "that we too were being held up as contemptible and dishonorable," Clodfelter said. "The majority of grunts condemned antiwar protesters, at least from 1965 to 1967, as reinforcements for the enemy." Hanoi Hannah's air-wave rhetoric penetrated the jungle, but it didn't induce in U.S. troops quite the effect she aimed for.

Plush overhead

From August 1966 to April 1967, marine Colonel Henry Aplington held a job with the unclassified title of "Department of Defense Special Representative" and was located at Tan Son Nhut air base. That meant he worked in intelligence, reviewing

Giants with dollars. *U.S. soldiers on leave amble down a Saigon street.*

and evaluating information about the enemy. Aplington picked up a lot of information about the U.S. effort in Vietnam too and evaluated it with an intelligence officer's impartial eye. Three things irritated him about the way the war was run.

"Quantification? Of course Mr. McNamara loved it so that's what he got. If he couldn't put it on a computer he didn't want to hear it." At briefing after briefing in the G-2 Ward Room at Military Assistance Command, Vietnam (MACV) headquarters, Aplington sat in the back row while officer after officer pulled out expanding pointers and listed statistics "which proved we were winning the war hands down. No one looked at the enemy situation map to the right of the briefers' easel which had not changed since the French were there.

"Security? Vietnamese civilians did all the menial jobs—it was cheaper than using U.S. troops." Aplington often visited the 7th Air Force Officer's Club at Tan Son Nhut after duty. American officers bellied up to the bar three deep and talked shop. All the bar girls and all the cafeteria girls were Vietnamese. The result of such practices throughout South Vietnam was that "We unintentionally built into the system the greatest VC low-level intelligence net that they could ever have wanted.

"Plush overhead? From generals' villas to PXs, USOs, movies, beer, you name it, we had it all." For many Americans, particularly for officers stationed at Saigon or other large cities, the comforts of home were often available. "You would have thought it was an occupation rather than a war," Aplington says.

A Vietnamese national

Walter Dunlap was a PFC in the army's 509th Army Security Agency Group, a communications unit, at Tan Son Nhut airport. Nguyen Muoi made beds, polished boots, swept floors, and washed clothes for PFC Dunlap and the twenty-three other soldiers in Dunlap's barracks. "She had a gold tooth, a wide smile which showed it off, seven children, and a husband in the Vietnamese air force," Dunlap recalled. Her salary was very important to her and her still-growing family, and when it became very apparent she was going to have her eighth child, the men of the barracks "wondered how long we would be without her smile and aid." The baby was born on Saturday and she was back at work on Monday. "It was a handsome baby—she brought it to show us," Dunlap said.

Over here

Whether a serviceman spent his whole tour humping "in the bush" or had it easy as a clerk and "skated" back in the rear, he knew at all times when he was due to return home to "the world." Those in the army, navy, air force, and Coast Guard were obliged to perform one year of duty in Vietnam, minus one week of R&R (rest and recuperation) leave in a neighboring country. Marines were required to serve thirteen months in the war zone and generally had only five days of R&R leave. But army or navy, air force or marines, any serviceman in Vietnam could say at any time exactly how many days he had left. Most soldiers started counting backwards soon after they arrived, and each day they subtracted one from the total days remaining to their DEROS—their Date of Estimated Return from Overseas. If a serviceman was "short"—if he had less than one month remaining until his DEROS—he probably could specify the number of hours he had left too. When the magic day arrived, he boarded the homeward-bound jetliner, or "freedom bird," with few regrets about leaving. But when he arrived back home he found home hadn't changed much, though he had.

Early in 1966 Richard Baker knew where he might end up, so he decided to outwit the government. A trumpet player in his high school's all-state band, Baker quit in his senior year and enlisted for the army band. He thought he'd keep away from Vietnam and out of combat. But one month after he finished basic training, Baker, Private Richard E., MOS 02B20, trumpet, cornet player, was aboard ship heading for a one-year assignment with the 4th Infantry Division band in Pleiku, South Vietnam. When he arrived they took away his instrument, gave him a rifle, and dropped him in the jungle.

Of his year in Vietnam Baker said "It was probably the worst and best experience I ever had." On guard duty once in a tower, MPs came in dragging an aged Vietnamese man. "He must have been eighty years old. I don't know what they brought him in for." The MPs tied him to a chair upside down and started to kick him. Then they taped his mouth shut and poured water down his nose. "Pretty soon he was dead. When you're only eighteen years old, it's hard to deal with something like that."

Back home in his native state of Washington, fifteen years after his twelve-month tour, Baker reflected. There were good things about being in Vietnam, about being a soldier among other soldiers, and being at war. "You had things there you could never have here—the friendship, the closeness," Baker said. "One man willing to give up his life for another man is a whole lot different than what you have back here. It makes here kind of a lonely place."

A marine near the DMZ at Dong Ha writes a letter home in late 1966.

"You're All Mine Now!"

Going in

You signed your name on the dotted line of DD Form 4—ENLISTMENT CONTRACT: ARMED FORCES OF THE UNITED STATES—and you were in the army, navy, air force, or marines. A bus ticket took you to a reception center somewhere, and when it stopped, the doors folded open and a big, stern man wearing a peaked campaign hat climbed on. He didn't much like what he saw. He scowled. He cursed. Then he roared: "You're all mine now!" For the next three days you were yelled at, tested, poked, processed, and fairly confused. Then the big, stern man you'd learned to call "Sergeant!" said you were shipping out for your basic training center. Separated from family, society, and the company of women, you had to remake a social order for the next two to four years in a world where everyone wore a uniform, and many went to war.

The U.S. Army provided 352 hours of instruction during eight weeks of basic training. Classes in military courtesy and sanitation gave way to classes in bayonet thrusting, rifle firing, and live-grenade throwing, with plenty of calisthenics and running mixed in. In the sixth week the trainee went out on bivouac to learn to live in the field

A band (right rear) strikes up as recruits arrive at the railroad station in Fort Jackson, South Carolina, in November 1965. The warm welcome belied the grueling training program ahead.

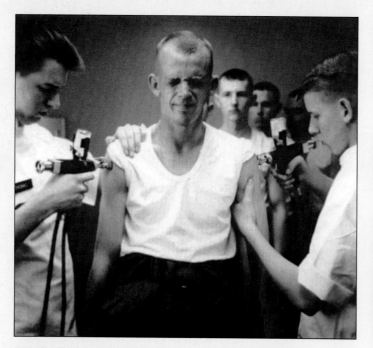

Tested, poked, processed. *A recruit at Fort Jackson receives two injections simultaneously.*

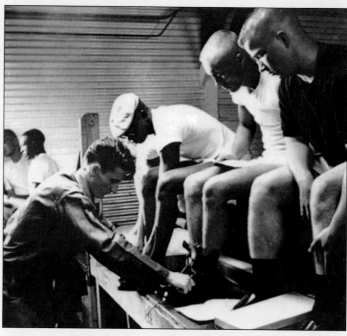

Trainees are fitted for boots *at Fort Knox, Kentucky. After 1965, U.S. troops in Vietnam wore canvas jungle boots that dried quickly.*

Draped in soiled sheets and clutching pillows, *six-day recruits at Fort Dix, New Jersey, move out to permanent barracks.*

and eat C-rations. During the seventh week trainers administered the Physical Combat Proficiency Test. At the end of the eighth week recruits graduated. After leave, all went on to Advanced Infantry Training (AIT). Some of the new soldiers trained further as clerks or cooks, typists or truck drivers. Those who trained in the various combat arms specialties, which ranged from infantry tactics to armored maneuver, underwent a nine-week course designed to qualify them for combat duty and, often, service in Vietnam. At combat arms training centers throughout the country various programs prepared soldiers to fight in Vietnam—and survive.

Combat arms

The goal of combat arms AIT was to give soldiers the experience of being in Vietnam before they arrived there. For example, at infantry schools trainers constructed realistic replicas of Vietcong hamlets, complete with thatched huts, tunnels, booby traps, barbed wire, punji-stakes, flocks of chickens, and "enemy" soldiers. Then the trainers set combat problems and confronted soldiers with them. At the three replica hamlets built at Fort Polk, Louisiana, training in patrolling, ambush, and counterambush received special emphasis.

Since much shooting contact with the enemy—the trainers who had fought in Vietnam called such contact a "firefight"—occurred unexpectedly at close range, and ended abruptly, frequently without sight of the foe, soldiers were trained in the techniques of "instant reaction" and "quick kill." Ordered to shoot at sound and movement without consciously aiming, men on mock patrols fired automatically at pop-up targets. Soldiers also learned the need for the buddy system. For example, when walking down a trail one man kept his eyes glued to the ground to check for trip wires while his companion kept a lookout for snipers.

At Fort Riley in northeastern Kansas, thick undergrowth offered a convincing version of Vietnam jungles, and hard-eyed trainers did nothing to dispel the illusion. All vehicles and personnel in the training sector

One day down, at least two years to go. *Draftee Dennis Lahey gazes out a barracks window at Fort Knox.*

The bottom line *in basic training: calisthenics.*

At Fort Jackson instructors demonstrate *"pugil stick" exercises, which prepare soldiers for bayonet fighting.*

"A soldier's weapon is his best friend." *A trainee aims an M1 rifle while another checks his trigger pull and a drill instructor watches, at Fort Dix, New Jersey, 1965.*

Trainees at Fort Polk, *Louisiana, in October 1966 wait for their sergeant's command to hurl practice grenades. New recruits also learned to throw grenades from standing, kneeling, and crouching positions.*

"Forget everything you learned back there. This here is the Nam. No substitute for bein' here."

American GI

were subject to ambush by "aggressor" forces at any hour. "We've got to make them aware that the roads are no longer safe and that they must be prepared to repel an ambush at any time," one officer said. Trainers also rehearsed a repertoire of counterinsurgency tactics. Patrols flushed enemy guerrillas who used friendly villagers as shields into "killing zones." "Quick-reaction" forces made twelve-foot jumps from throbbing helicopters into "hot" landing zones. At Georgia's Fort Gordon, trainees attacked the fortified village of "Vinh Hoa" only to find the enemy had slipped away into a maze of tunnels that led beyond the village. The men learned to detect enemy booby traps in the walls and ceilings of "hooches," the thatched houses of Vietnamese peasants.

They learned to set out booby traps of their own and to establish listening posts outside night defensive perimeters. At Fort Sill, Oklahoma, trainers introduced Vietnam-bound soldiers to the hazards of capture by the enemy. Interrogated while spread-eagled over a deep pit filled with snakes, the men learned that the best way to handle capture and interrogation was to avoid both.

With AIT behind them, and a thirty-day leave ahead, soldiers selected for duty in Vietnam had time to wonder how much of their training they would ever use. Some wondered how much of it was worthwhile. When they arrived in Vietnam, some were told "Forget everything you learned back there. This here is the Nam. No substitute for bein' here."

At Fort Polk's AIT center (above) in spring 1966, a column of soldiers marches past painted signs designed to instill aggressive spirit. "When they leave here, they are ready to fight," a training officer said.

During AIT at Fort Gordon, *Georgia, soldiers on patrol, their faces blackened, rush for cover from a mock sniper attack. The men are (left to right) Privates James C. Armstrong from Arlington, Virginia; Samuel R. Warren from Cadwell, Georgia; and Larry Hackworth from Creston, Ohio.*

Officer candidates learn *what to expect if captured by the enemy during the army's toughest prisoner-of-war course at Fort Sill, Oklahoma, July 1967. The "POWs" are ordered to "kiss the mud" as part of mock interrogation.*

"It certainly entered my mind that we were the 7th Cavalry Regiment and by God, we couldn't let happen what happened to Custer."

Colonel Hal Moore, commander of the 1st Battalion, 7th Cavalry, 1st Cavalry Division, at Ia Drang, November 14, 1965

Little more than a month after he had brought the colors of the 1st Cavalry Division to Vietnam, Major General Harry W. O. Kinnard took Army Chief of Staff General Harold K. Johnson's personal order—"Harry, I want you and your division to stop the enemy from cutting South Vietnam in two"—and carried it to the trackless mountains near the Cambodian border where his men clashed with two North Vietnamese regiments. Those critical Ia Drang Valley battles of November 1965 tested both the concept and the execution of airmobile tactics. In the month-long campaign, helicopters joined the action for the first time as something more than isolated gunships or airborne trucks. The 1st Cav's 434 helicopters not only transported supplies and men, but also delivered infantry directly to enemy locations. The widespread use of helicopter gunships, with their aerial rockets and machine guns, added a new dimension to the conduct of war.

But the Ia Drang campaign also tested the mettle of the U.S. infantryman—"the ultimate weapon"—and, in the three-day fulcrum battle for a nondescript forest clearing called LZ X-Ray, the soldiers faced their greatest challenge. On the morning of November 14, Lieutenant Colonel Harold G. ("Hal") Moore, commander of the 1st Battalion, 7th Cavalry, was bringing in his understrength battalion in successive helicopter relays when North Vietnamese regulars, in Moore's words, "boiled off

that mountain" in furious infantry charges backed by mortars and rockets. In fighting that General Westmoreland later called "as fierce as any ever experienced by American troops," Moore's men repulsed savage NVA attacks with every weapon available to them—from bayonets in hand-to-hand combat to close infantry fighting with the new M16 rifle, to artillery and tactical air support including B-52 bombing attacks on the Chu Pong Mountains. In the din and pandemonium of battle, Moore heard faint echoes of history reverberating from nearly a century before. "It certainly entered my mind that we were the 7th Cavalry Regiment," he said, "and by God, we couldn't let happen what happened to Custer." With the help of reinforcements and overwhelming firepower, the 1st Battalion ultimately forced the North Vietnamese to withdraw into Cambodia. When the Ia Drang campaign ended, the battle of LZ X-Ray proved to have accounted for nearly half of the 1,500 enemy casualties.

The 1st Cavalry Division had paid a heavy price for its success, having lost some 300 soldiers killed in action, half of them in one disastrous ambush of the 2d Battalion, 7th Cavalry, at LZ Albany. The enemy had closed so tightly that no perimeters could be identified, preventing the use of artillery or tactical air support for several critical hours. Moreover, the division's vaunted airmobility, though proven in combat, had nonetheless been stretched to its absolute limits, and many helicopters were in poor shape, while others were down for repair and awaiting spare parts. In addition, many of the soldiers, especially older veterans, had to accustom themselves to the peculiar concept of "victory" in Vietnam. As Associated Press correspondent Peter Arnett noted in a dispatch at the time, "Statistically, Ia Drang has been a victory for the U.S. forces. But

A moment in the battle of LZ 4, *which brought to a standstill the opening assault of the ambitious American Operation Masher. The command group of Company A, 2d Battalion, 7th Cavalry, takes shelter in a ditch near LZ 4 while Captain Joel Sugdinis (squatting) calls in artillery and 2d Platoon leader Lieutenant Gordon Grove (standing) peers out toward enemy lines.*

the troops at Ia Drang use the word carefully. Fighting on jungle battlefields, defending bitterly for several days and then abandoning them, they are deprived of the satisfactions of occupation." Arnett had identified a disconcerting truth about the nature of the Vietnam War.

As the 1st Cav returned to its An Khe base on Highway 19 in western Binh Dinh Province, General Kinnard faced the problem of where to look next for the enemy. Some in the intelligence section recommended a return to the western highlands early in 1966 in hopes of catching the enemy reassembling in the unpopulated jungles. But Kinnard chose to launch operations in northeastern Binh Dinh Province, a region of abrupt mountains and populous coastal plains. The ARVN 22d Division, responsible for that area, was spread thin in trying to keep Highway 1 open and secure and perform pacification tasks at the same time. The 1st Cav intelligence staff had confirmed reports of the Vietcong Main Force 2d Regiment and two North Vietnamese regiments—the 18th and 22d—operating in that sector. The three regiments comprised the NVA 3d Division, also known as the Sao Vang, or "Yellow Star," Division.

The Masher plan

Kinnard conceived of a series of mobile hammer-and-anvil operations in which troops launching from a central base could flush the enemy toward other friendly troops set in blocking positions. He chose the small airstrip and Special Forces camp at Bong Son as the hub of operations and carved the area around it into four sectors. The flat Bong Son Plain in the northeast was the operation's first target. The northwest sector contained the long and narrow An Lao Valley. To the southwest was the Kim Son Valley, known as the "Eagle's Claw" because its seven smaller valleys looked on a map like a bird's talons. In the southeast quadrant lay the rugged Cay Giep Mountains. To express the hammer-and-anvil nature of the plan, Kinnard titled the operation "Masher," but it was better known to the troops as the Bong Son campaign.

In planning the operation, the 1st Cavalry Division coordinated with the ARVN 22d Division as well as the Republic of Korea Capital Division, which had been stationed near Qui Nhon since October. In addition, the marines were organizing an operation to the north called Double Eagle, which was poised to sweep across the Quang Ngai-Binh Dinh provincial boundary to snare enemy units retreating from the advance of Operation Masher.

To spearhead Masher's important first phase, Kinnard chose the 1st Cav's 3d Brigade, under the command of Hal Moore. The former battalion commander, a recipient of the Distin-

guished Service Cross—the nation's second highest medal for valor—for his conduct at LZ X-Ray, had been on the promotion list to colonel; he received the colonel's eagles shortly after the Ia Drang campaign. Almost immediately Kinnard had assigned him to command the 3d Brigade, consisting of his own battalion, the 1/7, as well as the 2d Battalion, 7th Cavalry. For the opening phase of Operation Masher, the 1st and 2d Battalions, 12th Cavalry, joined the brigade, as did the 1st Squadron, 9th Cavalry, a reconnaissance unit of helicopter gunships. With artillery battalions and aviation companies, Moore's brigade totaled about 5,700 men.

Masher was scheduled to begin late in January 1966 after a three-day truce to mark the Tet holiday and Lunar New Year. January 25 would inaugurate the "Year of the Horse"— the Chinese calendar designation for 1966, a fact not lost on the soldiers of the 1st Cavalry Division, whose insignia features a horse's head.

The Communist heartland

A year earlier, the CIA had declared Binh Dinh, with its population of some 800,000, "just about lost" to the South Vietnamese government. Binh Dinh (the name ironically means "pacified") had been dominated by the Vietminh and Vietcong since World War II. When the Japanese departed in 1945, the Vietminh established control over the province and bedeviled the French there throughout the Indochina War. During the 1954 Geneva negotiations, the Vietminh petitioned to establish the line of demarcation below Binh Dinh on the grounds that they could not relinquish an area they had held throughout the war. Although they failed, Binh Dinh Province nevertheless remained the Communist heartland of the South.

Of the 90,000 regroupees from South Vietnam who went north in 1955, fully half of them came from Binh Dinh, and when the National Liberation Front (NLF) was created in 1960, some of those regroupees began to infiltrate back to renew familial ties and refine their political organization. They freed areas from government interference, where villagers fortified their settlements with an interlocking system of trenches and tunnels. The Vietcong drafted men who didn't volunteer, and soon many of the young men in the villages had gone off into the remote western mountains where the Vietcong trained and lived. It became a truism that in Binh Dinh Province, if a person was not a Vietcong, he was related to one.

The Vietcong overran three government district headquarters in 1964, and the government simply dissolved the districts, declaring them to be part of neighboring ones. In this way the government avoided having to admit the loss of the districts, but neither the Vietcong nor the villagers were fooled. The Vietcong assured the people that the sun would rise in the West before the government returned.

In January 1966, as the 1st Cavalry Division prepared to challenge that promise, the sun was unlikely to show from any direction. The southwest monsoon, which dumped up to an inch of rain per day, had passed. But the weather had shifted to the northeast, bringing a season of *crachin*, from the French word for "spit." A constant drizzle that could lighten to a mist or fall more heavily, *crachin* drifted down from slate gray clouds seldom higher than 3,000 feet. Visibility usually extended no more than three miles.

In the early morning hours, low stratus clouds dropped below a 1,000-foot ceiling, and the fog that resulted lifted slowly, dissipating by middle-to-late morning. Frequently, the fog persisted in the valleys, obscuring mountain ridges and peaks and creating perilous flying conditions.

For an airmobile infantry division that went to war through the air and protected itself with gunships and jets, the *crachin* often seemed an ally of the enemy. With tactical air support and gunships at times grounded or restricted, artillery, which provided the protective umbrella for infantry, was to assume a great importance. But rapid movement and emplacement of artillery batteries were themselves dependent on airmobility and decent weather, and some infantry deployments had to be delayed until the weather lifted enough for helicopters to bring artillery batteries forward. From a tactical standpoint, such caution was unavoidable. "Against that enemy firepower was our advantage," Colonel Moore explained. "To send infantry without artillery cover is to fight on the enemy's terms."

Staging the operation

On January 25, a gray and rainy Tuesday morning following the three-day Tet holiday, the soldiers of the 3d Brigade gathered their gear, weapons, and ammunition and began to move by highway and air to staging areas in eastern Binh Dinh Province. The day—"D minus three," or three days before the first blows of Operation Masher—got off to an inauspicious start.

The 2d Battalion, 7th Cavalry assembled on the An Khe airstrip just after morning chow to board a dozen C-123 transports for the ride to Bong Son. With about 80 percent of its assigned strength, the battalion totaled some 600 men. The first planes departed at 7:20 A.M., rising into the 300-foot cloud cover that shrouded the mountain peaks. One C-123, carrying 42 men—riflemen and mortarmen from Company A—had risen through the clouds above the mountain top when, for some unknown reason, it turned at a forty-five-

degree angle in the fog, lost altitude, and crashed into the mountain slope with a tremendous explosion. Intense flames ignited the plane's load of mortar rounds and grenades, and the rescuers who arrived at the scene within minutes had to keep their distance from the spraying shrapnel. After fifteen minutes, the ammunition stopped popping and rescuers were able to extinguish the fire. Every soldier and the four crew members had died. "The bodies were badly torn. It was not as bad to get killed on the battlefield, if one had to," observed Lieutenant Colonel Kenneth Mertel, whose men of the 1st Battalion, 8th Cavalry, took charge of the grim scene.

The other combat troops, maintenance platoons, and support personnel departed An Khe in truck convoys beginning at 8:00 A.M., driving east on the worn, potholed blacktop of Highway 19. The road ran flat atop the plateau of the central highlands and then dropped steeply toward the coastal plain, winding down through a narrow defile called the An Khe Pass. Huey gunships and OH-13 Scout helicopters (with plastic bubble cockpits) of the 1/9 Cav squadron reconnoitered ahead of the convoy and along both sides of the road, searching for potential ambushes.

The convoys drove some sixty kilometers to establish a forward supply base at Phu Cat on Highway 1, about forty-five kilometers south of Bong Son. Trying to convey the impression of establishing an area of operations well to the south of Bong Son, the 1st Battalion, 7th Cavalry, conducted wide-ranging search and destroy patrols for three days in that vicinity. Korean troops secured the Phu Cat base while ARVN troops patrolled Highway 1 north toward Bong Son. The 2d Battalion, 12th Cavalry, also came to Phu Cat.

Meanwhile, the 2d Battalion, 7th Cavalry, which had arrived at Bong Son, moved by helicopter to secure a wide, flat plain adjacent to Highway 1 as a landing zone. Called LZ Dog, it was located five kilometers north of Bong Son, and thus five kilometers closer to the projected Phase I area of operations. Division engineers rapidly began construction of an airstrip capable of handling C-123 transports. Artillerymen also arrived at Dog to set up battery of 155MM howitzers, with a range of 14.6 kilometers, which they trained toward the north.

One outfit that operated as a matter of course beyond the artillery umbrella was the Special Forces Project Delta, an elite U.S./South Vietnamese long-range reconnaissance group. In existence since late 1964, Project Delta had already earned acclaim from General Westmoreland for its ability to operate in enemy territory and provide firsthand intelligence on enemy positions and movements. Reconnaissance was an integral part of every operation, and before each large unit had its own men trained for long-range reconnaissance patrols (LRRPs), or "lurps," the job often fell to Project Delta.

To coordinate plans, Colonel Moore met at Bong Son with Delta commander Major Charles Beckwith. In six months as commander, "Chargin'" Charlie Beckwith had overseen twenty-five operations, and in order to know what to expect of his men, the fiery officer had himself led some of the operations. He had been at the head of the South Vietnamese Rangers who reinforced the besieged camp at Plei Me at the start of the Ia Drang campaign. Yet Beckwith's very impetuosity had contributed to his nickname. As one Special Forces colleague described him, "Charlie would always make the objective even if he had to go through the wall. Somebody else might go over the wall, or around it."

Colonel Hal Moore, *commander of the 3d Brigade, 1st Cavalry Division, which spearheaded Operation Masher. After the battle of LZ X-Ray in the Ia Drang campaign, Moore became known as "the man who can find the Vietcong."*

Moore and Beckwith agreed that the Delta recon teams would reconnoiter in the An Lao Valley, well to the northwest of the 3d Brigade's assaults. Because the Vietnamese soldiers in Project Delta were currently "standing down" for retraining and were unavailable for assignment, only Americans were on the Delta teams for this mission. The plan called for helicopters to insert them just before dark on the eve of the operation. If the Delta teams located the enemy, the Cav planned to insert a reaction force. "We can find the enemy if they're out there," Major Beckwith said. "If you find them, we'll come up and kill them," Colonel Moore answered.

Hammer and anvil

D-day for Operation Masher arrived on January 28, 1966, a dreary, wet Friday. The ARVN 22d and Korean Capital divisions tightened their holds over Highways 1 and 19, and the ARVN Airborne Brigade set out on search and destroy patrols in villages between Highway 1 and the coast northeast of Bong Son. Meanwhile, in the coordinated Double Eagle action, 4,000 marines stormed the beaches of southern Quang Ngai Province, just north of the Binh Dinh line. The marines were to link up with the Cav in two weeks for Phase II—the thrust into the An Lao Valley. Although Masher was to last for nearly six weeks and fall into four phases, it was Phase I, the few days during which the 3d Brigade encountered a North Vietnamese regiment and inflicted nearly half of the total U.S.-caused enemy casualties for the whole operation, that set the pattern, in tactics and the nature of the fighting, for the other phases.

The main push on D-day came from Moore's 3d Brigade assaulting north of Bong Son and LZ Dog, even though a light rain and gray, swirling, misty fog hampered helicopter movements and all but canceled tactical air support for the day. The weather threatened to frustrate the plan, which was to search for enemy units on the southern end of the Bong Son Plain and insert potential blocking forces farther north as the day progressed. Company B of the 1st Battalion, 7th Cavalry, landed at a point called LZ Papa, near the village of Luong Tho, to guard a CH-47 Chinook that had been shot down while transporting in a sling beneath it a 105MM howitzer. That company ran into scattered mortar and small arms fire, but it was quickly suppressed by artillery. The remainder of the battalion then moved by helicopter into LZ Papa. The 1st Battalion encountered harassing fire but few enemy soldiers. For the 2d Battalion, devastated at LZ Albany two months earlier and now filled out with many replacements, D-day was a radically different experience.

Southeast of LZ Papa, Lieutenant Colonel Robert A. McDade, 2/7 commander, sent two companies into landing zones that were three kilometers apart and separated by villages, rice fields, and a large cemetery. McDade ordered them to sweep the villages and link up. Company A, understrength at two rifle platoons because of the C-123 crash three days earlier, landed without opposition in an area designated LZ 2 and marched north through the paddies.

Company C dropped onto a sandy plain called LZ 4, surrounded on three sides by the hamlets and paddies of Phung Du Village. Each hamlet was a labyrinth of sorts, ringed by palm trees and fences, hedgerows and bamboo shrubs, and rice fields with their levees and dikes. To the south of Phung Du Village lay a large cemetery, with grave sites marked by rounded hillocks. To avoid hits on the village close to the LZ, no artillery had been laid down prior to the landing.

Rifle fire harassed helicopters carrying the lead elements of Company C as they approached LZ 4. Rather than use the "hot" landing zone, the remaining helicopters dropped their men slightly to the south, setting down the troops in four locations stretching over a kilometer. This proved to be a major blunder. As the company tried to regroup on the flat plain, enemy machine guns joined the rifle fire, and mortar rounds began to fall on the Americans. Entrenched in fortifications around the

landing zone, North Vietnamese soldiers had Company C pinned down in a crossfire. Watching his mortar platoon leader and radio operator fall, Captain John Fesmire radioed, "We're in a hornets' nest!" In a matter of minutes, U.S. killed and wounded stretched the length of the landing zone.

Despite concerns about civilians and refugees, the company called in artillery on enemy positions. One lieutenant, his leg smashed by machine-gun fire, lay against a hillock with his radio and guided the artillery men by the sound of exploding shells. But with the men of Company C so spread out, and their coordinates uncertain, only a limited number of shells could be fired without endangering the pinned-down Americans. Staff Sergeant William Guyer, who had taken over the mortar platoon, found himself and his men under fire from a machine gun. Guyer had a mortar tube and six rounds but no base plate or plotting board. Propping the tube in the sand, Guyer fired five of the rounds and watched them explode harmlessly. He adjusted the tube and kissed the last round before firing it. As it sped on its way, Guyer took a machine-gun bullet in the head and died instantly. Although he never saw it happen, the last round Guyer launched destroyed the machine gun.

Under intense enemy fire, *members of the 2d Battalion, 7th Cavalry, sprint past burial mounds in the village cemetery of Phung Du in Binh Dinh Province.*

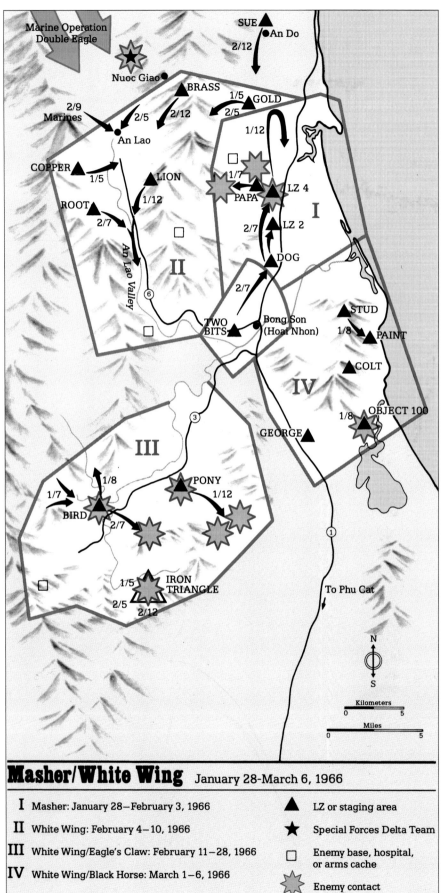

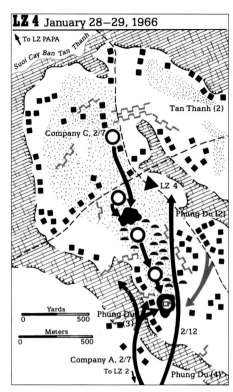

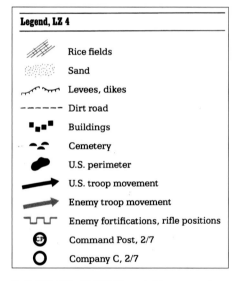

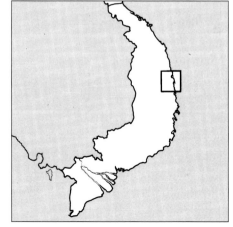

Masher/White Wing January 28-March 6, 1966

I Masher: January 28–February 3, 1966
II White Wing: February 4–10, 1966
III White Wing/Eagle's Claw: February 11–28, 1966
IV White Wing/Black Horse: March 1–6, 1966

▲ LZ or staging area
★ Special Forces Delta Team
☐ Enemy base, hospital, or arms cache
✶ Enemy contact

LZ 4 January 28–29, 1966

Legend, LZ 4

Rice fields
Sand
Levees, dikes
Dirt road
Buildings
Cemetery
U.S. perimeter
U.S. troop movement
Enemy troop movement
Enemy fortifications, rifle positions
CP Command Post, 2/7
O Company C, 2/7

South of the cemetery, Company A continued to move up without opposition until it reached the rice field immediately southwest of the landing zone. As the point squad waded into the paddy, enemy soldiers let loose with automatic weapons. The 2d Platoon put down a covering base of rifle fire, enabling the 1st Platoon to crawl across the paddy. The 1st Platoon then returned the favor, covering as soldiers of the 2d Platoon inched their way across under heavy fire, some of them struggling to carry casualties.

Once in the cemetery, the soldiers of Company A tried to consolidate. Some took refuge in a large trench that formed one side of a paddy dike. Others gouged out foxholes in the sand. One squad, roused by Sergeant William Bercaw, fixed bayonets and started to charge a machine-gun position in a line of palm trees. "I thought the shock effect of a well-determined force would turn the tables," said Bercaw, who was seeing his first combat. Moving evasively, the men rushed fifty meters and flopped in the sand close to the wood line, but they were summoned back by officers in the trench who had decided to call artillery on the position instead. Obeying orders, Bercaw told the men that he would cover their retreat by firing his M16 on automatic. He got to his knees and fired magazine after magazine toward the machine gun as tracers and bullets flew. His canteen got shot off, a slug creased his jungle boot, another passed under his chin and tore off the "D" ring holding his helmet strap. He fired eight magazines in all on full automatic, and to his astonishment, the enemy machine gun ceased firing. Bercaw hurried back, as his men provided covering fire. "I had a duel with an enemy machine gun," declared Bercaw, "and I won." Bercaw also won a Bronze Star for his actions that day.

In midafternoon battalion commander Lt. Col. McDade landed at the edge of the paddy behind the Company A position and made his way to the trench. "Every time you raised your head, it was zap, zap," said McDade. "The dirt really flew." A short time later, artillery units laid down a barrage of high explosives and a smoke screen, under cover of which six helicopters dropped into LZ 4 carrying reinforcements from Company B, which had been at LZ Papa. All six helicopters took hits; two were driven off. One platoon managed to jump off but its men found themselves in a heavy crossfire between U.S. and enemy positions, and they scrambled to get inside what passed for a U.S. perimeter. Those who made it could do little more than dig in. Heavy enemy fire continued. For the Americans, all maneuver had ceased. The 2d Battalion was stuck and effectively cut off. Worse, Company C was still scattered and isolated north of the cemetery.

Breaking out of LZ 4

Hal Moore was furious. His D-day offensive had bogged down in the white sand of LZ 4, and he'd seen no effective maneuver to regroup Company C and attack the enemy. He raised McDade on the radio. "I told him in no uncertain terms to get that landing zone cleared up, get that battalion organized, and get moving," Colonel Moore said. "I let him know I was very displeased with what was going on." At the same time, Moore recognized the difficulty of accomplishing that goal, and as night fell, he told the 2d Battalion, 12th Cavalry, to get ready to relieve LZ 4 in the morning.

Rain fell heavily during the night, and the wind picked up to fifteen miles per hour. Visibility closed to little more than 200 meters. The remnants of Company C, spread out over several hundred meters, took advantage of darkness to regroup. Beneath artillery fire, some of the men from Company A crawled the length of the cemetery to find the Company C stragglers and lead them back to the perimeter on their bellies, as the tracers of scattered sniper fire passed over their backs. The link-up was completed at 4:30 A.M.

In the morning the bad weather lifted slowly, permitting tac air—propeller-driven A-1 Skyraiders and B-57 Canberra bombers—to strike with bombs and napalm at enemy positions on the east of the landing zone. The first of three air strikes hit at 9:00 A.M., and artillery pounded the same area between sorties. At 10:45 two rifle companies of the 2d Battalion, 12th Cavalry— some 200 men—accompanied by Colonel Moore and his sergeant major, Basil Plumley, landed in a knee-deep paddy to the south and advanced northeast. They splashed through two paddies without opposition until they reached the edge of the cemetery. Then the NVA opened up, and the 2/12 returned fire.

Just shy of LZ 4, Moore's problems accumulated with an urgent radio call from his operations officer in Bong Son. The Special Forces Delta teams in the An Lao Valley had found the enemy—in force. Contrary to his bold assurances about inserting blocking forces into the valley, Moore had no reaction force available. The Delta teams had found the enemy too soon, before the Cav could move. Moore's brigade was pinned down on the Bong Son Plain. Instead of mounting an attack, Moore tried to organize a rescue. By radio, he directed the 1/9 Cavalry Squadron to locate the teams and extract them. He also sent Company A of the 1st Battalion, 7th Cavalry, to prepare an artillery position in the hills east of the valley and alerted the reserve battalion at Phu Cat—the 1/12—to prepare to move once artillery was emplaced. For the decimated Delta teams, however, only the rescue mattered any longer.

With the North Vietnamese and Vietcong in complete control of the An Lao Valley, the Delta teams had found no room to maneuver and their reconnaissance mission turned into disaster. One team had already been pulled out and a second had encountered three enemy patrols. In a series of firefights, three of six Americans were killed. With the three survivors on the run, the bodies had to be left and were never recovered. The last team of six men, spotted by a woodcutter shortly after infiltration, was ambushed and four men died. Although wounded, the two survivors, with the help of helicopter gunships, managed to keep the enemy at bay. Flying to the scene in his command helicopter, Major Beckwith was wounded by ground fire. Of the seventeen Green Berets who volunteered for the Project Delta

mission, seven were killed and three wounded, confirming what was already known—the enemy held the An Lao Valley.

Colonel Moore and Sergeant Major Plumley continued on to the cemetery at LZ 4 as soldiers from the 2/12 exchanged fire with NVA soldiers on the east flank. Moore and Plumley passed the trench filled with wounded American soldiers, some Vietnamese women and children, and ammunition and ration boxes. Beyond the cemetery and along the length of LZ 4 lay bodies of American soldiers. Moore met with Lt. Col. McDade for the latest reports. After they had conferred, Colonel Moore moved about the battlefield despite the heavy fire, organizing the troops for an attack on the enemy positions. "You can't do

With one comrade dead and another wounded, *four men from Company A's 2d Platoon wait for a letup in enemy firing before attempting to carry the wounded man to safety across a bullet-swept paddy southwest of LZ 4.*

your job in a damn trench," Moore snapped. "The Old Man was not pleased," Plumley recounted. "We moved around. We talked to the men. They weren't in too deep spirits although they had lost quite a few men. The biggest thing they needed was leadership and guidance to move them out of there."

Moore led the two companies of the 2/12 against the fortified enemy positions on the right flank. Originally at least a company of NVA soldiers had manned the trenches. But many of them had decamped and fled north during the night, leaving behind a platoon, planted in the artful network of fortifications, to slow the American pursuit. After some delays to uproot machine gunners, the 2/12 cleared the trenches and swept the hamlets of Phung Du Village.

North of LZ 4, Companies B and C of the 1st Battalion, 7th Cavalry, searched for any fleeing North Vietnamese. In midafternoon, they clashed with a dug-in North Vietnamese force estimated at three platoons. The fight lasted two hours, with the Americans calling in artillery, tactical air support, and helicopter gunships, before the enemy broke contact and withdrew. The blocking action of the 1/7 throughout the day accounted for forty-four enemy dead.

As darkness fell on Operation Masher's second day, the 1st Battalion, 7th Cavalry, moved a kilometer north of its battle site and bivouacked for the night. The 2/7 and 2/12

Driven back. *The enemy resumed firing as soon as the Company A men waded into the paddy, so they rush back toward cover. They finally evacuated the wounded soldier on their third try.*

Refusing evacuation to tend the wounded *at LZ 4, PFC medic Thomas Cole (right) ministers to Staff Sergeant Harrison Pell, shot beneath the ear. Both men recovered from their wounds.*

settled in for the night along the length of LZ 4 and the cemetery that they finally held. Colonel Moore bedded down in the field with McDade's men. "Those troops were pretty shook up," he said, "and I felt my presence would help their morale and self-confidence."

Combat support

On its third day Operation Masher began to unfold as planned, as the brigade set about combing through the paddies and villages, trying to trap remnants of the enemy battalion between attacking and blocking forces. Companies A and C of the 2/7, so battered for two days at LZ 4, swept north out of their cemetery bivouac at 7:30 A.M. on January 30. The relieving battalion, the 2/12, marched on the east flank in par-

allel formation. In one hamlet of Tan Thanh Village, just a kilometer north of LZ 4, they located an enemy company ensconced in what Colonel Moore called "a rat's nest of trenches and bunkers and spider holes."

Artillery and tac air pounded the enemy positions, and then the infantry moved through the hamlet yard by yard, firing rifles and machine guns and throwing hand grenades. Some 100 meters from the trenches, the two battalions split to stage a double envelopment maneuver. Some enemy soldiers bolted from the trenches and the Americans cut them down. Gunships

Weary and wounded soldiers *from Company C rest in a trench to escape the grazing fire of North Vietnamese automatic weapons. For battlefield identification, Company C soldiers painted circles on camouflage cloth of helmets; Company A used triangles.*

flying over the scene tracked down others. In spite of heavy fire from the trenches, the Americans suffered light casualties.

The 1st Battalion, 7th Cavalry, kept on the move northwest of LZ 4, shuttling between landing zones and patrolling on foot to intercept the withdrawing enemy. Late in the day of January 31, Company A encountered a reinforced enemy company in a hamlet of Luong Tho Village, and a furious firefight broke out. For over an hour the fight raged at distances too close to allow artillery or air support. Companies B and C from the 1/7 fought their way toward the village and provided enough fire to allow Company A to pull back its wounded far enough so that artillery and air support could be called in safely just before darkness fell.

Company A commander Captain Ramon ("Tony") Nadal had a dozen seriously wounded men. As darkness approached, Nadal reached Colonel Moore on the radio and requested a medical evacuation helicopter. But a night landing in a hot LZ, located in the center of a hamlet, had a negligible chance of succeeding. Moore told Nadal there would be no medevac until morning.

In his UH-1D helicopter, Major Bruce Crandall, commander of Company A, 229th Assault Helicopter Battalion, heard snatches of the conversation between Nadal and Moore. Crandall had to fly one more short mission to the north of Bong Son before he could park his Huey for the night, and out of curiosity he detoured over Luang Tho hoping to catch a glimpse of the stranded company.

As Crandall returned to base, Nadal raised him on the radio. The two were friends, and each had distinguished himself at the battle of LZ X-Ray, Nadal with his rifle company and Crandall flying in desperately needed supplies and evacuating numerous wounded. "Serpent 6, this is Firechief 6," Nadal called. "Do you read me? I got serious problems." "So what's new, Tony?" Crandall responded. "Every time you call me, it's trouble." Nadal explained the situation, and Crandall agreed to give it a try. After he refueled in the dark at Bong Son, the group commander came on the radio network and told him that he didn't have to go. Crandall acknowledged that the mission was voluntary. He had confidence that if he crashed, Nadal's men would cover and rescue him. At 7:30, lifting into the night sky without lights, Crandall proceeded north.

As the helicopter arrived over the hamlet, Nadal, carrying his flashlight and radio, crawled into the tiny landing zone, surrounded by palm trees and brush. The LZ was so small that Crandall would have to descend and ascend vertically, instead of approaching at an angle on the helicopter's normal glide slope. Such a vertical descent and ascent was possible only with a light load. Hunkering down as low as he could, Nadal turned on the flashlight and began to talk the pilot down. Tracer bullets flew across the pitch-dark landing zone.

Crandall couldn't see the trees. Or the LZ. He nudged the stick softly toward the needle of light that kept going dark as the NVA fired at it. Crandall heard Nadal talking, easing him down, bravely failing to mention the enemy fire that forced him to shut off the light and scramble a few yards away before flicking it on again. Peering down into the darkness, Crandall wished he could shine his search lights for just an instant to fix the trees. But that would allow the enemy to sight their aimless fire. He was almost down now. The light was close. As Company A laid down a tremendous base of suppressing fire, the helicopter, with the chop of its rotor adding to the roar, settled and hovered and touched down.

Men raced to the helicopter with the most seriously wounded. Because of the weight restrictions on the vertical ascent, Crandall could take but a half dozen. The loading consumed five minutes, as the firing continued, and then Crandall lifted off. "Coming out was tough because I had to pull up and take those people out without any forward movement," he said. The helicopter cleared the trees and banked south.

Crandall delivered the casualties to Bong Son, but the job was only half done. He returned to Luong Tho. Following the same procedure, he descended for the remaining casualties. This time everyone knew what to do and it went more quickly. Crandall spent perhaps two or three minutes on the hot LZ before getting out. Later he explained his heroism (he did not call it that but it earned him a Distinguished Flying Cross) in terms of mutual respect. "You always had great confidence in the infantry," he said. "You supported those guys as well as they supported you."

The day's combat had cost the 1st Battalion 13 men killed and 33 wounded. But the 1/7 had inflicted greater losses on the enemy, having counted 67 bodies, with another 100 estimated killed by artillery and tac air. The attacking and blocking tactics, made possible by air mobility, were proving effective.

Closing out Phase I

Contact with the enemy diminished in the first two days of February as the North Vietnamese continued their withdrawal to the north and west, slipping from hamlet to hamlet at night and during spells of bad weather that grounded reconnaissance aircraft. Some enemy soldiers were spotted near the village of An Do, fourteen kilometers north of LZ 4, near the province and corps boundary. The 2d Battalion, 12th Cavalry, flew to a clearing called LZ Sue, directly above An Do. They swept south but made no contact. There were reports also of a column of

North Vietnamese wounded, some carried on stretchers, heading west for a field hospital believed to be located in the hills above the An Lao Valley.

As contact with the enemy decreased, the battalions returned to their forward bases, and the 3d Brigade declared an end to the first, Bong Son Plain, phase of Operation Masher. In a week of combat, the Americans had killed 603 enemy soldiers by body count and estimated that an additional 755 had been killed as well. The brigade had lost 77 American soldiers killed on the battlefield and 42 in the C-123 crash. "Two battalions of the Quyet Tam [NVA 22d] Regiment, 7th and 9th, plus unidentified support element, were rendered ineffective as a result of Operation Masher," read the division report, adding, overoptimistically as it turned out, "The long-range results of loss of equipment, personnel, and prestige will be difficult to overcome."

The explosive battles against the entrenched enemy had necessarily ravaged the hamlets and villages, transforming many civilians into refugees. Women, children, and old men (males from teen-age years to late middle age were conspicuously absent) congregated around landing zones and battalion bivouacs, looking for shelter or transportation and scavenging for food. Their presence raised fears of sabotage by Vietcong sympathizers traveling among them. "We've been fired at by women many times," one soldier remarked. The number of refugees in Bong Son swelled to nearly 16,000 by the end of the operation. With no place else to go, as many as 12,000 additional war victims simply moved to Highway 1 and squatted there. Vietnamese and U.S. military and civilian agencies established medical aid stations and distribution points for captured enemy stores, especially rice and salt.

General Kinnard now moved the division's 2d Brigade under Colonel William A. Lynch, Jr., from An Khe to Bong Son to join Moore's brigade in the next phase of Operation Masher—an assault into the An Lao Valley. Several days had elapsed since the Special Forces Delta teams had inadvertently confirmed the enemy presence there. Although the North Vietnamese might have anticipated the operation from the reconnaissance activity and might therefore have fled the valley, the division had other indications that the enemy remained. Reconnaissance aircraft still drew hostile fire, for example, and the headquarters of the Sao Vang Division was believed to be located in the high ground north of the valley.

The assault was set for February 4 but had to be delayed until low clouds lifted off the mountains. When the assault took place, it carried a new name—Operation White Wing. Masher had garnered widespread press coverage at the very moment that Commander in Chief Lyndon Johnson was convening a conference in Honolulu that focused expressly on pacification programs. With the presidential emphasis currently on "nation-building" rather than the military aspects of the war, he bristled at the metaphorical military nomenclature. "I don't know who names your operations," he groused, "but 'Masher?' I get kind of mashed myself."

Word of the commander in chief's ire flashed to Vietnam, and the startled military officers, stung by the application of public relations to the business of war, began kicking about inoffensive titles. One cynic suggested "White Wing"—for the wings of the dove of peace. The name was sarcastic enough to catch on.

Operation White Wing

On February 7 four battalions landed on high elevations above the An Lao Valley and began to march down the mountain slopes to the valley floor. U.S. Marine units from Double Eagle and ARVN troops operated at the northern end of the valley, and an ARVN battalion blocked the southern exits. The three-day sweep was, in infantry jargon, "a walk in the sun." The enemy had evaporated. Their absence mystified the Americans, who discovered an extraordinary system of trenches and fortifications, along with elaborate traps and fields of punji-stakes. "The Charlies could have held us up here for days with one company," admitted Major Frank Henry, executive officer of the 2/7 Cavalry. "We would have had to wait until their ammunition ran out or our bombs flattened the jungle." U.S. officers doubted that such large enemy units could have evaded the intelligence and reconnaissance networks set out to locate them. Some speculated that the enemy had fled into the

nearly impenetrable mountains to the west and was hiding in caves there. A few enemy soldiers remained behind as a rear guard, however, and in several brief encounters the Americans killed eleven of them.

About half of the villagers in the valley asked to leave the VC-controlled area. In Chinooks overflowing with refuges, livestock, and some personal belongings, the division flew 3,491 people out of the valley and down to Bong Son refugee camps.

The third phase of Operation Masher/White Wing—an assault by the 3d Brigade into the Eagle's Claw area—proved far more successful. With the approval of General Kinnard, Colonel Moore reversed the tactics used in the An Lao Valley by emplacing artillery onto the floor of the Kim Son Valley and by sending infantry patrols through the canyons as "beaters" to flush the enemy into ambushes set along the likely escape routes.

On February 11 Lt. Col. Robert McDade's 2d Battalion, 7th Cavalry, landed at LZ Bird in the hub of the valley and routed first a Vietcong platoon, then a company that had moved in to assist the platoon. By midafternoon the area surrounding Bird had been secured, and an artillery battery arrived. Then, with their men carrying provisions to last forty-eight hours, other combat units landed in the valleys that radiated out from LZ Bird and set up ambush positions.

The 2/7 embarked on search and destroy operations the following morning, and although the companies encountered little resistance, they discovered caches containing weapons, ammunition, and grenades. Troops in their ambush position, meanwhile, began to snare enemy units on the run, and over the next two days the combination of ambushes, pursuit, and supporting artillery accounted for more than 200 enemy dead. In addition, Company A of the 1st Battalion, 12th Cavalry, located a base camp consisting of a hospital, mess hall, and hand grenade factory that contained two tons of scrap metal, fuses, and explosives.

Documents found on the body of one dead Vietcong soldier indicated the current location of a Main Force battalion —the 93d Battalion, 2d Vietcong Regiment—near the village of Hon Mot, in a valley unoccupied by brigade ambush forces. Moving hastily, Lt. Col. McDade sent two companies into the valley on February 15, and Captain Myron Diduryk's 120-man Company B ran into a Vietcong force, estimated as a reinforced platoon, entrenched near the village. "Unknown at this time," Captain Diduryk wrote in his report, "was the fact that the enemy consisted of two Main Force companies." To soften up the enemy fortifications, Diduryk called in firepower that included artillery from LZ Bird, mortar fire from the company mortar platoon, gunships, and air support from U.S. Air Force A-1 Skyraiders dropping cluster bombs. Diduryk meanwhile outlined a traditional infantry assault plan to his men.

As soon as the aircraft had passed, the men of the third platoon, with bayonets fixed, bounded forward, ultimately running and, said one soldier, yelling "like mad men." The assault scattered the more numerous enemy soldiers and some of them fled north—into the supporting fires of the 2d Platoon. Other enemy soldiers withdrew to the south and southeast. Company B's 1st Platoon, which had been acting as the reserve, joined in the pursuit, catching the Vietcong command group and capturing the wounded battalion commander, Lieutenant Colonel Dong Doan. Overall, Company B killed fifty-seven enemy soldiers while suffering two killed and six wounded.

In addition to having scored a significant tactical success, Diduryk's company had delivered an important Vietcong prisoner to the interrogators. "He was hard core," said Colonel Moore of the thirty-seven-year-old commander who had been fighting as a Vietminh and Vietcong since 1949. "He told me that day, 'You will never win.'" In spite of his belligerence, however, Doan was not unwilling to discuss his battalion's tactics and recent operations, and the division intelligence staff was able to pinpoint the probable location of a regimental headquarters in the mountains a few kilometers to the south. At this point the 1st Brigade of the 1st Cavalry Division, under Colonel Elvy B. Roberts, replaced Moore's weary men, who flew back to the An Khe Division base they had departed twenty-two days earlier.

While the 1st Brigade took over patrolling in the valleys around LZ Bird, the three battalions (1/5, 2/5, 2/12) of Colonel Lynch's 2d Brigade encircled the regimental headquarters in the rugged mountains and began to close in. The elaborate enemy defenses earned the region a nickname, the "iron triangle," borrowed from the forbidding Vietcong stronghold north of Saigon. Aided by artillery and air support, the three battalions continued fighting for four days against a tena-

Sky cavalry. *UH-1D helicopters (called "slicks") approach a landing zone in the Kim Son Valley to pick up 1st Cav soldiers during the Eagle's Claw phase of Masher/White Wing.*

cious enemy defense that finally collapsed after a B-52 strike.

In the iron triangle battles, the Americans killed 313 enemy while losing 23 of their own killed. Overall, the two-week Eagle's Claw-iron triangle phase of Masher/White Wing accounted for 709 enemy soldiers killed, with an equal number estimated killed. A great quantity of enemy materiel had also been seized.

By contrast, the final phase of the operation was brief and anticlimactic. The move into the jungle-covered Cay Giep Mountains between Bong Son and the South China Sea commenced March 1. Air force bombers blasted openings in the thick jungle canopy, permitting engineer teams to descend on rope ladders from hovering Chinook helicopters in order to hack out landing zones for the 2d Brigade. By the time the troops had disembarked and swept down slopes of the Cay Giep Mountains, however, the enemy had fled. According to local peasants, the 6th Battalion of the NVA 18th Regiment had been in the area, departing to the south two days before the Americans arrived. But apparently unknown to the North Vietnamese, the ARVN 22d Division had set up blocking positions in the lowlands to the south. These units clashed with the withdrawing enemy soldiers, killing fifty of them and capturing thirty.

The 2d Brigade spent several more days leapfrogging around the mountains in search of any remaining enemy units. But when the patrols in the fourth and final quadrant proved futile, the operation was declared closed on March 6, after forty-one days.

"So far as is now known …"

By all tactical measures, Operation Masher/White Wing had been a pronounced military success. With the destruction of the North Vietnamese 3d Division as its objective, the 1st Cav had proceeded to kill 1,342 enemy soldiers (with another 1,700 estimated killed), while losing 228 American soldiers killed and 788 wounded. ARVN and Korean troops had killed 808 enemy soldiers, to bring known overall enemy casualties to 2,150.

The 1st Cavalry Division had once again made effective use of airmobility and firepower. Helicopters airlifted entire infantry battalions a total of seventy-eight times and moved artillery batteries fifty-five times. Artillery fired a total of 133,191 rounds. The division also refined its use and coordination of firepower. Lieutenant Colonel Kenneth Mertel, commander of the 1st Battalion, 8th Cavalry, described one instance in which two of his infantry companies advanced behind a wall of perfectly coordinated, devastating firepower:

> C Company, on the left portion of the zone to the west, employed tactical air power, conducting air strikes close to their positions, as the company moved forward. In addition, C Company mortars … were

firing to the right side of the sector. In the B Company area … further to the east, tube artillery was falling. In between the B Company and the artillery and mortar targets of C Company, gunships provided firepower for a patrol working in that area. Thus within the same battalion zone, in an area 2,000 meters wide, simultaneously there was an air strike … mortar firing, tube artillery fire falling, and gunships in operation.

In forty-one days of contact, the Cav had clashed with all three regiments of the Sao Vang Division and claimed to have rendered five of nine enemy battalions ineffective for combat. In addition, the Cav had destroyed a mortar and recoilless rifle company of the Quyet Thang (NVA 18th) Regiment, the anti-aircraft company and signal company of the Sao Vang Division, and had seized three field hospitals. General Kinnard did not stint in his praise, rating the division's performance "at least 50 percent better than in our other long campaign in [the Ia Drang]. And we emerged from these forty-one days of sustained combat in far better shape than we ended our thirty-eight days of combat in [the Ia Drang]."

In accordance with U.S. strategy, Operation Masher had been mounted on the supposition that once the enemy forces' base areas had been destroyed by U.S. combat troops, the ARVN and Regional and Popular Forces would secure the countryside, and civilian agencies would institute pacification programs among the 140,000 Vietnamese "freed from VC domination." Stated General Kinnard's after-action report: "So far as is now known, the GVN [government of South Vietnam] intends to re-establish civil government in this area."

But in fact there had been little coordination at the command levels to insure any continuity between the military and pacification efforts. During the An Lao Valley sweep, a reporter had asked Colonel Moore about the coming crucial stages of pacification.

"I don't know what will happen next," Moore answered. "It's not my business. I'm a soldier and my job is to beat the enemy."

"Isn't it possible the Vietcong will reinfiltrate its old settlements after the U.S. troops leave?" the reporter persisted.

"It's possible," Moore admitted, "if the government doesn't really succeed in taking over. …"

It was more than possible. The South Vietnamese government was ill-equipped to carry out the functions of security and pacification. And before a week had passed after the conclusion of Operation Masher/White Wing, 1st Cav intelligence detected signs of enemy soldiers filtering back into the An Lao Valley and the Bong Son Plain. The Americans were finding that, in Vietnam, the fighting was not over when the shooting stopped.

The War on Canvas

"Untitled" by Pete Peterson

Peterson served with the 4th Psychological Operations Group, Headquarters Company, in 1970-1971. The group's headquarters was in Saigon, but Peterson was assigned to all areas of South Vietnam.

"Battery Adjust" by Leonard H. Dermott

Dermott joined the marines in 1965 and was an artillery officer before he became a combat artist in 1967. As a combat artist he was based in Da Nang. Dermott was discharged in 1967, having been awarded a Bronze Star with combat V.

"Thuong Duc Special Forces" by Barry W. Johnston

Johnston served in Vietnam from August to December 1968, as a combat artist for the army. He was attached to headquarters, Commandant Section, III Infantry.

"The Count" by Michael Kelley

Kelley was in I Corps from November 1969 through September 1970, with the 1st Battalion of the 502d Infantry, 101st Airborne Division.

"That's My Boy" by Michael Kelley

"Westy and Friend" by Michael Kelley

"Gunship on the Attack" by John Plunkett

"Enemies Passing in the Rain" by John Plunkett

Plunkett was with the 25th Infantry Division based in Cu Chi in 1969.

"Ambush Behind Thin Wood Line" by John Plunkett

"Meeting Red Ants in Bamboo" by John Plunkett

"We needed fifty years to do what we wanted to do in Vietnam. We had to change the Vietnamese national character, and that would take, at a minimum, three generations."

Army Lieutenant Colonel Donald Marshall

On January 17, 1966, the United States Marine Corps commandant, General Wallace M. Greene, Jr., returned to Washington, D.C., from a thirteen-day tour of the war zone. His conversations with analysts and infantrymen throughout South Vietnam had all led him to the same somber conclusion. "You can kill every Vietcong and North Vietnamese soldier," declared General Greene, "and still lose the war." For he realized that winning the war required something more than the skillful tactics and lavish firepower that the American army had used against enemy soldiers in the battle of the Ia Drang, Operation Masher/White Wing, and many other military campaigns, and that the marines had displayed in Starlite and other operations. "The real target[s] in Vietnam," General Greene was convinced, "were not the VC and the North Vietnamese but the Vietnamese people."

Targeting the people

To achieve victory the United States had to find ways of encouraging and enabling the people of South Vietnam to support and defend the nation and its government. But the ordinary South Vietnamese citizen's concept of the Republic of Vietnam as a nation was not well developed. Established slightly more than a decade before, the nation was jeopardized constantly by disaffected political and religious groups, military coups, and the die-hard Communist insurgency. Moreover, the South Vietnamese people's notion of allegiance to a national govern-

*Women use **don ganh** (shoulder poles) to carry their goods down the main street of Loc Dien, a contested village south of Hue.*

ment was vague, for the focus of the rural peasants who comprised the majority of the population was on the family, the hamlet, and the village. In the fight for the people of South Vietnam, the task of the United States was to build a nation —or at least help the government of South Vietnam do so— in the midst of a war. The U.S. needed to show the people that the nation and the government were worthy of their loyalty. Often referred to as "the other war," sometimes known as "winning hearts and minds," this effort was commonly called pacification.

Pacification was perhaps the most difficult challenge for the South Vietnamese and their American allies. Never one thing precisely, pacification was instead many things—a variety of programs developed by South Vietnamese and Americans, independently or jointly, to drive the enemy away from the people, to bind the people to the nation, ultimately to end the war. Some pacification programs were planned and executed primarily by military forces; others were devised and carried out mostly by civilian agencies. Some were conducted exclusively by ARVN troops and GVN cadres; others involved American soldiers and civilians; still others linked South Vietnamese and Americans in a common effort. But for all its permutations and combinations, the purpose of pacification was to reduce the enemy's control of the population, especially in rural areas where the Communists so often prevailed, and to extend the presence and influence of the GVN. Emphases varied at different times, techniques differed at various places, but in general pacification involved two major elements. The first was the provision of physical security for the population, accomplished by destroying or neutralizing the enemy's military and political power. The second was the development of social welfare and economic programs to improve the people's standard of living and increase their support for the GVN.

In its broad outline the process of pacification integrated military operations and civilian projects and occurred ideally in three phases. First, friendly troops mounted an operation to clear enemy soldiers and political cadres from a populated area, thus separating the guerrilla "fish" from the "sea" of people they depended upon for supplies, taxes, and political support. In this phase pacification meant killing as many enemy as possible and making those who escaped unwilling to return. It was carried out by ARVN troops, U.S. Marines, or U.S. Army soldiers. In the second phase of pacification these troops set up bases and worked to prepare defense against enemy attacks in villages and hamlets. This phase of pacification was designed to enable the population to resist attempts by the enemy to return and regain control. Frequently this phase involved equipping and training Vietnamese paramilitary forces—the Regional Forces (RF) and Popular Forces (PF)—who were recruited from the local area and assigned to defend it. This phase also included efforts by forces such as the National Police to collect intelligence about the dispersed enemy and to locate any enemy soldiers or cadres remaining in the area. The third phase of pacification called for programs aimed at persuading the people to embrace the GVN and to work to increase its authority. GVN and U.S. officials visited the countryside to assess the needs and aspirations of the people. In turn, they devised welfare and economic programs, such as distribution of emergency food supplies to bridge reconstruction or the development of local industries.

Trial and error

As the American build-up in South Vietnam began no one knew exactly how to provide physical security and a better life for a society caught in the crossfire of war. Everett Bumgardner, then field operations director for the Joint U.S. Public Affairs Office (JUSPAO) in Saigon, remembered the period as a time of creative confusion. "Everybody was experimenting."

Americans and Vietnamese military and civilians tinkered with scores of pacification plans, trying to find workable formulas. Pentagon experts studied the pacification problem and shook their heads over its complexities. Marine enlisted men stationed among the dangerous, enemy-infested hamlets of I Corps improvised a succession of schemes to enable rural villagers to resist the Vietcong. Idealistic Vietnamese spread out from province and district capitals into the countryside, determined to show the people that their government cared about their welfare and was willing to share their hazards. American agricultural experts labored to boost farmers' crop production

and persuade them that their interests lay with the GVN and its ingenious American ally. U.S. Army officers assigned as province advisers to the Vietnamese armed forces prodded their counterparts to provide the security necessary for successful pacification efforts. In the years after the war, few historians of pacification, and few actors in its complex drama, agreed about what worked, what didn't, or even what took place.

The PROVN study

Army Chief of Staff General Harold K. Johnson said he was "a pacification guy right from the start." But General Johnson felt that the U.S. military needed more information about South Vietnam in order to know how best to meet U.S. objectives there. "I just kept getting answers that didn't fit," General Johnson said. In May 1965 he commissioned "the broadest possible" study of the situation in South Vietnam. The secret study, titled The Program for the Pacification and Long-Term Development of South Vietnam, became known as PROVN. It was undertaken by a host of military and civilian experts in social sciences, military operations, and military intelligence whose mandate was "developing new courses of action to be taken in South Vietnam by the United States and its allies."

All members of the core study group, with one exception, had served in Vietnam or Southeast Asia. Led by army Colonel Tom Hanifen, each pursued a specialized line of inquiry. Army Major Arthur Brown studied the history of the Vietnamese people, Lieutenant Colonel Harold Emmons and Major Anna Doering probed intelligence-gathering functions, and Lieutenant Colonel Volney Warner, a former adviser in the delta, analyzed the problem of "leverage"—how to squeeze results from U.S. investments of personnel and resources in pacification.

Lt. Col. Warner developed a list of questions that he submitted to over 400 current and former military and civilian advisers returning from South Vietnam's 43 provinces and many of its 258 districts. Warner's questions ran a gamut of political, economic, and military categories, from the Chieu Hoi (Open Arms) program, under which the GVN offered amnesty to Vietcong defectors and often enlisted them in its armed forces, to the relief aid distributed to province chiefs. The questionnaire encouraged each adviser to suggest steps for the U.S. to take to bring the war to a successful conclusion while leaving the Vietnamese with a viable government capable of meeting the needs of the people.

Army Lieutenant Colonel Donald Marshall, an anthropologist, traveled to South Vietnam to analyze the military situation there and to assess, by interviewing U.S. and GVN officials,

Caught in the struggle. *Children are kept behind barbed wire at a VC holding area near Bien Hoa during a U.S. search and destroy operation.*

Vietnamese civilians, ARVN officers, and U.S. military advisory teams, just how pacification was working. The field team's findings, which included an in-depth analysis of the situation in Hau Nghia Province, showed an overall lack of cohesion among American advisory efforts.

A fifty-year war?

Collected in March 1966, ten months after their inception, the PROVN reports stated that "'Victory' can be achieved only through bringing the individual Vietnamese, typically a rural peasant, to support willingly the government of South Vietnam (GVN)." The PROVN study group continued, "The critical actions are those that occur at the village, district, and provincial levels. This is where the war and the object that lies behind it must be won." In addition, the group found "no unified effective pattern" to U.S. efforts in South Vietnam. In gray bureau-

cratic prose, the study recommended 140 courses of action. These included reorganizing U.S. efforts under a single manager, decentralizing authority to the province level and below, instituting South Vietnamese civil service reform, authorizing and encouraging the use of resources as leverage, and redirecting the military effort to achieve greater security for the Vietnamese villager.

PROVN's recommendations were offered as a means of reversing the situation in South Vietnam, which it described as "seriously deteriorated." But some of the contributors held strong doubts about the chances for success in Vietnam. Warner felt that "The key was always that our 'foe' was an illegitimate, inept South Vietnamese government. No amount of bombs dropped on the North would likely bring into being in the South a government that was much better than the one we had." Marshall, who briefed the Joint Chiefs of Staff, told them, "We needed fifty years to do what we wanted to do in Vietnam.

We had to change the Vietnamese national character, and that would take, at a minimum, three generations."

The Joint Chiefs of Staff gave the PROVN study an interested but noncommittal reception. PROVN was controversial because it questioned the U.S. policy of building up U.S. forces to fight a war of attrition. It argued instead that priority should be given to pacification. This argument threatened to fracture the military's uneasy consensus about how to prosecute the war. At the request of MACV, PROVN was reduced to a "conceptual document," and thereafter was treated with such delicacy that army officers who knew of its existence were forbidden to discuss it outside the Pentagon.

The spirit of PROVN, however, survived. Some of its authors ended up in positions where they could inject its conclusions into new programs. Someone leaked the PROVN study to Robert Komer, President Johnson's special assistant for pacification, and chief architect and director of the superagency Civil Operations and Revolutionary Development Support (CORDS), and Komer implemented many of the study's recommendations. Colonel Robert M. Montague, Jr., a member of Komer's staff who helped reorganize U.S. pacification support into CORDS said, "We always referred to the PROVN study." PROVN's clear-eyed statement of the principle that "success will be the sum of innumerable, small and integrated localized efforts," rather than "the outcome of any short-duration, single master stroke" proved prophetic.

The velvet glove

In his memoir of the Vietnam War General Lewis Walt, commander of U.S. Marine forces in Vietnam from May 1965 to May 1967, summed up what he believed to be the key to how to fight the war. "The struggle was in the rice paddies," General Walt wrote, "in and among the people, not passing through, but living among them, night and day … and joining with them in steps toward a better life long overdue." Beyond the three marine enclaves at Da Nang, Chu Lai, and Phu Bai in I Corps lay myriad villages containing over 2 million people. Most of these villages had long been under tight Vietcong control. General Walt proposed to regain them for the GVN by using "the velvet glove," a combination of friendly aid and physical security. Officially, the Marine Corps called its pacification program "civic action."

The first marine civic action efforts were spontaneous, informal projects begun by individual marines. In April 1965 First Lieutenant William Francis, the civil affairs officer for the 3d Marine Division, established a medical dispensary in a shanty-town called Dogpatch at the edge of the Da Nang air base.

Lt. Francis begged and borrowed medicines to equip the dispensary and assigned a Vietnamese nurse, a U.S. Navy hospital corpsman, and a navy lab technician to run it. The Vietnamese welcomed the project, but by the summer of 1965 Francis was frustrated. The marines, he felt, "were just sort of groping and feeling with inadequate supplies and personnel."

Lieutenant Francis's project attracted the attention of his superiors, however, and General Walt authorized his staff to expand it. By the fall marines established medical civic action projects, or MEDCAPs. MEDCAP units, made up of several navy corpsmen escorted by an armed marine squad, conducted regular sick calls in villages. While providing treatment for illnesses that ranged from malnutrition to parasite infections, the marines trained Vietnamese volunteers in rudimentary health care practices. Navy corpsmen like Josiah "Doc" Lucier of Birmingham, Alabama, braved booby-trapped trails to give injections, distribute drugs, and administer first aid in out-of-the-way hamlets. "Until we start treating these people like human beings, they aren't going to want to help us," Lucier said.

Some marines scoffed at civic action efforts, calling them "candy and pill patrols" that did little good. Besides, they were dangerous. "We try to help these goddamn people," one marine private explained, "and you know what they do? They send in their kids to steal our grenades and ammunition and use them to kill us. The hell with them!" General Walt replied to such criticisms by patiently explaining that "a soldier has to be much more than a man with a rifle whose only objective is to kill. He has to be part diplomat, part technician, part politician—and 100 percent a human being."

New directions

Late in the summer of 1965 the marines operated several programs aimed at providing villagers with security from violence and a chance to prosper. One of these, called County Fair, was designed to begin restoring security in rural areas. In a County Fair program marines worked with ARVN soldiers and GVN officials to flush out any Vietcong soldiers billeted in a village and to collect intelligence about VC military movements or propaganda efforts. A County Fair began with deployment of marine platoons around the outskirts of a village. After they cordoned it off they intercepted anyone attempting to leave or enter. Next ARVN soldiers herded residents into hastily constructed compounds. There GVN officials checked their identity papers and questioned anyone who seemed suspicious. Meanwhile ARVN troops searched for arms caches, tunnels, and people in hiding, marines administered rudimentary medical treatment, and GVN officials delivered speeches urging the people to help the government banish the Vietcong.

This program did not achieve good results. Peasants resented summary eviction from their homes and looting of their possessions by the ARVN. Frequently GVN officials chafed at the intrusion into their spheres of authority and refused to cooperate. The largest problem was the program's transitory nature. Conducted in two to four days, a County Fair operation left the peasants with no permanent improvement in security and did not enhance their economic well-being. Still, County Fair operations did serve as an indication to villagers that the GVN wanted both to expel the VC and to help the peasantry. These operations also enabled the marines and the ARVN to gain experience in the complicated business of pacification. Though U.S. Army units adapted the concept and developed their own version (called Hamlet Festivals), General Westmoreland felt that personnel assigned to such operations detracted from the "primary" U.S. responsibility of "destroying enemy main force units."

Another marine program proved more productive than County Fair. On August 30, 1965, Huynh Ba Trinh, the chief of Hoi Hai Village, visited the headquarters of the 1st Battalion, 9th Marines, to ask the marines to provide security for his people during their September rice harvest. Each harvest, the village chief explained, the VC demanded a sizable portion of the rice yield. What the VC took usually amounted to the only surplus the villagers could sell in the marketplace. Already, the village chief knew, the insurgents had moved into the area to collect the rice.

Lieutenant Colonel Verle Ludwig, commander of the 1/9 Marines, agreed to ward off the Vietcong and devised a project called Golden Fleece. When the rice harvest began on September 10, companies from the 1/9 saturated the area around Hoi Hai Village, conducted night ambushes, and set up cordons around the harvesters working in the fields. After a major unsuccessful fight with the marines on September 12, most of the VC left. The marines met only sporadic resistance during the rest of the harvest. Golden Fleece was an economic success because it preserved the harvest and it was also a psychological success. The marines proved they could defend the villagers, and they forced the Vietcong to increase their rice levy in other areas, thereby diminishing their popular support there.

U.S. Navy corpsman Robert Miller, *the bac si, or medic, for a Combined Action Platoon in Hoa Hiep Village, north of Da Nang, prepares to treat a worried young boy.*

Control over rice had been an important element of the war in Vietnam, and the success of Golden Fleece reinforced this fact among the marines. Soon other marine units, often working together with South Vietnamese troops, took up rice protection at harvest time. Emphasis on the technique also spread south among U.S. Army units. Not all subsequent Golden Fleece operations proved successful, in part because sometimes ARVN troops pilfered from the harvests they were assigned to protect. But the technique became a standard component of military operations conducted at harvest time.

Combined Action Platoons

The most ambitious marine pacification program took root in the summer of 1965. Captain John T. Mullin, Jr., the civil affairs officer for the 3d Battalion, 4th Marines, based at Phu Bai, saw an under-used resource in the marines' own backyard. Mullin thought that the Vietnamese Popular Forces soldiers, a poorly trained, ill-equipped local militia charged with defending villages, might be upgraded into an aggressive, effective fighting force if U.S. Marines took them under their wings. Mullin's idea impressed his commanding officer, Lieutenant Colonel William "Woody" Taylor. In July Colonel Taylor ordered his executive officer Major Cullen C. Zimmerman to draw up a plan for incorporating marines into PF units.

The plan called for combining a squad of fourteen marines plus one navy medical corpsman with three squads of PF soldiers, making a group of some fifty men in all. Called Combined Action Platoons (CAPs), these new units attracted a special breed of marine volunteer—highly motivated, idealistic, and sympathetic to the Vietnamese people. Lieutenant Richard Cavagnol, an artillery forward observer for the 3d Marine Division who witnessed the formation of CAPs, said all these men "really believed they could help the Vietnamese people, and by doing so, help win the war."

On the surface, the PFs were unlikely candidates to turn the war around. Some had been declared ineligible for service in regular ARVN units, and all lay at the bottom of the Vietnamese military structure. Pay was as low as 1,200 piasters per month, less than 10 dollars. Their weapons were limited to grenades and M1 carbines. Few were issued uniforms or other equipment, and many received no training. As a result, most PFs rarely defended their makeshift compounds and offered little security to villagers against VC attacks. Some made tacit "live and let live" agreements with the Vietcong or hid in towns, absent without leave. But General Walt believed the PF soldier was a potentially vital fighting force. "He was defending his own home, family, and neighbors. He knew each paddy, field,

trail, bush, or bamboo clump, each family shelter, tunnel, and buried rice urn."

Hoping to impress the PF soldiers by example, the marines showed them various techniques. Each marine kept a small notebook in which he recorded the daily activities of villagers in order to spot suspicious behavior. This intelligence-gathering practice aroused curiosity among PF soldiers. Marines patrolled after dark, took the point positions, and fired aggressively on the enemy when they found him, hoping the PFs would do the same. Some PFs caught on fast, responding with cunning and courage to the marines' examples. "They will fight if they know the system is competent and cares," one marine said. A CAP-trained PF soldier was the first Vietnamese decorated by the United States with a Bronze Star for heroism. But many PFs showed little improvement in their performance. Navy corpsman Gregory Flynn felt that the PFs he worked with "couldn't be trusted" with the jobs assigned to them, even after months of working with his squad.

In the end, the CAP program achieved only limited application. The eventual 114 platoons were scattered and frequently isolated. PF weapons and pay were little improved. Expanded NVA activities along the DMZ drew marine forces out of the villages, and by the first months of 1967 the CAPs came to be considered, as CIA officer Douglas Blaufarb later wrote, "a limited sideshow to the Main-Force war." With the decline of CAPs, Marine Corps pacification efforts ceased to attract the priority they enjoyed in early years of the war.

Xay Dung Nong Thon

As of mid-1965, almost two-thirds of the country's 12 million people were ruled by some 40,000 NLF cadres, protected by 130,000 Vietcong guerrillas. According to John Mecklin, a former director of the United States Information Service (USIS) in Saigon, the Communists operated by "stealing the people" away from the GVN. In Hau Nghia Province, southwest of Saigon, approximately 80 percent of the population was controlled by the NLF. In June 1965, the former province chief of Hau Nghia summed up the situation this way: "There are 220,000 people in Hau Nghia, and 200,000 of them are ruled by the Vietcong, which made me a hamlet chief, not a province chief." Northern provinces such as Quang Nam were all but lost to the GVN. William Nighswonger, the USAID province representative in Quang Nam, reported that pacification was "impossible" there. "The insurgent forces control most of the province by a combination of terror, propaganda, kinship ties, and substantial military power."

Leaders of the GVN understood well enough that pacification was a difficult business. But they tried to cooperate. In Saigon in July 1965 Premier Ky and chief of state Nguyen Van Thieu presented Ambassador Henry Cabot Lodge and Secretary of Defense McNamara with a pacification plan called *Xay Dung Nong Thon.* Often translated by Vietnamese as Rural Construction or Rural Reconstruction, Americans called the plan Revolutionary Development. Ky's plan created a ministry and proposed to send trained GVN cadres into hamlets and villages to institute reforms, and Ky appointed General Nguyen Duc Thang as minister.*

Under Thang's leadership the Ministry for Revolutionary Development produced a campaign plan for 1966 envisioning two phases of action. In the initial "peace restoration phase," a large force of ARVN troops was to expel VC forces from an area. Police would then move into hamlets to root out the VC infrastructure (VCI) as identified by GVN intelligence. Once this was accomplished ARVN and police forces were to provide security for a fifty-nine-man team of Revolutionary Development (RD) cadres (called *can bos* in Vietnamese). Once the RD team gained a foothold it was divided into two groups of military and polit-

ical workers. The military group, consisting of thirty-six men and women in three squads, was to prepare and occupy defensive positions and train a hamlet self-defense force. The political group of twenty-three *can bos* concentrated on eliminating the last vestiges of the VCI. At the same time they were to identify and report any corrupt GVN officials. During the "new life development phase" that followed, the team was to take a census of the hamlet, hear the residents' complaints, and initiate self-help economic projects. They also were charged to carry out land reform. Finally, before leaving the hamlet, they were to stage an election for local offices.

In March 1966 Robert Shaplen, reporting for the *New Yorker,* visited several hamlets in Binh Dinh Province to see how the RD program was working. In one hamlet in the middle of the province the team leader proudly showed Shaplen a preliminary census map his men had made. Of the

---

*(For an account of the origins of the Revolutionary Development program, see *Raising the Stakes,* another volume of The Vietnam Experience.)

American and South Vietnamese members *of the Echo Two Combined Action Platoon march into their compound near the village of Hoa Hiep after a mission during the summer of 1967. CAP installations like this one became a favorite target for enemy guerrillas.*

ninety-seven houses in the hamlet, ten were colored red because the families living in them had relatives in the Vietcong, fifteen were colored yellow because their owners had relatives in North Vietnam.

At the village of Hoai An he found the program less advanced. Surrounded by Vietcong, the village had not even been entered by the RD team, "a clear illustration of the fact that it would be a long time before all or even more of Binh Dinh was sufficiently pacified." In a village near Bong Son, Shaplen learned that a VC war memorial stood in the central village square. Government troops tried to penetrate this village but were ejected by Vietcong assaults. At the hamlet of Tau Nghia near Qui Nhon, Shaplen observed "considerable progress." By the end of June, cadres had completed a census of the people's needs and grievances, repaired roads, helped fishermen obtain loans for new motors and nets, set up a school, and turned over a sewing machine to a women's group.

Security problems

Revolutionary Development Minister Thang had set a goal of entering over 2,000 hamlets in 1966, but by the end of the year RD teams had visited only 440 hamlets, less than 25 percent of those targeted. As a result, the plan for 1967 did not expand, and Minister Thang concentrated on improving the original program by lengthening the cadres' training, doubling their pay, and reducing each team's quota of hamlets to be pacified from four to two. Some aspects of the revised plan succeeded. Expanded shipments of American materiel improved economic self-help projects and social services such as health and education. In the hamlet of Ap Bay in Vinh Long Province, south of Saigon, RD cadres constructed a new road, built several bridges, supplied a dispensary, distributed textbooks, and stocked fish ponds and pigpens.

Despite some successes, the Revolutionary Development

RD cadres learn house framing techniques *at the National Training Center at Vung Tau. RD-organized self-help projects succeeded better than programs to provide security and political reform.*

program foundered because the GVN proved unable to satisfy the rural villagers' fundamental desires for security and social reform. ARVN did not provide the villages with adequate military protection. At the hamlet of Tan Qui in Vinh Long Province the RD team leader was shot in the neck by a Vietcong sniper and died when ARVN troops refused to evacuate him. The Vietcong took advantage of poor security to wage an assassination campaign against key RD team members. In the first five months of 1967, almost 500 "Rev Dev" workers, out of a total of 10,000, were killed, wounded, or kidnapped. One U.S. official said in May that "The incident report in Quang Nam Province reads like the Cicero, Illinois, police blotter: hamlet chief kidnapped. Rev Dev cadre man wounded. Rev Dev man murdered."

The GVN's tolerance of corruption was another factor that prevented social reform. At the hamlet of Tan Thanh A in Long An Province, for example, though an RD team reported that a member of the National Police Force was extorting money, he was not removed. According to one RD team leader, the task of "eliminating oppressive individuals" was "the most difficult task of all. ... They are all tied with one another from the generals right down to the hamlet. We report them, but nothing happens."

The insensitivity of the GVN to rural villagers' desires for land ownership also militated against the success of the RD cadres. One of the professed goals of the RD program was land reform. In return for the support of villagers RD cadres promised that the GVN would redistribute property titles and prevent landlords' abuses of tenants' rights. But in many hamlets in Long An Province, according to Jeffrey Race, the GVN did not redress landholding inequalities. On the heels of the GVN security force that entered the hamlet of Hoa Thuan 2 came landlords, cast out by the Vietcong, who started collecting back rents. "The village chief approved of this state of affairs," Race wrote. "He indicated that the previous situation had been very hard on the landlords, because they could go into the hamlets to collect rents only on military operations." Thus the cadre team was unable to make any changes in the patterns of owning or renting land in the hamlet. To succeed, the RD teams depended on ARVN to provide security and on the GVN to institute reforms. When they lacked backing from either, the RD teams could do little to bring permanent security or increased prosperity to the countryside.

Fistfuls of dollars

Many, though not all, Americans believed that ultimate success in the pacification effort depended as much on relieving suffering and creating economic opportunities as on providing physical security. The idea was that when American assistance, channeled through the GVN, flooded the society, all the people would be raised to a level of prosperity superior to anything offered by the Communists and would fight to preserve it. The great cornucopian source of this assistance was USAID, the United States Agency for International Development.

By as early as mid-1965 the scale of USAID support for pacification had grown to some $500 million per year and was growing apace. In 1965 Edward G. Ruoff, a World War II marine infantryman, served as the coordinator for USAID programs in II Corps. Ruoff's list of USAID support reads like a county budget: American funds, distributed through GVN channels and disbursed by GVN officials, paid for school construction, teacher training, increased agricultural production, improved training of public officials, drilling equipment to increase the supply of water, and dam and bridge construction.

Other items on Ruoff's list reflected the inroads of war. USAID provided foodstuffs, cement, roofing materials, and medicines to refugees fleeing the fighting in their villages. The agency also rewarded Vietcong who abandoned the battlefield under the GVN's Chieu Hoi program. USAID developed radio networks to enable villagers to communicate information about enemy activity and retrained police forces to operate checkpoints, gather intelligence, and propagandize the people to resist the VC. In short, USAID support was supposed to bring a rural society of poor peasants into the twentieth century and help them win a vicious war at the same time.

Edmundo Navarro, USAID province representative in the III Corps province of Tay Ninh, told the U.S. Senate Subcommittee on Refugees in July 1965 that his staff had so much practice at assisting refugees that they had "perfected the art" of receiving them. Informed of an impending combat operation by the Republic of South Vietnam Armed Forces, Navarro "immediately put into action" what he called "the provincial machinery." Refugees driven out of their homes were led to areas where information teams welcomed them, and medical teams treated the sick and wounded. Within forty-eight hours Navarro hired Vietnamese contractors to build new houses, classrooms, and roads.

The situation in the northernmost province of Quang Tri, where Danny Whitfield served as USAID representative, was similar to that in Tay Ninh. "The people of Quang Tri are neither pro-Government nor pro-Vietcong," Whitfield told the subcommittee. "They are motivated by fear and the ability to survive." Living in one of the poorest of South Vietnam's provinces, with little productive farm land or industry, the people of Quang Tri were eager to accept U.S. aid. Still, the presence of people in the "new-life hamlets" built and sub-

Laurence D. Anderson, *a USAID representative in Bien Hoa Province, gives advice to a farmer.*

sidized by USAID did not guarantee that their hearts and minds had been won to the GVN cause. A State Department officer assigned to write political reports in 1965 put the matter bluntly. "A lot of pacification work was really just allocation of resources. We said [to the Vietnamese], 'If you cooperate you can get resources. If you don't you are likely to find yourself in a free-fire zone.'"

The rising tide

From the summer of 1965 to May 1966, Paul London worked as an assistant province representative with USAID in Soc Trang, the capital of the Mekong Delta province of Ba Xuyen. London found that USAID's efforts in the province were "not part of a structured system. We were just out there." USAID supplied a stream of commodities to Ba Xuyen, ranging from cement and tin roofing to rice and cooking oil. It all went into a warehouse to which London held a key. "The Vietnamese would come to us with an idea for a project and request mate-

rials. We would go out and open the warehouse for them. There really wasn't more to it than that."

Working without specific instructions, London became interested in assisting local businesses to develop and expand brick kilns, rice mills, and duck hatcheries. These businesses thrived. However, in one village London found that USAID materials were used to build a small school and a large house for the village chief. London felt that the USAID effort in Ba Xuyen was "materialist." "We thought that by giving people things, we'd get them to side with us." But USAID largesse did not override the politics of the Vietnam War and didn't win the people to the side of the GVN.

Nevertheless, sometimes American aid did improve the standard of living of many South Vietnamese, and sometimes greater military security accompanied greater prosperity. Clay Nettles, an AID representative in the II Corps province of Lam Dong, helped build a major tea-processing plant in the province. Nettles also allocated funds to create a silkworm breeding station, which distributed silkworm eggs throughout the province. When he left Lam Dong at the end of 1966 Nettles reported that there had been a "tremendous improvement in the military situation." Fred Ashley, a State Department officer reassigned to the AID staff in neighboring Tuyen Duc Province for most of 1965 and 1966, funded programs for improving the quality of pigs raised by farmers. By the time he left in January 1967, Ashley says, "We were almost ready to export. Our programs were successful because we had relatively better security, and the Vietnamese were doing things for themselves." The projects flourished because the VC did not operate in these sparsely populated provinces and because many who lived in them were anti-Communist refugees from the North.

Myron Smith arrived in Saigon in June 1966 to work as a soils adviser to the GVN's Ministry of Agriculture. Involved at first in distributing of fertilizer, Smith traveled through South Vietnam and saw that rice farmers were eager to increase their yields. "The farmer needed most of his rice production for his own survival," Smith said. "In a good year, he might have 10 percent or so of his production to sell. It used to take them several years to earn enough to buy a bicycle." But in 1967 at Vo Dat, in the delta province of Phuoc Tuy, Smith introduced a new rice seed developed in the Philippines. In the first season yields tripled. The GVN called the new rice *thon nang*, or rice of the gods, but to the farmers of Vo Dat who used their profits to buy motorbikes it was known as "Honda rice." "The program took off like a prairie fire across Vietnam," Smith said. But the new rice brought only a temporary blessing. It required intensive use of fertilizers, the price of which increased with inflation and eventually negated profits from increased yield. What started out a boom became a disaster because of a combination of increased fertilizer costs and lower rice prices because of overproduction.

Increased prosperity didn't guarantee that beneficiaries of American aid would support the GVN, but it encouraged some Vietnamese to lean toward the government. Mark Huss, a United States official who worked with the Office of Civilian Operations (OCO) and CORDS between 1965 and 1967, made two visits each year to every province in South Vietnam. "After a briefing by the province chief, when naturally, the inclination was to say that things had never worked so well before," Huss said, "you went out to investigate." Huss had his own means of learning whether aid was trickling down to the people. If the mortar between cement blocks was applied meagerly, he knew building supplies were being siphoned off. If the barbed wire around a hamlet was trampled down, that meant security was lax. If he saw someone with a fat pig in his backyard, he asked him where he got it. If the farmer replied that it came from the government he told Huss something he already knew. But if he volunteered that the government's program was a good one and he would go along with it, "then you knew pacification was taking place. Did the people look prosperous? What shape were their houses in, their clothes? How many motorcycles did they have? That's how you knew." One Vietnamese had a different strategy for determining whether pacification was working. According to Huss, Le Van Chat, the secretary general to the minister of the interior, always looked to see if flowers were planted in a hamlet. They were a sign of permanence, he thought, because the people who planted them expected to remain to see them grow.

Freezing the fish

American military advisers assigned to pacification roles recognized that security was crucial and each one was charged with making it a reality. Their challenge was to enable the people themselves to make their society safe from terror, because American troops could not be garrisoned indefinitely throughout the country to provide for that need. But since American advisers were individuals, and conditions varied from district to district, each adviser addressed the challenge in his own way.

Army Captain Harry T. Johnson, who served as Phu Cat district adviser in Binh Dinh Province in 1965, acknowledged that "you had to have security for pacification to work." But as he saw it, "all you had was insular security, little islands of security." If the people were the ocean in which Communist guerrillas swam, Johnson thought, "then you had to have solidification. If you freeze the water, they can't swim. You had

A peasant at a refugee village *near Da Nang sits before a USAID poster recommending good health care practices.*

to *ice* it." Johnson decided to create "a territorial force" from the companies of Regional Forces and the platoons of Popular Forces in his district.

Armed with M1 rifles, grenade launchers, and Browning automatic rifles (BARs), PFs remained at posts in their home villages, while RFs moved throughout a district. Johnson developed a program for upgrading these territorial forces in his district. "You would see that they were kept up to strength, check their weapons, see that they were getting paid and see that they were used for the purposes for which they were intended." Johnson spoke highly of the fighting ability of these Vietnamese soldiers. "You know what Vietnamese unit received the first American Presidential Unit Citation? A Regional Forces company from Binh Dinh province."

Early in 1966 Johnson was promoted to major and appointed senior RF/PF adviser for all of Binh Dinh. He made sure that district advisers set up programs for training and supplying the territorial forces and worked to establish a system of mutual support among them. "That was the glue that held things together." Operating with a limited logistics apparatus and inadequate communication equipment, RF and PF units often were not well coordinated. Efficient use of artillery or air support in their behalf was especially hard to achieve. Johnson began a lien doi, or command group, which carefully identified each commander's responsibilities, and ordered them in a hierarchy. He also installed radio networks that permitted better coordination among their units. But just as the *lien doi* system was becoming operational, Johnson received a visit from General Westmoreland, who reported that Washington had recommended that Johnson try a "constabulary" system instead. This system would require the territorial forces to act as police and collect intelligence in addition to their combat roles. "Any one of these things will work if you stick with them long enough to get the bugs out," Johnson argued.

"We would be back to the drawing board again, everything would be on hold," Johnson complained. The constabulary system would work no more efficiently, but it would call for reorganization and lost time. Although Johnson's arguments prevailed over the constabulary system, he criticized Americans for "lack of institutional knowledge," their failure to remember the past. "When you don't have institutional knowledge you play hopscotch. Every guy who comes in has a new idea, and you have to stop and get everything reorganized again."

Instant government

Colonel Sam Wilson of the U.S. Army saw many pacification programs come and go. Wilson had served as an adviser in the delta in 1963. From 1964 to the end of 1965 he worked as associate director of USAID's field operations. He believed that pacification efforts were fragmentary and poorly run. "Agencies at the top worked independently while agencies at the field level were competing." He concluded that everyone, Americans and Vietnamese, had to work together if pacification were to succeed. This notion had been discussed by American planners since General Westmoreland's trip to Malaysia in 1964 to evaluate the British experience in pacification there, but it had not been instituted. In January 1966 Ambassador Lodge appointed Wilson to the U.S. Mission and asked him to improve coordination among U.S. and GVN pacification programs. Wilson welcomed the opportunity, but by November he was "rather frustrated by the fact that we weren't getting people pulled together." Coordination could be achieved, Wilson insisted, only if one man in each province ran everything. A "single manager" with "complete control" over all American civilian personnel and resources, and plenty of leverage over Vietnamese staffs, should be appointed for each province.

Wilson persuaded Lodge and Westmoreland to let him test the notion in Long An Province in November 1966. His classification as a Class I foreign service officer with direct links to Lodge and Westmoreland helped Wilson gain control of the pacification programs in Long An.

Wilson found Long An a mess. Less than 25 percent of the population of 400,000 was under GVN control, and only 4 percent of the geographic area was physically secure. "During the hours of darkness," Wilson said, "this area dwindled to something on the order of 1 percent." Command responsibilities were so fractured that ARVN units rarely performed combat operations. When ARVN units did conduct patrols they "invariably avoided closing" with the enemy, and instead plundered the people, who "hated and feared them more than they disliked the Vietcong." Police operations against the VCI were "an unheard of thing," intelligence information was distributed haphazardly, and "the provincial government was doing little, if anything, to improve the lot of the people."

Once Wilson arrived in Long An, three battalions of the U.S. 9th Infantry Division were stationed in the province, and security improved immediately. By the spring of 1967, 30 percent of Long An's territory was secure. Visits by Prime Minister Ky, a friend of Wilson, sharpened ARVN performance. Command relationships were simplified to spell out the responsibilities of ARVN officers, and corrupt or ineffective officers were replaced. GVN officials were subjected to systematic reviews, and a system of periodic reports monitored the GVN's police retraining, public health, and Chieu Hoi programs. U.S. programs for gathering intelligence, conducting psychological warfare operations, and evaluating political conditions began to reinforce each other.

Early in March, Operation Take-a-Chance, conducted in the village of Long Huu, demonstrated the single-manager concept. Helicopters landed an "instant government" consisting of scores of Vietnamese and American civilians who set up schools, clinics, and police stations. "The U.S. effort has been focused at the provincial and district level and has ignored the village," Wilson said as the operation began. "We are still removed from the target—the village—and the Vietcong are sitting on the target." Operation Take-a-Chance made VC in the area get up and move. It was a sign that well-coordinated pacification actions had a chance to work throughout South Vietnam.

Colonel Wilson's rapid turn-around of conditions in Long An Province prompted Ambassador Lodge to ask him to write a detailed report, a shorter version of which soon reached President Johnson. After the president read it, he told Lodge "We want to do it this way all over the country." In May 1967, General Westmoreland asked Wilson to present a more detailed report during a meeting that Robert Komer attended. Appointed by President Johnson in April as his special ambassador for pacification, Komer was thereupon made the "single manager" of American advisory support to Vietnamese pacification.

A former CIA officer, Komer had served in both the Kennedy and Johnson administrations as an aid expert. A nonconformist and outspoken but efficient bureaucrat, Komer struck some as abrasive; Ambassador Lodge nicknamed him "Blowtorch." Komer thought Wilson's experiment in Long An was "a very good effort," but "the trouble was Sam didn't pursue it long enough." Soon after he arrived Komer reorganized pacification under the new structure of CORDS. It was to take time, but under Komer's leadership CORDS consolidated the many agencies responsible for assisting the Vietnamese and prevailed upon the GVN to improve the RFs and PFs, to strengthen the police, to accelerate the Chieu Hoi program, and to mount a new attack later known as the Phoenix Program against the VCI. CORDS also linked each program to the others. "We realistically concluded," Komer wrote later, "that no one of these plans ... could itself be decisive. But together they could hope to have a major cumulative effect." Still, pacification was at bottom a Vietnamese responsibility. The war to win the loyalty of the people would be won or lost only by the Vietnamese government.

Vietcong Village

How did the Communists go about winning the support of so many villagers in South Vietnam? A curious American, in pursuit of a Ph.D. thesis, decided to find out by examining the history of a single village. In 1974 James Walker Trullinger, Jr., who had worked for USAID in Da Nang, traveled to Thuy Phong ("Place of Waters"), a poor farming village eleven kilometers southeast of Hue. What he discovered, after months of interviews, is related in his book, *Village at War: An Account of Revolution in Vietnam* (Longman, Inc.).

It demonstrates how the Vietcong, working patiently for four years, built a movement in Thuy Phong. Vietminh supporters regrouped from North Vietnam to establish an NLF committee in the village in 1961, which organized residents into three-member cells. By 1965, three-fourths of Thuy Phong's 8,300 villagers supported the Vietcong, whom they knew as relatives and neighbors in the "liberation front." To reflect their control, the VC and their followers even changed the name of Thuy Phong, calling it My Thuy, or "Beautiful Waters."

The Communists had built their strong base of support by responding to local grievances against the GVN. According to one peasant:

> The Liberation had answers for all the most important problems. ... They had an answer about land reform ... about high taxes. ... They

also said they would help the poor, and this made them popular, because many people in the village were very poor.

In formal meetings, and in informal chats with villagers, local VC cadres preached passive resistance to GVN policies and programs. In 1964 the Communists began requesting taxes in the form of money or food. The villagers complied, believing VC promises that a General Uprising and subsequent Communist victory were close at hand.

But the quick victory never came to pass, and the arrival of U.S. Marines at nearby Phu Bai in April 1965 upset the Vietcong plans for "My Thuy." A Combined Action Platoon of thirty Vietnamese Popular Forces and fifteen U.S. Marines moved into a compound on Highway 1 in the center of Thuy Phong/My Thuy in August of 1965 and began to seek out the Vietcong. They and GVN security forces killed three political leaders and five of the village's twenty guerrillas. They also jailed two VC leaders and about twenty-five of their supporters. To the dismay of the cadres, village families began to withdraw support from the Communists.

The Vietcong fought back. Political cadres stirred up anti-imperialist sentiment that remained from French colonialism by launching an anti-American propaganda campaign. "The Vietcong ... did nothing but talk to us about the Americans," said one villager. "All the time. They told us how the Americans were destroying our country, how they were controlling the Government." The Vietcong also intensified their local military activities, with increased sniping and ambushing along Highway 1, and laid more booby traps throughout the village. Two women joined the guerrilla force. The Communists also launched terrorist attacks, carrying out at least five assassinations between 1965 and 1967. To escape the nighttime terror, many GVN supporters began moving to Hue each night.

The guerrillas' efforts culminated in a raid on the CAP compound in late 1967. A company of guerrillas "snuck in at night and fired on them [the CAP] very heavily," said one participant. The guerrillas killed "many" in the CAP before being repulsed, while only two or three VC died in the fight. The attack made the hoped-for impression on the village. A student recalled that "the people were very happy after they saw how brave the Liberation Front guerrillas could be in such an attack against the Americans. Many of us thought to ourselves, secretly, that we must support the liberation front." And a Popular Forces soldier who lost a leg in the raid reported, "That attack scared everybody for years. From then, we could not be sure about the defense [capability] of the army [ARVN]."

The CAP and GVN security forces remained in the village, but by the end of 1967 the VC had regained the near total allegiance of the villagers. The Vietcong had successfully overcome the American challenge, but in doing so, they and their adversaries had transformed the peaceful farming village of Thuy Phong/My Thuy into a battleground.

Battle of Dong Xoai

Rushing into the teeth *of heavy machine-gun fire, ARVN Rangers move forward during the battle to retake Dong Xoai on June 11, 1965. ARVN forces prevailed, but at a cost in men and morale so high that both sides recognized the battle as a tactical victory for the Communists.*

Left, top. ARVN Rangers *airlifted to join the assault on Dong Xoai take cover in a ditch. Moments later VC machine-gun fire raked their position.*

Left, bottom. "Every ten seconds a man would fall ..." *remembers Horst Faas, who took most of the photographs used in this essay. Here, an ARVN Ranger, shot in the legs, stumbles after his dropped weapon.*

Right. After being set down *by a helicopter, a ranger under heavy Vietcong fire scampers for cover across a soccer field.*

A commander of the Dong Xoai Popular Forces militia slumps to the ground in tears after learning his wife and children were killed in the crossfire.

Bodies of children are strewn at the entrance to a bunker where they sought shelter from the fighting. A Vietcong soldier killed by Dong Xoai defenders lies among the dead.

Shock and fear show *in these Vietnamese, some of the few who survived the battle.*

An ARVN Ranger *with a folded stretcher passes bodies of soldiers and civilians killed at the battle of Dong Xoai. Behind him a wounded soldier is helped to the aid station.*

"Peace? I never think about it. I have been a soldier since I was twelve years old. I am now forty-two. I think already I am too old to think about peace."

South Vietnamese officer

Before dawn on December 28, 1964, a battalion of the Vietcong 9th Division, its men clad in peasant clothing, moved toward the quiet village of Binh Gia. A prosperous agricultural community in Phuoc Tuy Province only 67 kilometers east of Saigon, Binh Gia's population consisted of some 6,000 Catholic refugees who had fled North Vietnam ten years before. The village was defended by a local force numbering no more than 100 lightly armed militia that depended for support on ARVN Ranger and marine reserve battalions stationed close to Saigon. As daylight broke on the twenty-eighth, the VC rushed into Binh Gia, quickly overpowered the militia, and seized the village church, where they established a command post. More soldiers of the 9th Division joined them and readied weapons to battle units of the armed forces of the Republic of Vietnam (RVNAF) charged with responding to the attack. Later that morning two ARVN Ranger companies were helilifted into the area. They moved within 300 meters of the village when a VC battalion attacked and forced them to withdraw. The next day the ARVN 30th and 33d Ranger battalions arrived by helicopter and took up positions. For the next two days the ARVN troops fought to dislodge the Vietcong. On the morning of the third day men of the South Vietnamese 4th Marine Battalion landed by helicopter. Their assault on Binh Gia met little opposition and soon the South Vietnamese units recaptured it, for the VC had withdrawn. But they left the lanes of Binh Gia, whose name meant "Peaceful House," strewn

Two RVNAF marines *charge a VC position as their comrades (foreground) deliver supporting fire during an operation in Vietnam's southern tip in early 1965.*

with the bodies of sixty ARVN and thirty-two Vietcong dead. Dazed villagers climbed out of fortified underground shelters while South Vietnamese relief forces collected their fallen comrades for burial.

But the battle of Binh Gia was not over. Later that day a U.S. Army spotter plane sighted a Vietcong force estimated to number two battalions (perhaps 800 men) in the rubber plantation southeast of the village. A reconnoitering U.S. Army helicopter gunship was shot down near the plantation and crashed, killing its four American crewmen. The next morning the commander of the South Vietnamese 4th Marine Battalion ordered one company into the plantation to recover the bodies of the American helicopter crewmen. The senior U.S. adviser to the Vietnamese commander, marine Captain Franklin P. Eller, argued against the mission, citing the likelihood of enemy ambush, but to no avail. At the site of the crash the South Vietnamese marines, accompanied by Captain Eller and two other American advisers, found several fresh graves. As they started to uncover them, enemy bugles blared a signal to attack. At the sound khaki-uniformed Vietcong soldiers executed a murderous ambush. As South Vietnamese soldiers and marines fell wounded around him, Captain Eller grabbed the handset of his radio and called for help. "These aren't guerrillas," Eller shouted, "they're regular troops!"

The other companies of the 4th Battalion reached the ambush site quickly, but the enemy ambushed them in turn. By late afternoon 29 of the 4th Battalion's 35 officers had been killed, including the battalion commander who ordered the mission. Of the 326 Vietnamese marines who fought that day, the Vietcong killed 112 and wounded 71. Two ARVN Airborne battalions arrived by helicopter the following day, January 1, but by then the enemy had slipped away, except for rearguard snipers who covered their withdrawal.

The Vietcong took victory with them as they disappeared into the jungle. Some 1,500 soldiers from the VC 9th Division had executed a shrewdly devised battle plan against twice as many South Vietnamese troops and killed or wounded more than 300 of them while suffering an undetermined fraction of those casualties. The South Vietnamese's casualties amounted to the highest toll in a single action to that point in the war. At Binh Gia the Vietcong accomplished an even greater triumph than that achieved at Ap Bac two years before in January 1963. "After the Ap Bac battle the enemy realized that it would be difficult to defeat us," said Le Duan, Lao Dong party secretary, in Hanoi. "After Binh Gia the enemy realized that they would lose to us."

On January 6, 1965, William Bundy, assistant secretary of state for Far Eastern affairs, sent a memo to Secretary of State Dean Rusk. In it Bundy characterized the RVNAF's defeat at Binh Gia as "discouraging" and predicted that "the situation in Vietnam is now likely to come apart more rapidly than we had anticipated in November." Later that month disheartened ARVN junior officers told a reporter for the *New York Times* that they lacked a sense of purpose. "I have to ask my men to go out and die," one ARVN officer said. "What am I supposed to ask them to die for?"

President Johnson's decision to send the U.S. Marines into South Vietnam in the spring of 1965, and the stepped-up bombing by U.S. Navy and air force planes throughout South Vietnam, initially had an encouraging effect on RVNAF forces. Some RVNAF servicemen saw the arrival of American combat personnel and equipment as the start of a new era. Khuc Hieu Liem served then as an ARVN combat engineer and held the rank of captain. "If the U.S. had not come in when they did," Liem said, "the war would have been lost." The coming of the Americans boosted the morale of Vietnamese soldiers and strengthened their fighting ability, he said, because it convinced them their predicament was desperate. "We realized we were in a situation of self-defense. The fear of an invasion from the North, which would bring poverty and suffering to the South, made us fight harder." Lieutenant Phan Thanh Long, an ARVN psychological warfare specialist, was impressed by the Americans' energy. "The Americans were good," Long said, "and they were dedicated to winning the war." As the first American combat troops arrived, that sense of purpose rubbed off on ARVN. During April 1965, ARVN troops fought and killed large numbers of Vietcong soldiers.

Death in the monsoon

But the surge in ARVN's fortunes subsided as rapidly as it had mounted. The long-awaited Vietcong monsoon offensive of May, June, and July 1965 reversed the gains of April and threw ARVN back on its heels. On May 9 a Vietcong mortar attack on Bao Trai, the capital of III Corps's Hau Nghia Province, killed 28 ARVN troops. The next day the ARVN 5th Division sustained over 170 casualties in the same area. And on May 11 at their base near the Phuoc Long Province capital of Song Be in III Corps, ARVN troops were overrun by a Vietcong assault force after putting up only a feeble resistance. The base was recaptured the next day when the VC withdrew.

During the last three days of May at Ba Gia, a hamlet near Quang Ngai, a force of nearly 1,000 well-armed Vietcong attacked three ARVN battalions. Panic-stricken, some of the ARVN soldiers fled from the battlefield, ripping off their uniforms and throwing away their weapons as they ran to hide out in nearby houses and rice fields. The attackers killed more than 100 ARVN and RF/PF soldiers before being driven out of Ba Gia by the rocket, napalm, and cannon fire of U.S. F-100 Super Sabres and A-1 Skyraiders. One month later, on July 4, after the ARVN had reoccupied the Ba Gia outpost, the Vietcong attacked again and regained the hamlet within ninety minutes. All day long bomb and rocket strikes by U.S. B-57 aircraft pummeled the enemy and eventually dislodged them. The ARVN were able to lay out their dead and wounded for evacuation by helicopter, but the Vietcong renewed their onslaught whenever aircraft approached. When two helicopters finally landed, terrorized ARVN soldiers trampled over the dead and wounded and rushed to board the aircraft. The helicopters' American crews had to fight them off to avoid overloading.

During this second attack on Ba Gia, General Nguyen Chanh Thi requested that U.S. Marines be thrown into the fight though units of his own troops were standing by on alert at Quang Ngai airfield. Earlier General Thi had questioned the need for U.S. combat assistance. But his confidence had eroded, and the American military leadership had anticipated him. One month before, General Westmoreland had concluded that without a huge increase in American combat responsibility RVNAF would lose the war. General Westmoreland's June 7 cable to the commander in chief of U.S. forces in the Pacific at Honolulu and to the Joint Chiefs of Staff at the Pentagon said, "ARVN forces are experiencing difficulty in coping with ... increased VC capability." Events three days later ninety kilometers north of Saigon confirmed this judgment.

Assault on Dong Xoai

Darkness had settled around Dong Xoai, a tiny district capital in III Corps's Phuoc Long Province. The evening hours of June 9 were still, except for the bursts of monsoon rain that soaked the scattered buildings and drenched the unfinished runway of the Civilian Irregular Defense Group (CIDG)-Special Forces camp. Montagnard CIDG guards patrolled the camp perimeter while twenty-four U.S. Seabees and soldiers rested after a hard day's work. Soon after midnight on June 10 the quiet was shattered by the crackle of the radio in the district chief's quarters. The muffled, shocked voice of the CIDG sentry stationed out on the airstrip hissed through the receiver: "The Vietcong are all over!" The next instant the blasts of exploding mortars and the muzzle flashes of recoilless rifles and automatic small arms lit up the darkness. Immediately wave after wave of Vietcong shock troops swarmed into the camp. Stripped for battle to breechcloths and steel helmets, and armed with AK47s and Chinese-made grenades and flame throwers, the attackers turned the soldiers' sleep into a waking nightmare.

As more than 1,500 enemy soldiers stormed the camp the executive officer of the Special Forces Detachment, Second Lieutenant Charles Q. Williams, roused the 23 other Americans and the 400 CIDG troops under his command. Realizing that the camp was nearly overrun, Lieutenant Williams ordered the confused defenders to fall back to defensive positions inside the district headquarters compound. The Vietcong assault forces rampaged through the abandoned camp, slaughtering some of the CIDG troops' wives and children as they huddled defenseless in shallow bunkers. Then the attackers advanced on the compound. "We beat back four or five attacks between midnight and 3:00 A.M.," Staff Sergeant Harold Crowe recalled. "There was assault after assault after assault."

At dawn U.S. and South Vietnamese pilots laid down

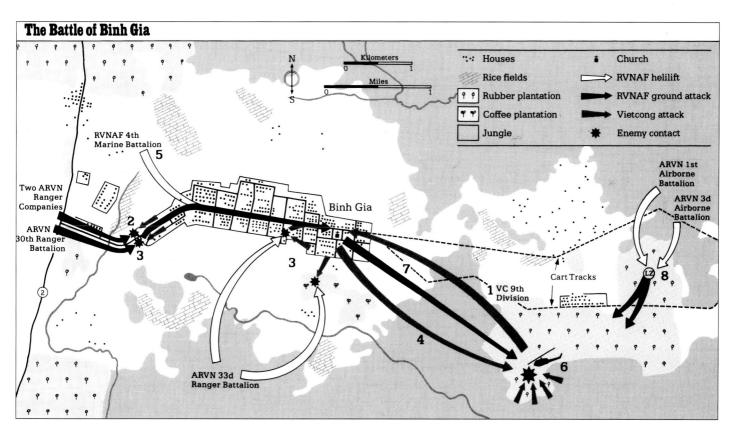

The Battle of Binh Gia

1. **December 28, morning.** *Battalion of the VC 9th Division overruns Binh Gia, sets up a command post in church.*
2. **December 28, afternoon.** *Two ARVN Ranger companies move within 300 meters of the village but are driven off by VC.*
3. **December 29, morning.** *ARVN 30th and 33d Ranger Battalions attack village; 30th occupies western portion; half of 33d takes village center.*
4. **December 30, dawn.** *VC withdraw.*
5. **December 30, morning.** *RVNAF 4th Marine Battalion sweeps village with ARVN Rangers, encounter no VC.*
6. **December 30, evening.** *U.S. Army helicopter shot down, four American crewmen killed.*
7. **December 31.** *RVNAF Marines sent to recover Americans' bodies are attacked by VC; more than half the marine battalion is killed or wounded by day's end.*
8. **January 1, morning.** *1st and 3d ARVN Airborne Battalions sweep rubber plantation, but VC have withdrawn.*

napalm and white phosphorous bombs on the Communist positions. Here, as at Ba Gia, air power played a significant role, but the attackers held their ground through the day. Intense flurries of Vietcong fire rebuffed an attempt to land an ARVN relief force by helicopter. One ARVN unit that did land was pinned down at once and wiped out, while helicopters carrying other units were driven off. The situation was perilous. Without reinforcements the compound's defenders would be annihilated. Late in the day ARVN General Cao Van Vien ordered forty helicopters loaded with troops of the ARVN 42d Ranger Battalion to land on a soccer field adjacent to the district headquarters building. The helicopters put down safely, the Rangers

clambered out, and immediately began returning fire. Fighting slackened as night fell. By dawn the next day the Vietcong had crept back into the jungle and disappeared into the rain.

After daybreak on the morning of June 11 the surviving Dong Xoai defenders returned to the camp. Anxious CIDG soldiers searched for their families among the rubble. Many were horrified by what they found. There were some 200 Vietnamese military and civilian casualties and 20 Americans killed or wounded—one of the highest U.S. losses in a single engagement up to that point in the war. But it might have been worse. During the night-and-day fighting Lieutenant Williams dashed through barrages of enemy gunfire to rally his troops, knocked

out an enemy machine gun using a 3.5MM rocket launcher with a faulty sight at a range of 150 meters, and guided evacuation helicopters to the wounded—despite wounds in both legs, his stomach, and his right arm. Williams's valor helped prevent a rout. Medevacked that afternoon, he was subsequently awarded the Medal of Honor for reflecting "great credit on himself and the Armed Forces of his country." MACV reports estimated ground actions and air strikes killed over 700 of the enemy.

All day long on June 11 and again on June 12 newly arrived ARVN Rangers scoured the countryside around Dong Xoai, tracking the enemy. Except for sporadic contact with rearguard trail watchers, the Vietcong eluded pursuit. Then the hunters became the hunted. As the light in the lowering monsoon clouds faded on the evening of June 12 the VC struck again, scattering the ARVN troops and forcing them to retreat to the Dong Xoai compound. Then the enemy regrouped to mount a charge through the compound walls. But before they could execute the maneuver the ARVN soldiers deserted their positions and ran off into the forest. The three U.S. advisers on the ground radioed for rescue and were airlifted out as the VC prepared to enter Dong Xoai.

Some evidence suggests that the Vietcong intended to hold the towns of Dong Xoai and Ba Gia after each attack long enough to proclaim each an NLF capital in a "liberated zone." At both towns they failed to accomplish this strategic objective. But the attacks were tactical successes. Ahiko Okamura, a Japanese photographer, was captured by the Vietcong in April 1965. Before the first attack on Ba Gia, Okamura heard a senior Vietcong official boast that his troops would attack and destroy large South Vietnamese military units. Huynh Tan Phat, deputy chairman of the Vietcong Central Committee, told Okamura "We are through with hit-and-run. Now we will attack in force to wipe out whole enemy units. These attacks will work well in the monsoon." Phat's prediction proved correct. Fifteen years later, in 1980, an official Socialist Republic of Vietnam history of the war stated that "The Dong Xoai victory pushed the puppet army a step further toward the peril of collapse and disintegration." In his own memoir of the war, General Westmoreland made a similar estimate. "Seriously disturbed by the trials of ARVN at Ba Gia and Dong Xoai," Westmoreland saw "the possibility that … I would have to commit American troops if a major ARVN force was to be spared utter defeat."

Why was it that the army, navy, air force, marines, and paramilitary forces of the government of South Vietnam, outnumbering their enemy, fighting within their own borders, supported by large numbers of foreign troops and large amounts of foreign arms, materiel, and money, did not fight victoriously? Why couldn't the RVNAF win, even with allied help? Why wasn't RVNAF winning on its own?

Numbers and ratios

At the time of the attack on Dong Xoai the RVNAF constituted one of the largest military organizations in the world. The regular ground forces consisted of the 227,000-man army and the 6,500-man Marine Corps. A still larger force was composed of

Bodies of South Vietnamese soldiers *killed at Binh Gia are carried away on an oxcart.*

paramilitary troops, including the Popular Forces at 150,000 men, the Regional Forces at 105,000, the National Police numbering 50,000, and the Civilian Irregular Defense Group at 15,000. The air force was composed of 12,500 men and 350 planes, including propeller-driven T-28 and A-1H Skyraider attack-bombers. South Vietnam's navy included 9,000 officers and men manning 600 vessels ranging from sampans and junks to converted landing craft equipped with machine guns and mortars.

Combined with 184,000 U.S. troops, and 23,000 troops from allied countries, the total forces of South Vietnam and its allies stood at more than three-quarters of a million men-at-arms by the end of 1965. At the same time the opposing side fielded 258,000 NVA and Main Force VC soldiers. Relative casualty rates as well as troop levels favored RVNAF: At the end of 1965, 4 enemy soldiers were reported killed for every RVNAF soldier. These favorable proportions increased as the war wore on. By the end of 1966, allied forces numbered more than 1 million and one year later totaled 1,188,000 while, according to some estimates, enemy forces had actually declined slightly to 257,000. By the end of 1967 the ratio of RVNAF to Vietcong and North Vietnamese soldiers was approaching 3 to 1, and 6 enemy soldiers were reported killed for every RVNAF soldier who died in battle.

At the beginning of 1965 American military advisers described the overall performance of South Vietnamese forces as "disappointing." Their reports pointed to "a lack of aggressiveness" in battle and characterized the military's attitude toward the war as "devoid of a sense of urgency." The officer corps was "short of able young trained leaders," they concluded, while the enlisted ranks were for the most part poorly trained, ill-informed about the nature of the struggle in which they were engaged, and lacked the desire to close with the enemy. To many Americans newly arrived in South Vietnam, these aspects of RVNAF's conduct of the war seemed both incomprehensible and unforgivable.

But unlike Americans, the South Vietnamese had been fighting the war for a very long time. Tran Tien My went to the war as a teenager in 1952 and fought as a guerrilla for the Vietminh. Captured by the French, My was converted to Catholicism, joined the French army, and saw combat in 1954 at Dien Bien Phu. After the defeat and withdrawal of the French he was absorbed into the army of the new Republic of Vietnam as a combat platoon leader in II Corps with the rank of first sergeant. The year 1965 was My's thirteenth of war. Many Vietnamese had been at war so long the idea of peace was difficult for them to imagine. "Peace?" asked one Vietnamese officer. "I never think about it. I have been a soldier since I was twelve years old. I am now forty-two. I think already I am too old to think about peace."

By 1965 the South Vietnamese military was suffering from a prolonged case of combat fatigue—society's war weariness had spread. "They've been at this war for more than twenty years," said U.S. Army Lieutenant Colonel Donald Roberts, an adviser in IV Corps. "They fought the French. They fought the Japanese. They fought the Vietcong. And now they're fighting the PAVN, the hard core troops infiltrated from the North. The American is here only for a year, and he wants to get on with the war." But the war the American shared was different for his South Vietnamese ally, Roberts said. "The Vietnamese soldier has no DEROS [date of estimated return from overseas]; he'll be fighting long after his American counterpart has gone home. There are no furloughs for him; no R&R [rest and recuperation] trips to Bangkok. You can't blame him for taking a placid, eternally patient, thoroughly oriental view of things. You can't blame him for getting discouraged and disgusted and just plain tired. You can even understand why he goes over the hill."

Born into war

Staff Sergeant Bud Traston arrived in Quang Tri Province in July 1965 and was assigned as a small weapons adviser to two ARVN companies headquartered at Cam Lo. Sgt. Traston thought the ARVN troops were as good as any other soldiers he'd seen in Germany or Korea and were as well-equipped as Americans. Their uniforms were in good condition, made of the same material and dyed the same color as American uniforms, but cut tighter about the inseam and legs. Some wore boots supplied by the United States, some sandals made from rubber tires, but each wore an American-made steel helmet. They carried supplies in Vietnamese-made ditty bags on their backs, strapped web belts containing ammunition and smoke grenades around their waists, and bore American-made M1 or M2 carbines, M60 machine guns, or M79 grenade launchers. Their diet was rice mixed with pieces of chicken, duck, or fish, and hot peppers. None had much money, few were married, most came from nearby hamlets where their families lived, and all seemed to be in the service for "a lifetime."

Soon after he arrived Traston was forced to change his estimate of the ARVN companies. The turning point was an operation conducted northwest of Cam Lo. One company of ARVN troops accompanied by a platoon of montagnards was ordered to take up positions on the north side of a river. To encourage the ARVN forces to develop independence, Traston and three other American advisers remained on the south side of the river with the second ARVN company. Suddenly North Vietnamese

With enemy soldiers in sight, *an ARVN officer radios an order to attack during action in the Mekong Delta in February 1967.*

soldiers began an all-out attack against the ARVN and montagnard troops on the river's north bank. The montagnards stood firm but the two lieutenants who commanded the Vietnamese troops bolted. Moments later the ARVN enlisted men abandoned their positions, jumped into the river, and swam for their lives. The platoon of montagnards was overrun and wiped out. "Had the ARVNs not broken and run," Traston said, "we wouldn't have lost the 'yards and we probably would have driven back the NVA."

Later that day the ARVN troops who fled the firefight drifted back to their base. As they came in, Traston said, "They just shrugged their shoulders." The company's commander took no disciplinary action against the two lieutenants or the enlisted men. The American advisers, under orders not to intervene in ARVN affairs, could do nothing. Traston began to realize that the ARVN soldiers did not want to fight. "A lot of them were born into the war. They'd been in battle all their lives." It was more important to the soldiers to protect themselves and care for their families than to die for their country. "They didn't know what they were fighting for. They didn't have any unity. They just wanted to be left alone to live a peaceful life."

Leaders of men

American advisers who worked with ARVN soldiers in 1965 all agree that the quality of an ARVN unit was in direct proportion to the quality of its leader. Lieutenant John L. Franck served as an adviser to a battalion of the ARVN 23d Infantry Division, headquartered at Nha Trang. The battalion commander was a

An ARVN captain *in the 21st Division stands with his U.S. adviser, 1967.*

forty-five-year-old captain named Soc. The ordinary soldier in Captain Soc's battalion wore a tight-cut standard Vietnamese uniform but decorated it with "gaudy extras" such as a colored neckerchief. He wore his ammunition supply in bandoliers that crisscrossed his chest, shouldered a small rucksack with little in it but a change of underwear, and carried an M1 rifle. Most of the soldiers appeared to be in their early twenties. Families accompanied the roughly 20 percent who had married, living in conditions no worse than those of the average Vietnamese. They served to defend their country and because service provided a small wage. Basically apolitical, they disliked the Communists but were not pro-GVN. Most were illiterate and none had a strong sense of mission or purpose.

Their leader, Captain Soc, had been fighting the war for fifteen years. Standing over five feet, eight inches tall, large for a Vietnamese, he walked with a cane because of a combat injury to one leg. Under Soc's leadership the ARVN battalion fought vigorously, according to Franck. "When given a mission, they would go out and perform it. When engaged with the enemy, they would close and fight to the finish. There was never any question that they might turn and run." On one major operation conducted south of Tuy Hoa, Soc ordered his men to take a hill occupied by Vietcong troops. The ARVN unit was beaten back again and again as it attacked the VC position. Then Captain Soc moved to the front line. While bullets whizzed past him, he used his cane to direct his troops. "They regrouped and attacked again," Franck said. "They were going to continue to do that until they got the darned thing." With the help of repeated air strikes the ARVN battalion gained the hilltop and killed every enemy soldier on it. Captain Soc made sure his troops obeyed him under fire. "If he gave an order, he saw that it was carried out," Franck said. "He had a good sense of humor, but was a demanding disciplinarian."

When superb leadership was combined with highly motivated troops, ARVN units were as good as any fighting forces in the world, according to most American advisers. Among elite units, such as airborne, Ranger, armor, and marine battalions, officers and enlisted men were uniformly excellent fighters. Captain George Livingston spent the last six months of 1965 as an adviser to the 8th Airborne Battalion, an elite unit headquartered at Tan Son Nhut air base outside Saigon. "My battalion was very good," Captain Livingston said. "It was well-led by its battalion commander, who had a lot of combat experience, was well-liked, and knew what he was doing." The battalion's professional leadership encouraged enlisted men to feel that they would be successful in battle. Good living quarters and allowances paid to dependent families strengthened their morale. The soldiers had the "macho mentality" of special units

and had no trouble recruiting despite heavy casualties. Many were ex-North Vietnamese or sons of those who left the North and opposed the Communists. Livingston felt they were "not necessarily for the GVN," yet "they didn't lack for guts." An American who served as an adviser to a Ranger unit echoed this view. "Elite units were eager for a fight," he said. But at the end of 1965 elite units amounted to less than 17,000 men, or approximately 5 percent of total RVNAF forces.

The name of the game

Despite the solid performance of elite military units, and the creditable service of some regular units, the bulk of RVNAF forces earned low marks. A catastrophic desertion rate was a symptom of a military in disarray. During 1965 more than 113,000 RVNAF soldiers were at some time listed as not present for duty and unaccounted for. Some of these unauthorized absences were temporary, made necessary by soldiers' responsibilities to tend to family matters, and made possible by primitive personnel record-keeping. But a large proportion of the ordinary soldiers absent without leave had lost the will to fight the war.

Partly at fault for RVNAF's low morale was the political nature of the conflict. "Politics is the name of the game," said one ARVN noncommissioned officer. "The war is an affair of politics. All the fighting, all the killing, all the victories and defeats don't mean a thing." Individual courage or dedication to national survival was misplaced, this soldier felt. An ARVN officer shared this view. "The Army is used as a pawn in a game of international politics, and the politics of the situation—not the courage or heroism of the Vietnamese soldier—will decide it. The soldiers see and feel this, and it damages their morale."

The day-to-day conditions of service also damaged the morale of ordinary Vietnamese servicemen. In 1965 a private earned 1,600 piasters per month, the equivalent of 13 dollars. One sergeant with more than ten years of service earned 15 dollars, just enough for his own needs. His wife worked as a tailor to support their children. Food allowances were paid to unit commanders to provide daily rations for their troops when on combat operations, but many diverted money for their own use, and many a soldier was forced to steal to eat. Families of Vietnamese servicemen accompanied them to their bases, but housing for dependents was usually not provided for them. At a typical base, the headquarters of the ARVN 21st Division at Vi Thanh in south-central IV Corps, families lived in makeshift huts built of discarded C-ration and ammunition crates. Sanitary facilities were primitive, there were inadequate schools for children, and during the rainy season knee-deep mud clogged paths among the ramshackle shelters crowded closely together.

Service in South Vietnam's military offered few attractions. Many servicemen entered the military because they were drafted, and they stayed in because they could not find employment elsewhere. For Le Duc Hue military service was an unsought career, not a crusade. Drafted in 1961 at age twenty-two, Hue served as a mechanic in the army engineer corps. Discharged from service early in 1965, Hue attempted to find a job in civilian society but could not, so he reenlisted, this time in the navy. By the end of 1965, he was assigned to a base in central II Corps where he served as an electrician and logistics technician. Hue felt discouraged about his country's chances of winning the war. "My experience tells me that the other side is more disciplined, and more willing to sacrifice." His own government and military seemed too weak. "The officials and the generals are too greedy. They don't think of the future, only of themselves."

Other soldiers agreed. Nguyen Van Chinh entered service in 1959 as a private soldier and four years later achieved his highest rank, that of ensign in the navy. Chinh saw combat in 1965 while serving on board a river patrol boat that operated on the Cuu Long River near Can Tho in central IV Corps. He thought that his superior officers didn't have clear goals. "They don't know where to go or what to do." He also thought that they didn't share the hardships of combat duty. "The generals always conduct the war from the safest place—as far from combat as possible. Sometimes they make a reconnaissance flight, but they appear for only a few moments. Then—zoom!—they disappear!" Chinh felt the war was being lost because of a lack of leadership. "Most of the generals have packed their bags and sent away their families and are ready to leave themselves at any time. The armed forces are like a snake, a snake without a head. It is all a waste."

Americanization

MACV responded to RVNAF's weakness in combat and its low troop morale by increasing American troop levels everywhere but in IV Corps. There, because of GVN sensitivity about foreign troops in that most populous area of the country, and the absence of NVA units, three South Vietnamese divisions retained responsibility for combat operations as before. By the end of 1966 U.S. troop levels had risen to 385,000, more than twice the number of a year before. Increased American responsibility for combat operations took pressure off beleaguered ARVN units and permitted them to concentrate on defending themselves against enemy attacks. In addition, American fund-

ing for RVNAF in 1966 increased to $738 million, a jump of $177 million from the previous year. These funds were used to expand RVNAF troop levels and to provide more training facilities and programs. By the end of 1966 RVNAF forces had increased by 50,000 men. Also, the U.S. conducted negotiations with the government of South Vietnam over the assignment of ARVN units to pacification support. The shift occurred during late 1965 and the first half of 1966.

While the influx of American troops and money relieved ARVN of some of the danger it faced from the enemy, the build-up also brought with it new problems. Despite MACV's efforts to control inflation caused by the large increase in American spending, prices for basic goods soared. As a result, life got harder for the Vietnamese soldier. He resented the better weapons, better equipment, and better medical treatment given to American soldiers. He grew envious of the higher pay, more comfortable housing, and larger quantities of food supplied to soldiers he regarded as foreigners. One RVNAF serviceman was astonished by the Americans' wealth. "They are the most powerful, the most sophisticated, the richest army in the world—especially the richest. Each soldier has three servants!" The Vietnamese soldier saw his own commander wait for the decision of his American counterpart before issuing an order. He saw his wife go out to work at housekeeping, laundering, or other tasks for the Americans. He saw his children sacrifice their self-respect to beg among them. He heard himself called by names Americans used for their common enemy—"slope" or "dink" or "gook." But many ARVN soldiers were impressed by the skill of their American allies and seemed to appreciate the sacrifices they made.

The Saigon government hoped to help its cause by expanding RVNAF. But the army's rapid growth—projected to jump from a total of 571,000 at the end of 1965 to 643,000 by the end of 1967—meant that new recruits had to be trained and more officers schooled to lead them. The RVNAF Joint General Staff acted to alleviate a shortage of trained and competent field-grade officers, particularly at the company and platoon level, by instituting a vigorous program of training junior and noncommissioned officers. The JGS also published a handbook for small unit commanders containing guidance in combat tactics and supervision of enlisted men. Previously, promotions had been more a function of personal or political ties than of leadership abilities. The JGS took steps to improve promotion policies and procedures and began to require efficiency reports on junior officers' performance. As a result the JGS laid a foundation for basing promotions on military competence rather than political connection. A program called "New Horizons" set clearer guidelines for provision of daily rations, more equitable

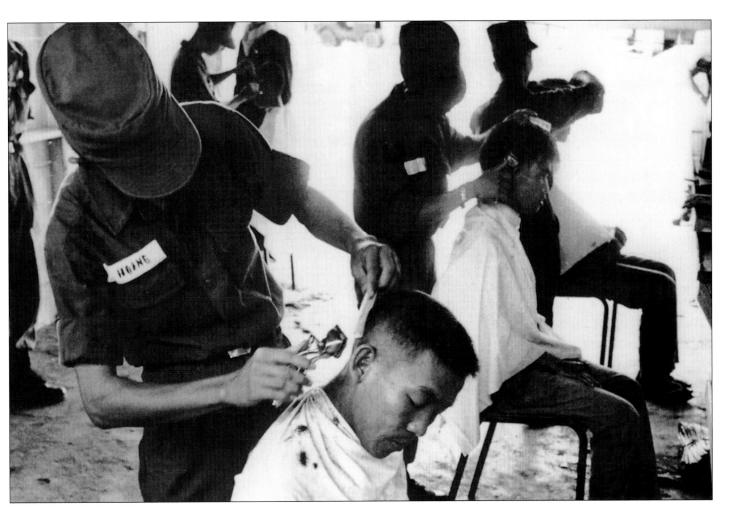

New RVNAF recruits receive their first crew cuts *in summer, 1965. That year, South Vietnamese draft call-ups increased dramatically, quadrupling during July, and training for recruits was shortened from twelve weeks to nine.*

leave policies, and better housing for dependent families. RVNAF leaders also made a more concerted effort to explain the nature of the war in order to increase soldiers' dedication to the goal of national survival. Improved training and increased benefits began to pay off in better morale. In 1967 the RVNAF desertion rate fell by more than one-third.

ARVN pacification

By the fall of 1966 approximately fifty ARVN battalions, roughly half of all ARVN units, had assumed the role of conducting pacification operations. Previously some ARVN units performed pacification tasks, but because of poor management and a lack of enthusiasm their efforts were largely counterproductive. "The behavior of the army toward the people was not good," said one ARVN lieutenant. "Soldiers stole property and grabbed women. They horrified the people, who hated them." To reduce ARVN abuses Saigon's military leaders reorganized pacification

tactics and retrained ARVN soldiers to execute them better.

ARVN units assigned to pacification support employed the tactical concept of "clear and hold." Focusing their efforts on villages and hamlets outside provincial capitals and district towns, ARVN forces conducted clearing operations to drive out enemy troops. Next ARVN units established permanent fortified bases on their outskirts and conducted routine patrols and periodic sweeps away from the population to blunt the threat of attack by large enemy units. Meanwhile locally recruited Regional Force companies and Popular Force platoons stationed closer to the people assumed responsibility for protecting them from attacks by smaller enemy units. When this shield was in place civilian workers in GVN programs such as Revolutionary Development attempted to carry out their duties. Mobile Training Teams (MTTs) including Vietnamese and Americans instructed ARVN battalions in the goals of pacification and ordered them to cooperate with the local population. But many ARVN commanders resented assignment to pacification. General Ngo Quang Truong claimed that the need to provide for pacification support weakened ARVN units for combat activities. "After a long period of operating from fixed positions, the combat spirit of a unit was greatly reduced. Combat aggressiveness either decreased markedly or was completely gone."

As ARVN responsibility for pacification increased, American advisers assigned to ARVN units took on the duty of monitoring their activities. In 1966 and 1967 Colonel Nathan C. Vail served as deputy senior adviser with the ARVN 7th Division at Ben Tre in IV Corps's Kien Hoa Province. On the basis of his personal experience Colonel Vail concluded that ARVN support for pacification was unsuccessful. ARVN troops required to live in combat zones looked out for their own safety. "Operations were compromised and there was a live and let live kind of environment," Vail said. Some ARVN soldiers were dedicated to the cause of their government, but many were not. "Most wanted to wait until the situation cleared up, until they could be sure which side would win."

The enemy within

Participation in pacification operations by ARVN combat units could result in greater security. But the assignment of ARVN units to static positions near populated areas also increased military control—already pervasive—over the lives of citizens. After the coup of June 1965 that installed Air Vice Marshall Nguyen Cao Ky as president, the armed forces of South Vietnam gained predominant authority over the affairs of the nation.

In each of South Vietnam's 43 provinces the head of government was a military officer, usually an ARVN lieutenant colonel appointed by President Ky, to whom he owed political fealty as well as military obedience. District governments within each province were also headed by an ARVN officer, who usually held the rank of major. In addition to conducting combat operations and pursuing pacification objectives, these province and district chiefs performed civil duties such as tax collection, disbursement of funds, or administration of aid programs. Since only the military possessed means for maintaining security, establishing order, and carrying out other duties of government, military governors set civilian as well as military policies. But while ARVN's increased role in pacification consolidated its civil authority, it multiplied opportunities for bribery, extortion, and graft. A parent who applied for a child's birth certificate customarily paid a small fee under the table to expedite the application. A small businessman who wanted to build a rice mill found that zoning restrictions evaporated when he politely presented government offi-

cials with cash gifts. During the American build-up of 1966 and 1967, such corruption grew enormously and became a serious obstacle to South Vietnam's goal of nation-building.

In the war-ruptured society of South Vietnam huge amounts of American money and resources fostered a wide variety of illicit practices. Money spent by the United States military to acquire land for bases prompted questionable real estate dealings. Military administrators diverted American-supplied commodities for sale in the black market. Opportunities for acquiring illicit income persuaded some ARVN commanders to use their troops as laborers and concessionaires. By the fall of 1967 an ARVN Ranger battalion near Pleiku was supplying the U.S. 4th Infantry Division with beer, prostitutes, and laundry services. Next to the sprawling U.S. air base near Bien Hoa another ARVN Ranger battalion built a red-light district known as "Tijuana East."

Such corruption weakened GVN efforts to win the loyalty of the people. A farmer who depended on using a bridge to bring his produce to market welcomed ARVN guards who protected it from VC sabotage. But he balked at their demand that he pay a "tax" to cross. A poor family that suffered a bad harvest and needed rice to feed itself was pleased emergency supplies provided by the U.S. Agency for International Development were available but resented being charged for bags of rice marked "not for resale." Corruption also weakened ARVN's combat performance. Despite attempts at reforms, inexperienced and incompetent officers sometimes gained promotions over capable officers because of political connections. And honest military officers who served under superior officers they knew to be corrupt frequently mistrusted their orders. Colonel Sidney Berry, a MACV senior adviser to the ARVN 7th Division in the spring of 1966, said that his counterpart, Colonel Nguyen Viet Thanh, "questioned the motives" behind the orders of his commanding officer, General Doan Van Quang. Rumor held that Quang had made a fortune by trading rice and opium on the black market. Quang was dismissed for corruption by President Ky later in 1966, but in 1968 he was appointed assistant for military and security affairs by his close associate, Nguyen Van Thieu, when Thieu succeeded Ky in the presidency.

Soldiering on

Despite the obstacles they faced, some ARVN units continued to perform with distinction in battle. First Lieutenant David Fishback, an assistant adviser to the ARVN 52d Ranger battalion in the fall of 1966, said that its soldiers were excellent troops. "These guys were killers. I never saw any of them run." Many had been recruited out of Saigon jails, choosing military service over prison. Thus motivated and well-equipped, the battalion was led by officers who had accumulated years of combat experience. Captain Douglas Rogers, an armor officer who served as adviser to the 1st Troop, 4th Cavalry Regiment, thought that its soldiers were both aggressive in battle and technically proficient. "They drove their armored personnel carriers as well as Americans, and maintained them better." Superbly led by their commander, a captain named Ly, Rogers said that the 1st Troop was "quite brave" in combat with the Vietcong and "really stacked them up."

Though certain units of ARVN troops were "as good as any American units, and some were better," as one adviser put it, the overall performance of ARVN troops in combat was inferior to that of American troops. According to figures included in *The Pentagon Papers,* during the first nine months of 1966 only 46 percent of ARVN combat operations by units of battalion size or larger resulted in contact with the enemy. Ninety percent of combat operations by U.S. forces of this size resulted in enemy contact. Some of this disproportion is attributable to the diminishment of ARVN units' combat effectiveness caused by their

An ARVN soldier directs *the relocation of Vietnamese out of a village near Da Nang. Resettlement operations were intended to dry up the sea of people in which Vietcong guerrillas swam.*

assignment to pacification duties. During this same period the number of enemy troops killed by ARVN troops fell from a weekly average of 356 to 238, while the weekly average for U.S. troops rose from 476 to 557. American battalions were not only killing more enemy soldiers than were ARVN battalions, but they were also being killed more often: The "friendly kill rate" per ARVN battalion per week was .6; the comparable figure per U.S. battalion per week was 1.7—nearly three times higher. For the eleven-month period from August 1966 to June 1967, Vietnamese forces were rated about half as effective as U.S. forces in killing Vietcong and North Vietnamese Army troops. While American combat units searched and destroyed, some

U.S. officials complained, certain ARVN combat units searched and avoided.

The ARVN unit most notorious for poor performance was the 25th Division, commanded by General Phan Truong Chinh, which operated in southwestern III Corps after relocation from I Corps. ARVN Chief of Staff General Cao Van Vien described the 25th Division as "not only the worst ARVN Division, but possibly the worst division in any army." In all of 1966 the 13,000-man division conducted over 100,000 combat operations (most routine small unit patrols) but made contact with the enemy fewer than 100 times—a ratio of one-tenth of 1 percent. During this time the 25th Division claimed to have

Aussies, ROKs, and Other Allies

Although the United States and South Vietnam bore the major burden of fighting the Communists, in Vietnam they were not alone. Other countries sent military units in response to President Johnson's "more flags" campaign during which he pressured members of the Southeast Asia Treaty Organization (SEATO) to join the struggle in Vietnam. Thailand, the Philippines, New Zealand, the Republic of China (Taiwan), and Spain contributed to the "Free World Forces" in Vietnam with military personnel that served primarily in support roles, and thirty-nine other countries sent economic, humanitarian, and technical aid. Australia and Korea, however, each sent several combat maneuver battalions, which earned a reputation for bravery while facing the same battle hazards as the U.S. and RVNAF forces.

Australia deployed units beginning in 1965; by the end of 1966, 4,525 troops were stationed in Bien Hoa and Phuoc Tuy provinces, including two battalions, an armored carrier troop, a field artillery regiment, and air service and signal support units. One of the Aussies' largest battles took place at a French rubber plantation called Binh Boa seventy kilometers southeast of Saigon. On August 18, 1966, 1,500 North Vietnamese and Vietcong ambushed

the 108 men of Delta Company, 6th Battalion, Royal Australian Regiment. In the initial exchange of fire, the Aussies sustained heavy casualties. In the monsoon rain, Delta Company fought the attackers to a standstill. Braving heavy enemy fire, Aussie helicopter pilots resupplied ammunition, while armored personnel carriers provided support fire with .50-caliber machine guns. After four hours, the Australians drove the enemy from the battlefield, forcing them to leave behind 245 dead.

Next to the United States, the Republic of Korea (ROK) sent the largest military force to aid South Vietnam. By the end of 1966, 44,897 ROK troops fought against the Vietnamese Communists. Positioned along the coasts of Ninh Thuan, Khanh Hoa, Phu Yen, and Binh Dinh provinces, the Korean Capital Division, the 9th Infantry Division, and the 2d Marine Brigade carried out orders to protect the Vietnamese population on both sides of Highway 1. Since the ROKs did not have helicopters and were not highly mobile, they performed clearing and holding operations instead a large-scale offensive sweeps. As Lieutenant General Chae Myung Shin, commander of Korean forces in Vietnam, explained, "We hit and stay, not search and destroy."

Renowned for their fierceness and courage, ROK troops were drawn from the elite units of South Korea's armed forces. In the Korean Capital "Tiger" Division almost all junior officers had graduated from the Korean Military Academy and were hand-picked by senior

Capital Division officers. The 2d Marine "Blue Dragon" Brigade and the 9th Korean Infantry "White Horse" Division—famous for decimating two Chinese divisions in 1950 during the Korean War—made up the other two elite units. The White Horse Division underwent an antiguerrilla training program described by General Dwight Beach, commander of U.S. troops in Korea, as "the roughest course I have ever seen." In addition to learning hand-to-hand combat, soldiers gained expertise in a deadly form of karate called *tae kwon do*. Not long after their arrival in Vietnam, stories circulated describing ROKs who killed Communists with a single stroke of the hand. Americans respected the ability of their Korean allies. During the Korean War, South Koreans had relied heavily on Americans for leadership and tactical support. In Vietnam sometimes they surpassed their American "teachers" and accumulated a higher captured weapons count in search and clear operations than Americans engaged in similar actions. Lieutenant General Chae did not greatly exaggerate when he boasted, "Where the ROKs are, it is 100 percent secure."

During August 1966, a Korean battalion working with the 4th Infantry Division near the Cambodian border had divided into three companies for small unit patrolling. On their sixth night, the 101st North Vietnamese Regiment of approximately 600 men ambushed one of the Korean companies. Five times the North Vietnamese attacked in waves but were repulsed by the 150-man ROK company.

inflicted 17 enemy casualties but reported a total of 70 casualties among its own troops. Fifty of these were due to truck and jeep accidents. In the same period the U.S. 25th Division, which shared the ARVN unit's tactical area of responsibility (TAOR), suffered more than 1,000 wounded and approximately 200 dead. When Lieutenant Colonel Weldon Honeycutt, the American adviser to the ARVN 25th Division, pointed out its deficiencies in his monthly reports to MACV, General Chinh accused him of destroying "the spirit of cooperation between Americans and Vietnamese." General Chinh was well-connected to higher-ranking ARVN officers, and his protests elicited apologies from MACV. Colonel Honeycutt was reassigned to the United States. The affair had a chilling effect on other American advisers, who grew wary of exercising leverage over their counterparts.

Combined operations

Many deficiencies in combat effectiveness could be traced to ARVN's lack of tactical assets equal to those of U.S. units. Helicopters for moving troops quickly into battle and air and artillery support during engagements were less readily available to ARVN units. Demands on small arms stockpiles and logistics equipment by U.S. units delayed modernization of ARVN forces.

When the NVA withdrew the next day, they left 182 dead on the battlefield. The Koreans lost only 7 men. Three U.S. Army tank personnel who assisted them had "endless praise" for the Korean company.

Not all Korean operations ran so smoothly. Fired on by VC hiding in a hamlet in Binh Dinh Province, a Korean unit swept the area. The next day a U.S. naval officer entered the hamlet and found scores of dead civilians, including the bodies of the hamlet chief, his wife, and children who had been tied to stakes and eviscerated. One survivor claimed that a Korean officer had ordered him "to leave this place, and tell people what happened."

Although ROKs were known for employing brutal tactics against the VC, they often succeeded in implementing peaceful pacification programs. To win people's allegiance the ROKs told tales of Communist atrocities during the Korean War and of the progress South Korea had made since the Communists had been thrown back. Pointing to their refrigerators and their electric fans, they proudly explained, "This was made in Korea." Although these tactics often worked, some envious Americans grumbled at their deviation from U.S. pacification operations. "You get the feeling," said one irritated U.S. official, "that they stay awake all night trying to think up new ways to do things around here."

More Flags

	1964	1965	1966	1967	1968	1969	1970
AUSTRALIA							
Strength	200	1,557	4,525	6,818	7,661	7,672	6,763
Number of maneuver battalions		1	2	2	3	3	3
KOREA							
Strength	200	20,620	45,566	47,829	50,003	48,869	48,537
Number of maneuver battalions		10	22	22	22	22	22
THAILAND							
Strength	0	16	244	2,205	6,005	11,568	11,586
Number of maneuver battalions		0	0	1	3	6	6
NEW ZEALAND							
Strength	30	119	155	534	516	552	441
THE PHILIPPINES							
Strength	17	72	2,061	2,020	1,576	189	74
REPUBLIC OF CHINA							
Strength	20	20	23	31	29	29	31
SPAIN							
Strength	0	0	13	13	12	10	7
Total strength	467	22,404	52,566	59,450	65,802	68,889	67,444
Total maneuver battalions	0	11	24	25	28	31	31

In order to upgrade the effectiveness of ARVN units, and to familiarize them with American combat tactics, General Westmoreland and his staff at MACV experimented with a limited system for on-the-job training of ARVN. MACV urged American commanders to adopt ARVN units and to cooperate with them in combined combat operations. One of the first such operations, Lam Son II, occurred in June 1966. It joined troops of the ARVN 5th Division with soldiers of the U.S. 1st Infantry Division. The largest, Operation Fairfax, called *Rang Dong* by the Vietnamese, began in November 1966 and lasted through December 1967. Operation Fairfax combined elements of the U.S. 1st, 4th, and 25th Infantry Divisions with Vietnamese forces drawn from the ARVN 5th Ranger Battalion and the 3d and 5th Airborne Battalions. As the operation continued, these units were replaced by other U.S. and ARVN forces.

Conducted in three districts of Gia Dinh Province, located east and south of Saigon, Operation Fairfax was troubled at the outset by command coordination problems. But once these were corrected and mutual trust was established between cooperating U.S. and ARVN units, allied forces conducted joint maneuvers. After several months both allies assigned roles to local RF and PF units and cooperated with them in pacification activities such as County Fairs. By the spring of 1967 provisional security had been established, and American units began to run training programs for regular ARVN and RF/PF troops. These programs culminated in a five-day test held in September 1967 during which ARVN soldiers demonstrated marked improvement. By December the bulk of U.S. forces were withdrawn from the three districts, and ARVN forces accompanied by a small number of American advisers assumed independent responsibility for maintaining security. At the conclusion of the operation more than 1,000 Vietcong had been killed, and 40 VC had defected to allied troops. Operation Fairfax was considered a success by both American and South Vietnamese leaders and used as a model for subsequent combined operations in 1968.

Some American officers spoke highly of Operation Fairfax, but others questioned the idea. According to Brigadier General Robert C. Forbes, the commander of the 199th Infantry Brigade in November 1966, the ARVN 5th Ranger Battalion was more a hindrance than a help. One U.S. officer said "They became dependent on us for rations, for medical support, for calling in air strikes, even for leadership." Though ARVN troops were not placed officially under U.S. command, it was not uncommon, he said, for a U.S. company commander to wind up commanding two companies, one American, one Vietnamese. "You just can't stop the war to start training people, and that's what this boils down to," said another American. Elsewhere close

cooperation between U.S. and ARVN units sometimes had extremely adverse effects. Fist fights broke out between American and South Vietnamese Special Forces troops deployed in areas near the Cambodian border. At Quang Tri in April 1967 disloyal ARVN troops betrayed American positions to the enemy, led VC and NVA troops through minefields, and killed their own commander. Four U.S. Marines died and twenty-seven were wounded in that incident. In Binh Dinh Province in December 1967 American machine gunners manning armored personnel carriers (APCs) of the 50th Mechanized Infantry became enraged when ARVN troops fled a fierce battle with the Vietcong, leaving the APCs without ground support. When the ARVN troops started firing at the enemy from a position some 200 meters behind the APCs, directly through the American positions, the APC gunners "turned their weapons on them," according to the MACV operation report, which says no more about the matter. Such instances of ARVN misconduct in battle made many U.S. troops distrust their Vietnamese allies. And the spectacle of ARVN corruption, which joint operations permitted Americans to witness firsthand, had a damaging effect or American morale. Increasingly U.S. troops wondered why they should risk their lives in a war that the South Vietnamese seemed unwilling to fight for themselves.

War without end?

As American troops took over more of the fighting, respite from battle and improvements in leadership and training stemmed the deterioration of South Vietnam's military. The shift of ARVN forces to pacification extended security to the population in some areas, but it also resulted in increased corruption. Efforts to upgrade the combat effectiveness of ARVN units through combined operations met with limited success. Meanwhile American casualties mounted, and the war appeared to some observers to be a stalemate. If in 1965 the American people accepted the president's decision to send American boys to do the fighting Vietnamese boys should be doing themselves, by the end of 1967 their patience was wearing thin. The persistence of weakness and corruption among the ARVN and GVN, contrasted with the tactical skill and political determination of the enemy, combined with the mounting toll of American deaths to raise the prospect in Congress of a bloody, endless war. A growing clamor arose among the American public for a more spirited and honest South Vietnamese contribution to the war effort.

Operation Fairfax, *August 1967. Helicopters of the U.S. Army's 199th Infantry Brigade (Light) lift off after dropping ARVN Rangers into a landing zone in the Mekong Delta twenty-five kilometers southwest of Saigon.*

"Our comrades felt no pity.... We had been told to slaughter as many imperialist soldiers as we could since, if the number of American dead mounted, the American people— who dislike this war—would overthrow their government."

North Vietnamese soldier

The typical North Vietnamese regular fighting in the South was twenty-three years old—four years older than his U.S. counterpart—and came from a farming cooperative where after years of food shortages he and his family finally had enough to eat. He stood five feet two or three inches and weighed 115 to 120 pounds. A Buddhist and a bachelor, he had already logged three years of compulsory service, undergoing military training and also instructing local militia and participating in public works and agricultural projects. Fewer than half the soldiers belonged to the Lao Dong (Communist) party or its youth groups. Yet they were believers in the social and political order of North Vietnam and likely to come from a family actively involved in "building socialism" on the cooperative. He was ready to fight at the behest of his government, if initially reluctant to do so in South Vietnam, so far away from his family. The first soldiers to travel South were volunteers but, like "volunteers" in every army, they had essentially been chosen or coerced and they didn't entirely like it.

Early in the war, many did not learn that they were going South until just before departure. Some did not discover their destination until they were en route. Few soldiers had home leave before the separation, which was likely to endure for years, and those who made it home and who knew of their destination were advised not to inform their families. "My family assumed that I was going abroad to study," said one senior lieutenant who was granted leave. Afterward communication with the family was a rarity. It took three or four months for letters mailed from the North to reach a unit in the South and at least as long for mail to travel in the opposite direction. "Mail call" seldom took place more than once every two months, and some NVA* units never received mail.

A soldier going to the southern battlefield reported to a staging area in North Vietnam for as much as four months of military and political training. The political phase included intense indoctrination on a soldier's duty to the fatherland, on the evils of the American "invasion" of the South, and on the necessity of reunifying the two Vietnams. The essential theme was reunification by means of armed political struggle.

This doctrine of struggle—*dau tranh*—was central to the North Vietnamese psyche. In fact, the English word "struggle" fails to convey the quasi-religious dedication of *dau tranh*. For a Vietnamese, *dau tranh* was an enormously emotive force. Military, or armed, *dau tranh* included warfare, both guerrilla and Main Force, but it also legitimized assassination and kidnapping in pursuit of reunification. Political *dau tranh* covered the organizing and proselytizing activities among the people and VC/NVA military, to persuade them or force them to adhere to Hanoi's goals. People's war as defined by Ho Chi Minh and

Civilians in North Vietnam *stand aside as an army detachment parades past. For many North Vietnamese regulars, the march led to southern battlefields.*

*(North Vietnam called itself the Democratic Republic of Vietnam, DRV in American shorthand, and gave its military the title of People's Army of Vietnam, or PAVN. But the Americans grew sensitive about perpetuating their enemy's propaganda by employing such titles, since North Vietnam was undemocratic and its military was not a people's army but rather a conventional force. Thus in 1966 the American Embassy directed that the country be referred to, simply, as North Vietnam, or NVN, and that its army be called the North Vietnamese Army, or NVA.)

General Giap held political and military *dau tranh* to be the pincers between which the enemy would be crushed. Although disagreements over strategy and the allocation of resources occurred regularly among Hanoi's leaders, the basic premise of reunification by means of *dau tranh* was an article of faith.

At the northern indoctrination centers—Xuan Mai, southwest of Hanoi, was one of the largest—cadres presented lectures and courses on the soldiers' military role in the reunification of the fatherland. Often the recruits acted like soldiers everywhere. "When the political cadre gave his lecture ..." said a nineteen-year-old private, "he was standing up there talking, and we were down here pinching one another, smoking cigarettes and fooling around." But the lessons nevertheless sank in. "The soldier's supreme duty is to fight on the side of the revolution," another private summarized. "The revolution has given independence to one half of the country, but there still remains the other half. The revolution is going on in the South. North Vietnamese fighters go there to fight on the people's side to free them from the yoke of American imperialism. Vietnam is indivisible."

Anti-Americanism increasingly constituted a significant part of the soldiers' indoctrination. They learned that the aims of the American "invasion" were to oppress the Vietnamese, to control the plantations as the French had, and to use South Vietnam as a springboard to take over North Vietnam and other countries. With only vague notions, if any, about North Vietnam's role in the South, most soldiers were totally perplexed about the "wanton" American bombing of North Vietnam. They were enraged about the killing of their countrymen by bombs, about construction projects demolished, about transportation disrupted. "All the construction works the people had completed in ten years by tightening their belts were destroyed by the Americans," one soldier complained. The Americans were represented as virtually the only foe. Soldiers became so accustomed to the idea of fighting Americans that it often shocked them on arrival in the South to discover that they had to fight fellow Vietnamese as well.

In spite of the intense indoctrination, many soldiers remained hesitant about leaving their families. They feared they never would return home since they knew relatives or neighbors who had infiltrated a year or two earlier and had neither returned nor sent news. Some soldiers who turned in their weapons asked to go home. They were instead "re-indoctrinated and re-educated." A half dozen from one company deserted and returned to their native villages, but the army sent a truck for them. "The women and the boys in my village made fun of me," said one. "They said it was ridiculous for a youth like myself who had the good fortune to be chosen to go south to refuse to leave the North and to escape home. So I had to go." Political cadres continually motivated soldiers whose enthusiasm wavered, reminding them of their duty to their countrymen in the South. "My comrades were all very sad at first," reported a soldier. "But the cadres mobilized their spirits and then they began to feel all right about it. They were all enthusiastic and willing to go south in the end."

While the cadre functioned as a politicized first sergeant—indoctrinating and exhorting the troops and occasionally stiffening a backbone—another mainstay of Communist control was the three-man cell. Each soldier was part of such a cell, and the trio worked, marched, ate, and fought together. This tight bond bolstered morale and helped to soothe feelings of isolation the men experienced in being away from their families, fighting in what was for most a foreign land. The reliance of cell members on one another also fostered tenacity in battle. The appointed cell leader, often a combat-tested veteran or newly promoted sergeant assigned to a "green" unit, directed his two comrades in battle. The younger soldiers relied heavily on the leadership of the veterans. "If a cell member split from his cell during combat," one soldier said, "our actions would become uncoordinated and our casualties would be higher."

Criticism/self-criticism

As much as the cells constituted a "home," they were a prison as well since the members had to watch each other and criticize any untoward behavior, either military or political. A soldier shirking his duty or losing his devotion to *dau tranh* found himself upbraided by his comrades in criticism/self-criticism *(kiem thao)* sessions or reported to the cadre by his cell mates. For the NVA soldier, to indulge in the normal grumbling of the infantryman was to take a political risk.

In *kiem thao* sessions, the soldiers offered judgments of their comrades and listened to evaluations of their own performances. The meetings sometimes featured discussion of tactics from the unit's recent engagements or suggestions on such topics as antihelicopter warfare sent from the army command. *Kiem thao* sessions could become extremely heated and emotional. For some soldiers the sessions were especially traumatic, as they heard their weaknesses and failings denounced publicly and then had to respond to those charges. Serious military offenses, such as attempted desertion or refusal to fight, were often dealt with by means of *kiem thao* sessions. The public humiliation and disapproval of his comrades would sometimes suffice to force the soldier to rectify his attitude and behavior.

For a few weeks prior to their departure for South Vietnam, the troops received especially nourishing food to strengthen them for the journey. In addition to the normal staples of rice and fish sauce *(nuoc mam)*, the soldiers feasted on beef, pork, fish, fruits and sweet cakes, sugar, and milk. During this period they also began to assemble the gear they would take South. Every man received a rucksack and a variety of uniforms—green or brown army uniforms and a pair of black pajamas—as well as black and yellow underwear, socks, a sweater, a belt, and a khaki hat. A pair of rubber-soled sandals completed the clothing issue. His bivouac equipment included a sheet of nylon about eight feet wide that served as a ground cloth or tent, a long length of rope to suspend the tent, a linen hammock, a mosquito net, an entrenching tool, a canteen, and a mess kit—a tin bowl, water cup, and spoon. The medical kit contained bandages and cotton, water puri-

fying and antidiarrhea pills. All-important antimalaria pills were often in short supply. Finally each received a quantity of ammunition for his Chinese-made AK47 rifle or carbine; soldiers were not likely to waste ammunition they had transported on their backs. In addition to his weapons, each soldier ultimately carried up to seventy pounds of gear and ammunition in a rucksack.

The journey south

The troops left the training centers and traveled by train or truck to the coastal city of Dong Hoi in southern North Vietnam where they received a week's supply of dry field rations—sugar, salt, tea, cans of condensed milk and salted meat, and rice. More rice was available at way stations along the route. To avoid detection by American aircraft, the troops

North Vietnamese officers, *with map cases hanging from a strap across their chests, take a break in their training day to hear news of the battlefront read from People's Army newspaper.*

marched at night along paved and dirt roads to the south and southwest, toward the demilitarized zone and Laos. At the settlement the soldiers called "Ho Village" in the northwest corner of the DMZ, they rested for several days in grass-roofed barracks.

Some men reacted to their imminent departure with a sense of finality. One early infiltrator, a sergeant and assistant squad leader who knew he would fight for the duration of the war, remembered, "I went to the South to liberate the southerners and had no hope of returning. Either I would die there, or if I were still alive, I would have to wait for national reunification to return north." Despite their forebodings, however, the majority of soldiers seemed to have been deeply affected by the training and indoctrination for their patriotic mission. "My heart is filled with joy and with an intense love for our kinsmen," one NVA soldier jotted in his diary upon setting out for the southern battlefields. "I pledge to achieve victory before returning to my homeland," wrote another.

By company or battalion, the soldiers departed at two- or three-day intervals for the so-called Ho Chi Minh Trail. Within a few days of marching along beaten paths up and down mountains, they crossed into Laos. A diverse system of thousands of paths and roads, the Ho Chi Minh Trail extended for hundreds of miles through Laos and Cambodia. The network consisted of narrow footpaths and wider roads improved as the years passed by engineers and civilian labor gangs (made up of North Vietnamese, Laotians, and montagnards) to handle trucking. Trails that led over mountains were often built up with bamboo steps and hand railings. Some paths crossed streams strung with crude rope and bamboo bridges, and more than one river had a bridge built inches below the water's surface to conceal it from aerial reconnaissance. Ferries shuttled the soldiers across some rivers. In the early years, the soldiers usually marched during the day, shielded from U.S. aircraft by the high and thick jungle canopy. They often saw loaded trucks grinding south and empty ones rattling back toward the North. They passed labor crews at work on the roads and witnessed peasants pushing bicycles laden with sacks containing military supplies and rice.

On a typical day the soldiers rose at three-thirty in the morning, marched from four until eleven, and, after breaking for lunch, they set out again until six in the evening. They rested ten minutes for each hour walked and took one day off out of perhaps every five. Led by armed liaison agents, who knew only their section of the trail, the soldiers covered some fifteen to twenty-five kilometers per day, depending on terrain. Grouped in their three-man cells, they marched in a column,

with one trio walking point fifty meters ahead and three other men stalking an equal distance behind. They often stopped for the evening at way stations—simple clusters of two or three thatched-roofed shacks guarded by a squad of soldiers and located as much as a kilometer deep in the forest. The way stations contained rice stores to replenish the soldiers' rations. Other nights the soldiers bivouacked off the trail. After stringing their hammocks and digging foxholes, they cooked and ate dinner, prepared rice-ball lunches for the following day, and went to sleep, usually just after dark.

The hardships of the journey took their toll immediately. "Marches obviously are hard," read a 1967 article for cadres. "The heat makes you tired and the rain makes you tired; there are many streams and many ferries. … There are many high passes in the mountains; if you move by night you do not get to sleep and if you move by day you must stay up late and get up early." Weighted with heavy packs, many of the men turned their ankles or developed blisters from their sandals. In the tropical climate, sores failed to heal and tended to become infected. But the most serious threat came from mosquitoes; an estimated 10 to 20 percent of the northerners died of disease on the march south. (In contrast, only an estimated 2 percent of infiltrators were victimized by air strikes.) His comrades in the three-man cell aided a soldier if he faltered, shouldering his pack and weapon and lending an arm. Those too ill to continue were left at way stations to recuperate, a mixed blessing since it meant the rupture of the three-man cell and the breaking of ties with other soldiers in the unit.

Malaria might result in death or a temporary reprieve from the march, but it never amounted to a ticket back home. "At least one-third of my company asked for permission to return home on the pretense of sickness," said one assistant squad leader early in 1965. "I myself contracted malaria. I too asked permission to return north to convalesce for a while, but the cadres rejected it." After recovery, the soldiers joined up with other units passing to the South.

An officer who in 1966 spent nearly six months in transit with his 400-man battalion reported that the unit lost half its strength en route. Even though officially combat effective, the 200 remaining soldiers were scarcely in a fighting mood. "Owing to the long journey," the officer said, "the bad food, and the malaria which daily became more serious, because of the insufficiency of medicine, the troops became demoralized and confused."

The taxing journey could result in disruption of entire units. The men of the 250th Regiment, assigned to the NVA 7th Division northeast of Saigon, arrived in October 1965 in such poor physical condition that the regiment was deactivated and, in the spring of 1966, its recovered able-bodied soldiers were sent on as replacements to the Vietcong 9th Main Force Division. The NVA 52d Regiment, also part of the 7th Division, was dispersed in the same manner in early 1967.

Command and control

After arrival in South Vietnam, usually at the end of a backbreaking hike through the central highlands, the soldiers earned a period of rest to regain their strength and acquaint themselves with their areas of operations. That period of rest often resulted in rude discoveries for the soldiers, who learned quickly that South Vietnam was not almost entirely "liberated," as they had been told. Rather, so much of the country was contested that they had to camp in the jungle and move frequently to evade U.S. and ARVN infantry and air patrols. Instead of joining their "kinsmen" in a "fraternal uprising," NVA soldiers in regular units found themselves cut off from the people. Those soldiers assigned to Vietcong Main Force units had more contact with the villagers, but it was not always satisfactory. "I thought the North had sent us to liberate the South," grumbled a private attached to the Vietcong, "and yet people in the South expelled us from their houses."

As the numbers of North Vietnamese regulars in the South grew—nearly 27,000 soldiers had been committed by the end of 1965—Hanoi organized new field headquarters. The B-3 Front, established in September 1964 as the first NVA regulars prepared to march south, took charge of the central highlands. In 1966 the B-4 Front grouped northern I Corps (Quang Tri and Thua Thien provinces) into one front while the B-1 Front took responsibility for the populous coastal provinces of Quang Ngai, Binh Dinh, Phu Yen, and Khanh Hoa. These latter two commands reported directly to a North Vietnamese Army headquarters located north of the DMZ.

Only the southern half of the country remained in the hands of COSVN—the Central Office of South Vietnam (or, as Hanoi literally called it, the Central Office of the Southern Region). The original Vietminh jungle headquarters during the French Indochina War, COSVN was reactivated by Hanoi by 1961 and was directly subordinate to the North. Commanded by NVA General Nguyen Chi Thanh since early 1964, and dominated by northerners, COSVN directed the political and military affairs of the VC.

Located in War Zone D north of Saigon in the early 1960s, COSVN later shifted to War Zone C in heavily forested Tay Ninh Province bordering Cambodia, north of the Parrot's Beak. The allies' Operation Attleboro, conducted in War Zone C in

late 1966, caused a further dislocation of COSVN, and some elements fled across the border into the sanctuaries of Cambodia. Some functional sections ended up in such widely scattered locations that visitors at one time reported it took four days to travel by foot from the organization department to the finance and economy section. Quite unlike an American headquarters, the main COSVN command was a simple site consisting of a few buildings and underground tunnels, guarded by perhaps a regiment. Trails leading to it were camouflaged and booby trapped, and COSVN leaders had separate houses with underground shelters and escape tunnels. The nerve center itself was located underground to shield it from B-52 attacks, although any strike within 500 meters would have been devastating. (The July 1967 death of General Thanh was believed by the Americans to have resulted from a B-52 raid on COSVN. The four-star general, U.S. reports said, was wounded in the chest and carried hurriedly overland to Phnom Penh, Cambodia. From there he was flown to Hanoi, where he died. His death, officially announced in Hanoi July 6, was attributed by the North Vietnamese to a heart attack.)

In a speech to the April 1966 COSVN Congress, Hanoi Politburo member Nguyen Van Vinh, head of the Lao Dong party's reunification department and hence the immediate link between Hanoi and COSVN, gave an apt evaluation of the deployment problems facing the Americans. "In South Korea, the enemy sent all his troops to the front," Vinh said. "In South Vietnam, he has introduced between 300,000 and 600,000 troops who must fight on the front line and, at the same time, protect the rear. But [they] can fulfill only one of these tasks. If they oppose our movement in the South, they will be unable to stop reinforcements from North Vietnam. If they concentrate their force to stop reinforcements from North Vietnam, they cannot stand firm on the front or in the rear." To exploit the Americans' problems, Vinh emphasized, the questions of strategy and tactics were all-important. "In a war of position, they can defeat us," he said. "But with our present tactics, we can win and they will be defeated."

In pursuing their strategy of protracted warfare, the North Vietnamese relied on precepts summed up in Mao Tse-tung's maxim, "The strategy of guerrilla war is to pit one man against ten, but the tactics are to pit ten men against one." In other words, the North Vietnamese and Vietcong, although numerically inferior, had to discover the weaknesses in allied formations and defenses and then mass for attacks on smaller concentrations of enemy troops or lightly defended posts. Their tactics emphasized surprise, speed, and elusiveness, and they chose not to fight unless they held the advantage in numbers. Until they were ready to fight, the units had to evade major allied operations as well as routine U.S. and ARVN reconnaissance patrols.

Living underground

To avoid contact the North Vietnamese and Vietcong kept out of sight, remaining in sanctuaries in Laos and Cambodia and bivouacking deep in the jungles in South Vietnam. An extensive network of tunnels and underground shelters permitted many local guerrillas to elude allied patrols. Perhaps the most extensive tunnel system existed sixty kilometers from Saigon in the district of Cu Chi, home of the U.S. 25th Infantry Division. Begun during the French war and expanded during the American war, the complex of tunnels and underground rooms measured perhaps 200 kilometers in all. Extending beneath virtually every village and hamlet in the district, the tunnels contained living rooms and storage areas for food and ammunition connected by passageways. Ventilated by bamboo air shafts, the tunnels were reached by a variety of entrances including camouflaged trap doors and holes dug beneath the water lines of river banks. When the Americans used German shepherds to locate the entrances, the Vietcong sprinkled U.S. government issue mosquito repellent on the trap doors and left American soap and cigarettes just inside, thereby covering their own scent and making the dogs think only Americans were present.

In jungle bivouacs the soldiers exercised care not to disturb the area or leave signs of their presence. Rather than digging fire pits, they built small stone fireplaces that they dispersed after the meal. They avoided stepping on plants. A battalion bivouac was divided into three companies in triangular formation, with each company located in effective small arms range. The three men of a cell bivouacked together, stringing their hammocks between small trees. To lessen the possibility of being spotted by aircraft, the soldiers were forbidden to have white clothing or utensils that might reflect light. Before departing, the soldiers policed the bivouac to clear up indications of their camp. Sometimes the units separated for the day to hide or take shelter from patrolling aircraft and returned to the bivouac before dark.

When they moved, the North Vietnamese generally marched in column formation without smoking or talking and without breaking branches or brush along the trail. If aircraft appeared overhead when the soldiers were in dense forest, they kept moving. In areas with less overhead cover, they dove into any nearby bushes. If they were in the open when aircraft flew over, the soldiers, whether standing or sitting, simply froze, and hoped to blend with the terrain.

To compensate for American superiority in airmobility and firepower, the North Vietnamese and Vietcong developed an expertise in cover and concealment; this in turn allowed them to move close to the enemy without detection and to lay effective ambushes. The typical NVA soldier wore a circular frame on his back, to which he attached twigs and grass. When he crouched in a foxhole, the camouflage formed a cover; when he lay prone, it concealed his head and shoulders and allowed the soldier to turn his head without moving his camouflage. By contrast, the U.S. infantryman early in the war, with branches and grass stuck into the camouflage band on his helmet, often resembled what one observer called "an eight-foot-tall potted plant" whose every movement attracted the eye.

The North Vietnamese and Vietcong often booby trapped likely helicopter landing zones, and, to counter these tactics, the Americans took to "prepping" a landing zone prior to assault with artillery and tactical bombing. During the bombing, however, the VC/NVA "stay in their bunkers deep in the jungle," reported Lieutenant Colonel Le Xuan Chuyen, a northerner serving as chief of operations of the Vietcong 5th Division, "or sometimes they place a heavily armed squad in the middle of an open spot where the helicopters land. After the bombing and artillery fire is over, the VC move their troops to the jungle's edge in order to attack the landing troops." Earlier in the war, the soldiers had fired at passing helicopters, thus revealing their own locations and bringing heavy fire in return. As their tactics improved, however, they began to wait until the choppers had landed and troops were deployed before firing.

One slow, four quick

When they finally chose to attack, the North Vietnamese and Vietcong Main Forces massed their troops to gain the tactical advantage of "ten men against one." They sent an entire regiment against a battalion (1,500 to 2,000 men against 500 to 600), for example, or a battalion against a company (400 against 100 to 120). In battle, 10 soldiers might attempt to isolate and rush 2 or 3 enemy. Whether assaulting a fixed position or laying an ambush, the North Vietnamese rigidly adhered to a tactic known as "one slow, four quick." The "slow" meant meticulous and methodical planning, possibly for months, with reconnaissance, sand table exercises on scale models, and rehearsals. During the planning period, logisticians sent ammunition, food, and medical supplies to be cached near the intended battlefield. Only when all was in readiness did the infantry embark on its four "quicks": movement, attack, battlefield policing, and withdrawal.

The infantry moved in dispersed groups to the battle area, joining in formation only at the scene. With ambush parties positioned on the flanks to intercept any relief effort, the units launched the ambush or attack. The action often came at night or in bad weather when U.S. air activities were reduced. In combat the North Vietnamese closed with the defenders as tightly as possible, sometimes engaging in hand-to-hand fighting so that tactical air power and artillery could not be called in against them. The soldiers tried to bring down the spotter planes of the forward air controllers who located targets for fighter aircraft.

When the tactical objectives had been met, or if the attack was failing, the NVA began to break contact. As they did so, they continued to pepper the enemy with rifle fire as any abandoned weapons were collected. After the wounded and dead, in that order, had been evacuated by the transportation unit—the dead usually dragged by means of a thong or wire tied about the ankle—the NVA fell back in the order of heavy weapons, infantry, reserve elements, and flank guards. A rear guard often remained on the battlefield to keep the enemy pinned down and slow any pursuit. The preplanned route of withdrawal always differed from the path of advance, and an alternate route led in yet another direction. Reserve forces covered both avenues. The soldiers retreated to a location twelve hours away from the battlefield, regardless of terrain, marching in column formation with point and flank security.

The NVA's inflexible withdrawal tactic struck two major psychological blows at the enemy. Coming as it often did just as pinned-down U.S. or ARVN forces were massing for a counterattack, disengagement thus deprived the opposing forces of an opportunity to avenge their dead. Moreover, the VC/NVA practice of removing slain comrades from the field proved frustrating to a foe preoccupied with body counts as a measure of progress.

The recovery of bodies also served as a motivating factor for the Vietnamese soldiers, whose Confucian-Buddhist heritage instilled a pious regard for family and ascribed a great importance to a grave site that family or descendants could one day venerate. Even if the soldiers were buried in South Vietnam, far from the family, the possibility always existed that relatives could make a pilgrimage after reunification.

But the problems of retrieving bodies grew as the United States continually improved response times of helicopter gunships, artillery, and tac air. With quick reactions, the United States might turn the tide of battle rapidly and prevent a thorough policing of the battlefield. North Vietnamese soldiers

A Communist photograph *shows a Vietcong Main Force unit advancing into battle in late 1966. Only when they knew they held a sizable advantage did VC/NVA forces attack.*

reportedly expressed shock when their dead and wounded comrades had to be abandoned on the battlefield in the Ia Drang campaign. "The cadres said we don't have enough time to take the killed and wounded from the battlefield because our unit's movements would be delayed and aircraft would come and bomb its position," a twenty-year-old private had lamented earlier. "This discouraged and demoralized the fighters a lot."

The NVA soldier fought with a tenacity that struck his American foe, who marshaled such an array of firepower against him, as fanaticism. Americans marveled at North Vietnamese regulars who continued to advance into heavy concentrations of fire and who, when wounded, persisted in fighting with small arms and grenades. Wounded NVA soldiers at the battle of LZ X-Ray, for example, inflicted many U.S. casualties. The phenomenon of bandaged NVA soldiers taking the field became commonplace, which among Americans often earned a soldierly admiration, mixed with apprehension, about such a driven foe. Some Americans believed the North Vietnamese regulars' tenacity was drug-induced. The soldiers "appeared to be hopped up," read the LZ X-Ray after-action report from the battle of the Ia Drang Valley, while another from the battle of Dak To in fall 1967 repeated stories of soldiers who "bounced off trees" as they charged and who sported "strange grins" when they fought. Before some attacks, Americans reported smelling marijuana smoke, and one infantry lieu-

tenant spoke for many other U.S. combat soldiers when he declared after the war, "I will never be convinced they weren't using drugs."

But even if drugs were occasionally used, as indeed they were increasingly used by some American troops, such practice was not widespread, and little evidence has surfaced to prove that the North Vietnamese and Vietcong soldiers' toughness derived from any artificial substance. Rather their motivation seemed largely to stem from a sense of purpose instilled by indoctrination and heightened by the political cadres. The soldiers lived *dau tranh*. They knew their duty, and they carried it out. "Our comrades felt no pity," one soldier explained after a successful ambush. "They knew

they had to kill as many Americans as possible. We had been told to slaughter as many imperialist soldiers as we could since, if the number of American dead mounted, the American people—who dislike this war—would overthrow their government."

NLF—the village war

The National Liberation Front was a body whose head resided in Hanoi. Established to help accomplish Hanoi's goal of reunification, the NLF's role was to develop an effective political and military organization in the South. Seemingly independent, the NLF was in fact largely controlled by COSVN and hence by Hanoi. Its own ruling arm—the People's Revolutionary party—was the southern branch of the Lao Dong party. The NLF built an identity separate from Hanoi's, among many other practical reasons, to present the struggle in South Vietnam as a rebellion—a "war of national liberation" in Communist terminology. As one party member who defected in 1965 explained, "the front is only a dummy, a disguise designed to win [over] organizations in the country and to win the support of the neutralist countries on the international scene."

Yet the NLF was far more than a "front" organization for Hanoi, as generally understood. It had spent years agitating effectively among the people and building a militia, guerrilla force, and army. Its political base was so pervasive, its followers so numerous, its military so formidable, and its international profile so visible, that the NLF indeed had a very substantial life of its own—one that later in the war Hanoi itself had to confront and overcome.

Between 1965 and 1967, the Vietcong faced a set of worsening crises brought on by the introduction of U.S. troops: problems of maintaining its political base among South Vietnam's villagers, of appropriating taxes and rice, and of continuing to fill out its army. The infiltration of North Vietnamese units continued steadily after it began in late 1964, and yet the NVA did not outnumber Vietcong in Main Force battalions until late 1967, when the combined Communist Main Force strength was set by U.S. analysts at 120,000 soldiers. In spite of heavy losses, the Vietcong managed to keep troop levels constant—the number of soldiers in Main Force battalions remained about the same from 1965 to the

Using the side of a destroyed U.S. vehicle as his jungle blackboard, a VC guerrilla instructs recruits—many of them female—on operating the B40, an 82MM antitank grenade launcher.

The Village War

Revolutionary art. *With its printing presses in the jungle, the Liberation Publishing House produced leaflets, pamphlets, postage stamps, and books. These drawings, published by the NLF house, celebrate Vietcong women war heroes.*

Propaganda duty. *Vietcong cadres distribute leaflets to peasants in Binh Duong Province, a "liberated" area that the Vietcong renamed Thu Dau Mot Province.*

Morale booster. *Performers from the touring group "Liberation Art Troupe" entertain soldiers and residents of a village in Tay Ninh Province.*

Recruitment. *Ba Lan (above, left), a Vietcong soldier, encourages a montagnard of the central highlands to support the Liberation Army. The Vietcong competed with the U.S. Civilian Irregular Defense Group program for the loyalty of the montagnards.*

eve of the Tet offensive. This they achieved through a combination of recruitment and conscription.

Where possible, the Vietcong tried to continue the patient practice of wooing potential soldiers to their side. "I was visited fifteen times by Mr. An," one soldier said in explaining his decision to join the Vietcong, "and no one else ever came to see me." But the recruiters also combined patience with cunning. "[They] came to me and said they had heard I knew how to fire a rifle," related one former Vietcong soldier. "I said yes, and they were pleased by that. Nguyen came back to see me many times and we became friends. One day he came by and said they were going off to fire a few sniper rounds at the nearby government outpost. ... I went with him and after he had taken a few shots he gave the rifle to me and asked if I wanted to fire. I fired a few shots and then we went home. That night he told everyone in the village that I had fired at the outpost and so of course I was no longer safe, and that night I joined the Vietcong."

The NLF had also instituted a compulsory draft order in 1964 in areas it dominated. Conscription was straightforward: The Vietcong simply chose available "recruits" from villages. Some VC soldiers called for a young man in Binh Dinh Province, for example, and when he answered the door, they took him along, after ordering his family to put together five days' provisions for the group. Another time they called for a young man who wasn't home but took his younger brother instead. Arriving home a few minutes later and hearing the news, the man ran after the party to exchange himself for his brother. But rather than release the brother, the VC took them both. Once a soldier participated in an action, the cadres informed him that he had become a criminal in the eyes of the government and was thus unable to return to GVN protection. The soldier was trapped.

Cadres also encouraged women to take on greater responsibilities, including the shouldering of arms against the U.S./ RVNAF forces. If "the women's role is developed appropriately," said a ranking general in the South in 1966, "guerrilla forces can be increased by 50 percent and militia forces can be doubled immediately." In some areas up to one-fourth of the local Vietcong force consisted of women who acted as sentries, couriers, cadres, even as soldiers in self-defense militia. Women also buried mines and set booby traps around their villages.

The Mekong Delta, dominated by the Vietcong until the arrival of U.S. combat troops there in 1967, continued to be a recruiting and training ground for VC Main Force battalions sent north. According to one party cadre in Chuong Thien Province, his village normally had two squads of guerrillas armed and clothed by the front, and each hamlet in the village had a squad of volunteer militia. In the early 1960s the village was required every three months to supply one squad to be integrated into Main Force battalions. Occasionally, an urgent call had come for two or three squads to be integrated on an emergency basis. But beginning in the fall of 1965 the demand for troops increased, and almost every month his village staged a sendoff ceremony for local soldiers going north.

Taxing the peasants

By mid-1967, with nearly half its force made up of draftees, the Vietcong found its policy of conscription backfiring—many of the soldiers turned out to be uncommitted, both politically and militarily. The rate of desertion soared. In 1965 some 11,000 Vietcong had turned themselves in to the government, and in 1966 more than 20,000 deserted. In the first few months of 1967, Vietcong were "rallying" to the government side at the rate of 1,000 per week, mainly through the Chieu Hoi program, by which the GVN offered amnesty to Vietcong defectors. Many of the defectors, however, were marginal Vietcong, those without a profound political commitment who grew war-weary. The political backbone of the Vietcong—the so-called infrastructure—remained essentially unchanged.

As the war expanded, the Vietcong hiked taxes, often beyond a villager's ability to pay, and resorted more and more to coercion in order to collect. Early in 1966, for example, a young cadre, accompanied by five armed Vietcong, arrived at a village in Binh Duong Province to sell "Liberation Bonds." After assembling the villagers, the cadre lectured them on the need for voluntary contributions to the anti-American, anti-imperialist, anti-Saigon front. When the villagers ignored the lecture, the cadre shouted, "All right! I came here to get money for the Liberation Bond drive. And that's what I'm going to do. No more talk, but pay up!" With five Vietcong rifles trained on them, the villagers did exactly that. A higher tax levy placed a great burden on peasants in "liberated areas" to whom the VC had recently given acreage under their land distribution program; by 1966 taxes in some areas had risen above the 30 percent formerly charged by the landlords. But land distribution had engendered good will, and front representatives assured the people that the levies were only temporary and were being used to help the front launch a general offensive.

The Vietcong likewise appropriated an increasingly greater share of rice harvests for their own troops as well as for the North Vietnamese, and cadres spurred the people to improve their production output. "No matter how tense the situation may be, we still must maintain optimum production," read a 1966 COSVN directive which estimated that up to 80 percent of the available land had been cultivated in spite of U.S./South Vietnamese military sweeps and pacification programs. Farmers were exhorted to plant every available plot of soil. "Crops such as seed rice, third-month rice, early rice, late rice, tenth-month rice, sweet potatoes, early maize, cassava, potato, taro, etc., should be planted as much as possible in the fields, around houses, in yards, along roads and pond banks," read the COSVN directive.

In the competition between the NLF and U.S./RVNAF forces for the hearts and minds of the people, the villages became the battleground, and the people themselves stood in the crossfire. The Communists suffered considerable attrition among the peasants from the punishment of war, which the National Liberation Front was often powerless to counteract. A 1966 COSVN document condemned U.S./RVNAF pacification programs, which resulted in destruction of the countryside. "They conducted air and artillery strikes, and sweep operations.

They sprayed toxic chemicals to defoliate the fields, destroy villages, and throw farmers into confusion. At the same time they also carried out cunning political and economic measures aimed at moving the people and forcing youths to enlist in their army."

In village after village the population slept in the fields rather than in their homes for fear of potential shelling. One despondent VC political cadre in a village in Bien Hoa Province confirmed the peasants' fear of retaliatory bombing. The people, he said, "are afraid that, by conducting attacks near their own villages, they may cause the enemy to fire at their villages and launch air raids and bomb their dwellings. This fear has become more and more pronounced especially whenever the U.S. aggressors launch raids or mopping-up operations. The enemy has dropped leaflets threatening our people with destruction of their villages if they resist or fight." According to this cadre, the "fierceness of enemy attacks" had driven two-thirds of one village's residents to government-controlled areas.

The flight of the rural population to government-controlled

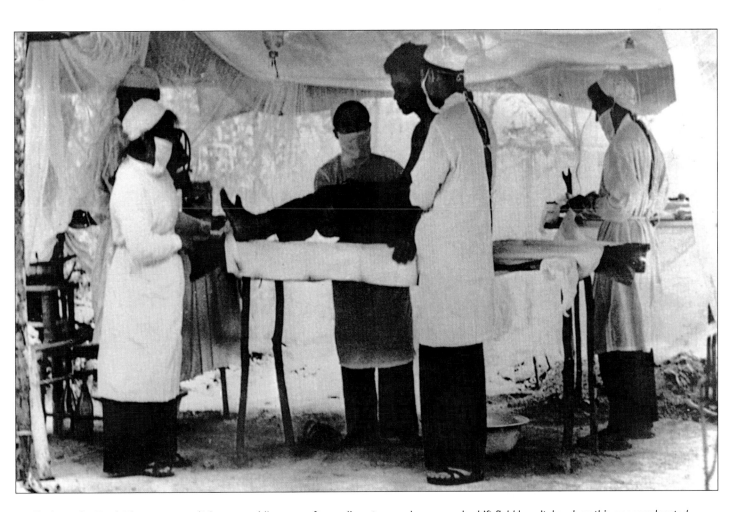

Medical care for North Vietnamese *and Vietcong soldiers was often rudimentary, and even a makeshift field hospital such as this one was located several kilometers from the battle action.*

refugee camps or cities represented a critical problem for the Vietcong. In 1966 and 1967, some 1 million peasants per year were relocated from rural areas, resulting in a vast loss of popular support and potential resources for the front. Although the refugees were not necessarily converts to the government, their homes, taxes, food production, and young men were lost to the Vietcong.

Many of those still living in contested areas began to lose faith that the Vietcong would prevail. As war weariness grew, and any hope of an early Communist victory disappeared, the mystique of the Vietcong faded among the villagers. Many in fact held the front responsible for the great dislocation of society. "The front is deteriorating every day," complained one Vietcong who rallied to the side of the South Vietnamese government. "It had promised a great deal but it can't keep its promises. Each year it says, 'This is the year of decision.' It is because of the front that the people die in bombing and fighting, that their families are scattered, their property is damaged, and they cannot till their land."

Even some of the highly motivated Vietcong and North Vietnamese Main Force troops became despondent—at fighting the Americans, at keeping on the run from spotter planes and bombardments, at living in the jungle where the thick canopy shielded them from U.S. firepower but also blocked out the sun day after day. Some soldiers defected simply because they had tired of being chased. But most stayed enthusiastically within the fold. One North Vietnamese soldier, a medic in the Quyet Tam (NVA 22d) Regiment, exhibited the attitude that the party cadres had worked so hard to instill. Although his unit had been in almost continual contact with the enemy in Quang Ngai Province, the soldier trusted in the omnipotence of the Lao Dong party. "We were out of rice, ammunition, bandages, and cotton," he jotted in his notebook. "How long would it take us to break up the 8,000-man sweep operation of the enemy? I don't worry. The party will provide leadership."

Although the North Vietnamese and Vietcong shared a common purpose, they did not always work together in full harmony. At the highest levels officers of the party often disagreed on matters of strategy, and debates took place between the NLF and COSVN and even between COSVN and Hanoi on the best means of combating the Americans. Squabbling also occurred at lower levels as a pecking order developed among cadres. Political cadres outranked military officers in both Vietcong and North Vietnamese units because political goals took precedence over military objectives in the Communist theory of revolution, and mission orders normally arrived through political channels. Once the mission was given, of course, the military officer took tactical command of the troops, but the situation offended many experienced and able officers. North Vietnamese cadres who had come early to the South felt superior to those who had come later, and both in their turn looked down on Vietcong cadres because they had not received their training in the North. "Each person thinks he has worked more for the National Liberation Front and the country," said Lieutenant Colonel Le Xuan Chuyen, the VC 5th Division chief of operations. "The contradictions between northern cadre and southern cadre are truly hard to solve because at present there is envy and dispute."

Regional rivalry and differences extended down into the ranks as well. VC and NVA soldiers often served together, with northerners filling out VC Main Force units and local Vietcong introducing NVA units to the unfamiliar terrain of their area of operations. Many Vietcong, still convinced that the NLF could win on its own, actually resented the reinforcements from North Vietnam. They complained that the NVA soldiers were arrogant and received preferential treatment. Some VC mocked the northerners' accents and called them doltish and slow-moving as they took time to acclimate to the new environment. In turn the NVA referred to the southerners as *gia song* (bean sprouts) and the Vietcong retaliated by calling the northerners *rau muong* (raw spinach). Southern shopkeepers made things worse by sometimes taking advantage of the NVA soldiers' "clumsiness and lack of experience" to add 10 or 15 percent to food prices when the northerners came to buy.

The bickering was serious enough for the party in the South to step in with a homily urging an end to "regrettable mistakes" and love for the "comrades and brothers ... helping us to defeat the American aggressors and their lackeys more quickly in order to liberate the South and unify the country." The party further praised all the people of the North—"the 17 million northern compatriots who are tightening their belts and sharing their food with the South, who are doing everything for the South."

The large rear base

The party was not speaking lightly. The "large rear base"— as the party sometimes called North Vietnam—had been actively supplying the South for years, and the lines of communication connecting South and North formed the vital life line that kept the Communist struggle alive. The logistical system had been in place since the Lao Dong party formed Group 559 (named for the date of its creation in May 1959) to establish a route connecting North and South. Beginning with a few hundred troops and cadres equipped with no more than cargo bicycles, Group 559 expanded into a large force of transportation troops, engineers, infantry, and antiaircraft artillery involving tens of thousands of people and thousands of cargo trucks. Group 759, established two months after 559, organized maritime infiltration to South Vietnam. Its first ship reached the Ca Mau Peninsula with weapons cargo in the fall of 1962.

The troops of Group 559, often with enforced help from local laborers, built trails and roads and constructed way stations through the jungles of Laos and northern Cambodia. Although totally unimpeded by its enemy in early years, Group 559 worked clandestinely. The high canopy of trees in the dense jungle concealed most trails and installations. Transportation units and support regiments filtered down the trails, organizing jungle military posts, called *binh tram,* and improving roads and bridges. They built straw and bamboo structures as depots for munitions and food. Rice, sugar, condensed milk, dried fish, and tobacco came through Cambodia on trucks and in boats that traveled at night and were tied up and camouflaged during the day. Different groups took responsibility for road maintenance, security, and movement of supplies. In time some of the more sophisticated jungle posts had field hospitals and theatrical groups who staged performances and showed films. Hanoi was later to boast about the "strategic route bearing the name of the great Uncle Ho which crossed the Truong Son (Annamese) Mountains, connected the battlefields, and amounted to a relatively complete land route, pipeline, and river route network."

For United States military strategists, the route bearing the name of Uncle Ho—the Ho Chi Minh Trail—was in a way the mocking symbol of the war, dramatizing as it did the defiance of the enemy as well as the frustrating political restrictions that forbade the Americans to attack the flow of enemy forces and supplies. Officially the United States was restricted to South Vietnam and could not enter Laos or Cambodia. But neither could the enemy's infiltration be allowed to continue unimpeded.

North Vietnamese porters *on the move south ford a river along the Ho Chi Minh Trail.*

The North Under Siege

Between February 1965 and October 1968 American aircraft dropped 1 million tons of bombs, rockets, and missiles on North Vietnam. Transportation routes in the southern panhandle were hit early in the air war; deep craters pitted all roads south of Hanoi. Houses had been reduced to rubble and their inhabitants evacuated north. Before long a U.S. pilot described the panhandle region as a "moon-valley" showing few signs of life.

In 1966 U.S. aircraft moved north to bomb cities and industrial complexes. By April 1967, when the bombing campaign expanded to Hanoi and Haiphong, air raids had substantially destroyed the country's other urban centers. Few outsiders knew the effect of the attacks on the North Vietnamese. On the following pages the photographs of Lee Lockwood, whose 1967 trip to North Vietnam was the first by an American photographer since 1954, provide some glimpses of North Vietnam under siege.

The government ordered the evacuation of children and elderly from Hanoi in February 1965. Homesickness and the economic hardships of life in the country, how-

On a bombed dike *in the southern panhandle, North Vietnamese soldiers on a training run pass peasants carrying earth for filling bomb craters.*

In downtown Hanoi *residents wait for the "all-clear" during an air alert. Concrete cylindrical shelters, two-and-one-half feet across and five feet deep, line the city streets at six-foot intervals.*

ever, brought many residents back to Hanoi. When U.S. bombers moved closer to the city in 1966, Hanoi ordered a second evacuation of all citizens not "truly indispensable to the life of the capital." The government made the transition easier by providing ten dong (three dollars) for each preschool child moved and by establishing rural camps in the country for children without relatives. Eventually about one-third of Hanoi's 600,000 residents left the city, although many returned on weekends and holidays.

Those remaining in the city, mostly workers, rose at five in the morning and worked from six to ten-thirty and two-thirty to five, dispersing at midday during the peak bombing period. "The impression I had," wrote Harrison Salisbury, an American journalist who visited North Vietnam in December 1966, "was of a city determined, rather grim, businesslike, with little time for relaxation, play, or leisure."

During a visit in March 1968, the novelist Mary McCarthy found the city drab and life there austere and strenuous. The central market was closed, there was little to buy in the stores, and few people ate in the restaurants. The government-run department stores and rationing centers operated only in the early morning hours when few air raids occurred. But McCarthy also observed a well-tended city, where sprinkler trucks regularly cleaned the streets and construction crews repaired bomb damage. Travel on roads outside Hanoi was hazardous: At night drivers used parking lights or shielded headlights, during the day they camouflaged their vehicles with paint or a mesh of leaves and branches.

About 500,000 young people joined roving "youth shock brigades" to repair damaged transportation routes. Groups of up to 150 filled bomb craters and resurfaced roads, using tools, gravel, cement, and boulders that lay piled beside the roads every one or two miles. Often the job was done in an hour or two. Repairing bridges proved more difficult. Youth brigades replaced most of them with pontoon bridges made by tying together flat-bottomed canal boats and topping them with bamboo poles or boards.

Bicycles moved supplies when trucks and railroads failed. With a passenger pedaling, a bicycle carried 150 pounds of cargo and when pushed, up to 600 pounds. The only mode of transportation available for most Vietnamese, bicycles were in short supply. They cost an average worker nearly a year's salary and had to be rationed by the government. "The best present you could give your girlfriend in Hanoi," wrote Harrison Salisbury, "was not a box of candy, a bouquet of roses, or even a diamond ring. It was a new bicycle chain."

The North Vietnamese claim to have built 21 million bomb shelters and dug 30,000 miles of trenches between 1965 and 1968. During a bombing alert in the city, loud-speakers and sirens signaled the proximity of *may-bay-my* (U.S. aircraft), at which people dove into shelters and militia scrambled to rooftop firing positions. The all-clear sounded when the danger was past.

In the countryside foxholes and trenches dotted roadsides and dikes. Peasants sta-

Bomb damage on Nguyen Thiap Street *in downtown Hanoi after a raid on December 14, 1966. Although the target was probably a railroad overpass ten meters from the street, the attack destroyed some fifty houses.*

tioned in high towers sounded an alert with drum rolls or gongs and flew colored flags, or lamps at night, for those too far away to hear. Local party officials organized residents into "civil defense groups" whose priority was to rescue those buried alive in shelters, then to put out fires, administer first aid, deactivate bombs, and eventually to repair damaged shelters and homes.

The evacuation of large population centers sent thousands of children and workers into the countryside. The government transferred urban teachers to the country to set up new schools; agricultural cooperatives also provided the young evacuees with schooling and jobs.

To avoid massing children in large buildings that could be perceived as bombing tar-

Children wear thickly woven hempen helmets *as protection against bomb shrapnel. These boys are crossing a dike on their way to school in Phong Loc, a Catholic village in the Red River Delta.*

Just before shipping out, *North Vietnamese soldiers take a last look at a window display in Hanoi's main department store. The mannequin's Caucasian features are a vestige of colonial days.*

Workers camouflage *Russian-built Moskvitch automobiles in Hanoi prior to a Cuban military delegation's inspection trip to the southern panhandle.*

A flower-seller *hauls dahlias and reeds for basket weaving to market.*

Opposite. Factories moved to the countryside, *taking over buildings such as this temple in Phat Diem, where fifty employees, including women and children, weave mats and rugs from hemp.*

Female militia members, *their rifles stacked nearby, repair an irrigation ditch near Phat Diem. The white posts along the road guide unlighted vehicles at night.*

At an agricultural cooperative *in Thanh Hoa Province, a worker sounds an airraid warning gong made from a dud 750-pound U.S. bomb casing.*

Water buffaloes *received special protection from U.S. bombs, since they cost the equivalent of about $142—almost twice the yearly salary of a North Vietnamese peasant.*

Vu Cat and his seven-year-old son, *who lost a leg when a bomb fell on the village of Phu Vinh on November 2, 1966. Fourteen villagers, including Vu Cat's wife and five of their seven children, died in the raid.*

"The astonishing thing is the way the North Vietnamese seem to take all this in stride.... The people seem ... calm, as though they could go on like this forever."

Lee Lockwood

gets, the North Vietnamese dispersed and disguised their schools. In Xuan Dinh, a suburb of Hanoi, classrooms were scattered throughout the village in peasant huts connected by trenches. In the schools, survival was emphasized over learning. Building air-raid defenses and performing "patriotic tasks," such as tending livestock and gardens, took priority over lessons.

Phat Diem, a community of 5,500 in the Red River Delta, had suffered over sixty bombing attacks by 1967. Much of Phat Diem, an agricultural area without military targets, lay in ruins. "It was plain from the ground that these buildings, though they might seem substantial from the air, were serving no military purpose," Harrison Salisbury wrote. "I wondered whether it might be that the targeting authorities, hunting vainly over the dreary rural scene for something to attack, had decided that substantial buildings *must* have some military significance."

Residents who remained in Phat Diem seemed willing to carry on despite the hardships. Airraid bunkers and trenches dotted the landscape, and villagers carried woven hats or helmets to protect against shrapnel fragments. "Women were chattering gaily in the rice fields," observed Lee Lockwood.

"When bombs started to fall two miles away, making the ground shudder, they worked on seemingly unconcerned."

"The secret of the North Vietnamese success," concluded Salisbury, "lay in a massive investment of manpower, labor, and materiel, and a careful utilization of national resources." But more than that, success lay in a determination to endure. "The astonishing thing," wrote Lee Lockwood, after surveying the bomb damage, the dislocation, and the shortages, "is the way the North Vietnamese seem to take all this in stride. ... The people seem ... calm, as though they could go on like this forever."

"Nobody on my team runs. Anybody who runs gets left, and they know that. Running, you break bush and you make noise. One noise and they find out where you are and the chase is on."

Special Forces NCO Tim Kephart

For three days in October 1965, the reconnaissance team of two Americans and four Vietnamese prowled the Special Forces camp at Kham Duc, near the Laotian border, waiting for the rain to let up and for the clouds to break. They killed time by unpacking and repacking their gear, test firing and cleaning their 9MM Swedish K submachine guns, studying the maps again, and poring over the briefing information. Tension during the idle days hung thick as fog, for their highly classified mission could open a new phase of the war. They were about to embark on the first U.S.-led cross-border operation into Laos, code named Shining Brass, to reconnoiter and interdict infiltration along the Ho Chi Minh Trail.

Seeing ill omens in the weather, two or three of the Vietnamese were falling prey to second thoughts. Sergeant Major Charles "Slats" Petry and Sergeant First Class Willie Card, both combat veterans, reassured them. The team had trained together at Long Thanh, a base near Saigon, sweating their way into top physical condition. They'd honed their reconnaissance and tracking skills and had drilled in helicopter infiltration and extraction—the entire team bursting out of the helicopter and getting off the landing zone within seconds so that the chopper scarcely had to touch down, thus lessening the risk of detection. The team knew that a mission is most often compromised at the landing zone; they would feel secure only when they slipped into the enveloping jungle. The Vietnamese were not combat veter-

---

The crack of rifle fire *sends members of SOG Reconnaissance Team Michigan scrambling for cover during a long-range reconnaissance mission into Laos.*

ans. But after "graduation," which consisted of three reconnaissance patrols in South Vietnam, Petry and Card judged the team to be at the peak of readiness. Then the rain and clouds blew in over the border the night before D-day, October 15, 1965.

The border in those jungle-covered mountains, rising to 1,400 to 1,800 meters above sea level, was more a vague idea than an exact line of demarcation. Widely scattered montagnard tribes constituted the only population, and the terrain was so rugged that most of the 1,300-kilometer frontier between South Vietnam and neighboring Laos and Cambodia had never been accurately charted.

That North Vietnamese men and supplies were entering South Vietnam through the Laotian mountains was indisputable, yet MACV had little tangible evidence of the extent of infiltration. By mid-1965 the MACV Studies and Observations Group (SOG), an innocuously named group established a year earlier to conduct clandestine unconventional warfare against North Vietnam, was attempting to fill that intelligence gap. From photo reconnaissance SOG had accumulated a list of 500 potential "targets" in Laos that might provide evidence of infiltration. Some targets were firm, such as suspected way stations or truck parks, and others were more speculative, such as dying leaves on an otherwise healthy tree, which might indicate a cache of arms or supplies buried among its roots. SOG wanted ground reconnaissance teams to verify the targets, and General Westmoreland, the Commander in Chief of the Pacific (CINCPAC) Admiral Ulysses S. G. Sharp, and the Joint Chiefs of Staff applied a continual pressure in Washington. However, for political and diplomatic reasons—notably the 1962 Geneva accords, which declared Laos neutral and forced the withdrawal of U.S. troops—the White House and State Department refused to permit American troops to cross the border.

The May 1965 appointment of Colonel Donald D. Blackburn to command SOG added a new voice to those arguing for covert cross-border operations by Americans. Blackburn knew Vietnam, having already served as an adviser in the late 1950s. He was also no stranger to unconventional warfare. Trapped when the Japanese overran the Philippines in 1942, Blackburn refused to surrender at Bataan and escaped to the jungle. There he organized a guerrilla force of Igorot headhunters who operated with great success behind Japanese lines. Returning from the war a twenty-nine-year-old full colonel, Blackburn gravitated to Special Forces, eventually commanding the 77th Group at Fort Bragg. Operation White Star, the 1959 Special Forces program to organize Meo tribesmen in Laos as a resistance force, was Blackburn's handiwork, but it had ended with the 1962 Geneva accords. Now Blackburn agitated for a covert return of American Special Forces to Laos.

SOG was already conducting several operations against North Vietnam, including penetration of the North by Vietnamese agents and coastal raiding and shelling (Operation 34). A psychological warfare section (Operation 33) ran several diverse projects, among them the beaming of radio programs into the North. Under Op 35, also called the Ground Studies Group, Blackburn developed a three-phase plan for operating in Laos. The first was reconnaissance to verify the use of infiltration trails and sanctuaries. Phase Two involved the insertion of commando units supported by air power to "exploit" the targets. The third phase was a classic Special Forces mission: organizing a resistance movement among the same tribesmen who had participated in White Star.

Anticipating approval from Washington, Blackburn assembled a formidable team of volunteer Green Berets to mount Op 35. As commander he named Colonel Arthur D. "Bull" Simons, an irreverent, hard-charging World War II ranger whom Blackburn had sent to Laos as head of White Star. Simons got things done by bulldozing obstacles, including regulations and the people who made them. His gruff manner got results. "He's the only man I know who genuinely hates people," said one admirer.

Major Larry Thorne, a native Finn, was named operations officer. Thorne had led his own commando unit during the Russo-Finnish war and had operated with audacity behind Soviet lines. On one occasion "Thorne's Company" attacked a convoy and killed 300 Russian soldiers without losing a man. His exploits made him a national hero and twice earned him the Mannerheim Cross, Finland's equivalent of the Medal of Honor. Under provisions of the postwar Lodge Bill, which allowed foreign nationals to join the U.S. Army to earn their citizenship, Thorne enlisted as a private, volunteered for Special Forces, and soon won a commission. Old hands in Special Forces often referred to him as "the great" Larry Thorne.

Major Sully Fontaine, the assistant operations officer for all of SOG, took charge of recruiting for Op 35. An American of French parentage, Fontaine had parachuted into France in 1944, before his seventeenth birthday, to work with the Resistance. Having joined SOG shortly after its inception, he had already carried out dangerous missions. Speaking French with native fluency, Fontaine had shed his uniform and traveled three times to Cambodia. Posing as a French agricultural engineer, he had toured rubber plantations in eastern Cambodia, gathering evidence of the infiltration of North Vietnamese soldiers.

Major Fontaine, together with Colonels Blackburn and Simons, recruited volunteer NCOs from Special Forces assignments around Vietnam. Some veterans arrived from the 1st Special Forces Group in Okinawa. The premium was on combat experience and length of service; in Op 35's early days, no enlisted man below the rank of E-7—Sergeant First Class—was accepted. At Camp Long Thanh, the Americans trained with volunteers from the Vietnamese Special Forces (Luc Luong Dac Biet, or LLDB) attached to SOG's Vietnamese counterpart, whose cover name was the Strategic Technical Services.

Approval for Op 35—with the code name Shining Brass—finally came on September 21, 1965. Like many programs in Vietnam, Shining Brass was begun on a limited scale, using what CINCPAC Admiral Sharp characterized as "the creeping approach." The operation was saddled with three restrictions: Penetrations were not to exceed twenty kilometers, they were permitted in only two areas along the border, and crossings had to be made on foot. The twenty-kilometer limit remained in effect, but the other two restrictions were overcome by a process Blackburn called "erosion by indifference." The requirement to cross on foot posed the slightest problem: Commanders deliberately chose inaccurate maps, those which showed the borders located farthest west. Helicopters were used from the start. And the area of operations expanded soon after the first

---

A SOG reconnaissance team *makes a final equipment check. Hanging from the American's Stabo rig (with "V" ring at the shoulder) is a field dressing pouch. Below that are a universal pouch containing M16 magazines, a smoke grenade, and a canteen. The Nung team member has a coil of rope affixed to a "D" ring for use in emergency extractions and carries an AK47.*

Three times daily while on mission *a SOG recon team announced its position and situation to a FAC, who relayed the information to the base. The team leader depicted here, balancing his map and folding-stock Swedish K submachine gun, calls in on a PRC-25 radio carried by a Nung team member. The assistant team leader with an XM177 rifle (more commonly called the CAR15) keeps a watchful eye.*

Shining Brass recon teams returned from Laos with solid intelligence of infiltration.

Over the fence

Chosen to lead the first mission, Sergeants Petry and Card flew with their Vietnamese team members to the Special Forces camp at Kham Duc, which was to serve as a forward operating base for SOG's early Laotian operations. Colonel Simons fixed the inaugural mission for October 15, but the rain and fog prevented the launch and set the men to chafing with frustration.

On the third day the rain stopped over Kham Duc, but visibility was still poor on the Laotian border to the west where mountain peaks poked above the clouds. Conditions remained treacherous for flying, and just finding the landing zone would require a stroke of luck. Timing was also essential. The infiltration would come at last light, at what the military called EENT (end of the evening nautical twilight), and no time could be wasted searching for the LZ. The Vietnamese helicopter pilots were among the most daring and experienced pilots in Vietnam. They agreed to try an infiltration despite the unfavorable flying conditions. Thus, toward the end of day, two CH-34 helicopters, unmarked and sprayed with camouflage paint, climbed above the clouds over Kham Duc and banked to the west.

Petry, Card, and their four Vietnamese teammates sat on the floor of the lead chopper, the drop ship. Dressed in camouflage fatigues and soft bush hats, they carried no identification and all their gear and weapons were "sterile"—non-U.S. government issue. Though it had Washington's approval, the mission was "deniable" by the U.S. and South Vietnam. Without military identification, the men could be treated as spies instead of soldiers. But if captured, they were to say that they were soldiers who had innocently strayed while on border patrol. In fact, their five-day mission was to reconnoiter what appeared in aerial photographs to be a trucking terminus fifteen kilometers inside Laos.

The second helicopter, carrying only the pilot, copilot, and Major Thorne, doubled as the command ship and recovery helicopter. Thorne was in command of the infiltration and would remain aloft near the landing zone. If the LZ got hot, Thorne's chopper would come in as a gunship. The two helicopters were soon joined by a forward air controller, an air force major flying a single-engine Cessna 0–1 Bird Dog spotter plane.

In the vicinity of the landing zone, the three aircraft circled above the clouds looking for an opening. A descent seemed hopeless. But in the last minutes before darkness would have scrubbed the mission, a hole opened in the clouds, and, improbably enough, the landing zone, a clearing among 100-foot pines, lay directly below. The drop ship slammed into the hole and Thorne followed.

The drop ship settled downward, the prop wash bending the elephant grass. Before the wheel even bounced, Petry leaped. Card and the Vietnamese jumped after. Seconds after touching down, the ship kicked back up. The hole in the clouds was blowing closed though, and the pilot couldn't see Thorne's helicopter. It might still be descending. "Get out!" he ordered over the radio. "I can't see you. Wait for me upstairs."

The second pilot acknowledged the call, and the drop ship continued its ascent out of the valley, through the clouds. When the helicopter broke through the clouds, however, neither Thorne's bird nor the FAC were in sight. Nor did they respond to the radio calls. Both helicopters had used a lot of gas in circling, but the FAC had plenty of fuel. With his own fuel low, the lead ship couldn't stay and search; besides, the light was almost gone. Reluctantly he turned for Kham Duc.

Thus at 2020 hours, October 18, 1965, Larry Thorne vanished. He'd battled the Soviets and survived, only to be swallowed by a cloud bank on the border of Laos and South Vietnam. The disappearance of two aircraft and four men, without so much as a radio distress call, was never explained, nor was any wreckage found. Op 35 had claimed its first victims, and a shot had yet to be fired.

Operation Shining Brass

Happiness, went the saying in Vietnam, is a cold LZ, and no one was shooting at Petry and his team as they crouched at the edge of the clearing. Sounds of the jungle rose as the chop of the helicopter rotor faded. They listened for any voices or movement but only heard rainwater falling through the foliage, dropping with a loud, hollow patter on the broad leaves. Before total darkness closed in, the team moved a few hundred meters off the landing zone and strung hammocks. Movement was impossible at night since the noise of breaking blindly through the jungle would advertise their location. With visibility often limited to about ten meters, an animal or person would be heard long before being spotted. The men ate the first of their LRRP rations—individual plastic bags of instant rice and shrimp, beef, or pork that fluffed into an edible meal minutes after the addition of cold water. Two men stood guard while four tried to sleep.

Shortly after dark the rains came again. It rained intermittently but heavily for the next five days, making sleep nearly impossible and transforming the jungle into a muddy morass in which the men sank to their ankles. Not only did that slow the march, but it also prevented the team from concealing its trail.

Danger lay in discovery by the Vietcong or by montagnard hunters or woodcutters, many of whom worked for the enemy as trail watchers.

For three days the team advanced through the muddy suction of the jungle toward the target. Rains washed away the insect repellent with which they had doused their clothes. Leeches dropped from tree branches or from leaves the men brushed in passing. In spite of the muggy heat, the men wore long-sleeve shirts buttoned tight at the wrist and collar. Bush hats, pulled low, kept the leeches off their faces and necks. They plodded up and down mountains with the Vietnamese soldiers rotating at point, and Petry walking second, followed by the other three Vietnamese at ten-meter intervals, keeping the man ahead just in sight. Card came last in the patrol, stalking behind to protect the rear and watch for trackers. In thinner jungle, the spaces between the men lengthened. The spread-out patrolling protected the team from being ambushed all at once. They were most vulnerable at night, with all six close together. The team kept total silence—"noise discipline"—and communicated with hand signs.

After three days, they had traveled nearly fifteen kilometers. The target lay in a valley beyond the next mountain peak. Darkness was settling as the team neared the peak, and they halted and listened. In the distance they heard the sounds of trucks—wheels spinning, motors racing and whining in low gear as drivers evidently struggled to extricate vehicles from the mud. The sounds moved in two directions, which confirmed the photo analysis: The trucks were dropping off supplies and reversing direction, indicating a depot in the valley.

The team had found the target, but they had also found numerous fresh trails, obviously used by enemy patrols. Petry decided to close in on the target the following morning, and he backed the team down the mountain. In the morning he planned to probe the enemy's perimeter in an effort to learn what supplies they were transporting and exactly where they were stored. Then he would call in a bombing strike on the enemy sanctuary.

It was raining hard as the team members roused themselves before first light. Petry quietly briefed them on the plan and on the route he wanted for the final leg, telling the point man specifically not to climb the mountain again. They would avoid the area they had climbed through yesterday, where they had left tracks, and go around the waist of the mountain. As day broke, the Vietnamese point, an excellent scout, set out correctly, but after a short distance he picked out a path that bent upward. Petry tried repeatedly to get his attention, but the point man was too far ahead, his alertness straining forward and the rain muffled any sound. Then the ambush sprang.

A blast of fire shattered the morning, and the point man fell dead. Petry answered with a full magazine—thirty rounds—from his Swedish K. He snapped in a second magazine. The two Vietnamese behind him, instead of rushing forward to build up a base of fire, ran back toward Card. They had panicked, and Petry found himself alone, without help. He couldn't risk moving closer to the point man; he'd seen him riddled with automatic weapons fire and knew him to be dead, but without help he couldn't attempt to recover the body. Petry withdrew cautiously, and in the thick jungle, no one pursued.

Petry regrouped the team. Then he climbed alone by another route toward the top of the mountain to complete the mission. Making an educated guess, he radioed the forward air controller to bring in an air strike where they had heard trucks the previous day. Soon four F-105 fighter-bombers from Udorn Air Base in Thailand arrived and made a bombing run over the target. The guess proved accurate. Secondary explosions occurred in the wake of the bombs indicating that enemy ammunition had been hit. As more bombs laid open the jungle, the pilots saw more targets; they had discovered a depot. Defenders opened up with antiaircraft artillery, and more jets scrambled from Udorn. Eighty-eight F-105 sorties eventually attacked the base. Petry and his men withdrew and the next day found a hole in the jungle canopy large enough to call in a helicopter for extraction.

An exhausted Petry and Card returned to Da Nang for a debriefing and a muted celebration. Blackburn, Simons, and Fontaine were exultant. Petry's team had located the Ho Chi Minh Trail and had coordinated perfectly with American air power in an interdiction strike. But the SOG commanders had to look at the balance sheet. They had lost two aircraft and five men—two Americans and three Vietnamese—and they hadn't recovered a single body. Operation 35 was bound to be costly.

A mine of intelligence

Master Sergeant Dick Warren, team leader, and Sergeants First Class David Kauhaahaa and "bac si" Donaldson took a second Shining Brass group into Laos shortly after Petry had returned. After an uneventful infiltration, the team of three Americans and four Vietnamese set off toward a suspected way station. In the middle of the second afternoon, the Vietnamese point man, following an overgrown trail through the jungle, came face to face with five flank guards from what appeared to be a Vietcong battalion moving toward the same way station.

The SOG team fired on the Vietcong, driving the guards back and gaining for themselves a few moments. Then they broke through the jungle for half a kilometer, the noise announcing their location but also putting some distance between them-

Although SOG recon teams *usually avoided camouflage fatigues as too recognizable in enemy territory, these men use standard tiger suit fatigues. The first man, a montagnard armed with an M3 "greasegun," wears Bata boots, American copies of French patrol boots with rubber soles and canvas uppers.*

Special Forces/ Special War

Part of Special Forces *detachment A-303 poses on Christmas 1966 before the start of Operation Blackjack 31. Front row from left are NCOs Dale England, Patrick Wagner, Dennis Montgomery, and James Howard. Standing from left are James Donahue, Captain James Gritz, George Ovsak, and William Kindoll.*

> *"The enemy is beginning to realize that he no longer has exclusive dominion over his safe areas."*

Colonel Jonathan F. Ladd, 5th Special Forces Group

With the introduction of U.S. combat troops and North Vietnamese regulars, the Special Forces and their paramilitary strike forces took to the offensive, giving a new emphasis to unconventional operations in support of the conventional combat effort. By the fall of 1965, some sixty Special Forces camps, stretching from the DMZ to the Ca Mau Peninsula, and usually located in enemy-dominated territory, contained nearly 25,000 montagnards and Vietnamese in the Civilian Irregular Defense Group (CIDG) program. Trained guerrillas able to move rapidly through the jungle without artillery support, the Green Berets and their CIDG troops met the guerrilla enemy on his own terms and his own turf.

With the benefits of more than three years' experience in Vietnam and a familiarity with the language and culture, the Special Forces, aided by the irregular troops and their families, gathered timely, accurate intelligence. They hunted down elusive enemy units so that conventional units could engage them. They performed this expanded role so well in fact that by mid-1966, MACV estimated that half its ground intelligence reports originated from Special Forces programs.

The more venturesome CIDG forces, and the remote camps themselves, remained vulnerable to large-scale enemy attacks. The Special Forces thus created quick reaction forces, called Mobile Strike, or Mike, Forces, able to relieve a threatened or besieged camp or to reinforce troops fighting a superior enemy unit. Four Mike Forces, one for each corps, were created in July 1965, and a fifth was stationed at Special Forces headquarters in Nha Trang for use as a reserve anywhere in Vietnam. Composed largely of montagnards from the CIDG program, the Mike Forces grew slowly, however, and after a year, none had reached its authorized battalion strength of nearly 600 men.

That changed when Colonel Francis J. "Black Jack" Kelly assumed control of the 5th Special Forces Group in June 1966 and assigned a high priority to the Mike Forces. "The Special Forces were out there at the end of nowhere," said Kelly. To Lieutenant Colonel Charles M. Simpson, his newly arrived deputy for the CIDG program, he gave a clear-cut order: "While I am group commander, none of my corps will be taken by the enemy. If one appears threatened, be it day or night, the Nha Trang Mike Force will be parachuted into that camp to prevent its defeat, and you will lead them!"

After this introduction, Simpson discovered to his great dismay that the Nha Trang Mike Force consisted of but 350 montagnards, none of whom had ever jumped out of an airplane. He immediately began an expansion program. Working with the Mike Force commander, Simpson brought the roster up to five companies totaling 850 montagnards, all of whom were given airborne training. Too short to reach the overhead cable when the order came to hook up, they had to be lifted by the U.S. trainers. But Simpson found that the doughty montagnards "went out the door like a shot" when the order came to jump. The four other Mike Forces were also brought up to authorized strength, and all the soldiers had earned jump wings by September 1967.

The continuing need for intelligence on enemy capability and movement remained paramount and led in August 1966 to the creation of two other Special Forces long-range reconnaissance units to supplement Project Delta, which had been organized in late 1964. Delta provided reconnaissance teams of Americans and Vietnamese to prowl behind enemy lines and "roadrunner" teams of Vietnamese who, dressed as Vietcong, moved more boldly among the enemy. The two new units, Omega and Sigma, operated in II Corps and III Corps, respectively, and consisted of 120 Americans and some 900 CIDG troops, including a Mike Force battalion as a reaction force. From their formation, each group, with sixteen reconnaissance teams of six men (two U.S. and four CIDG), and eight teams of roadrunners, was in great demand to gather on-the-ground intelligence on the enemy. In their first nine months, these units spent an average of 60 percent of their time on operations.

In the fall of 1966, Colonel Kelly put the Special Forces guerrilla training to practical use when he devised American-led mobile guerrilla forces to harass the enemy's rear for weeks at a time. The Special Forces guerrillas were to infiltrate enemy-controlled areas to attack couriers and patrols and reconnoiter base camps and way stations for possible attack by air strikes. They were to destroy food and ammunition caches and rig booby traps and delayed action explosives in their wake. They would make the enemy react to them, instead of the reverse.

For each corps, Kelly organized a guerrilla force—a Special Forces twelve-man "A" detachment in command of a company of montagnards or other ethnic minority men. The first guerrilla force operation took place in the central highlands near the Cambodian border in October and November 1966. With Captain James A. Fenlon and his team leading a 249-man montagnard company, the operation called Blackjack 21 (the numerals signified II Corps, first mission) continued for thirty days. The second operation, Blackjack 22, led by Captain Robert Orms and including 173 Rhade tribesmen, lasted for thirty-four days in December and January in the highlands between An Lac and Buon Mi Ga. They finally exited the jungle with two Vietcong Main Force battalions in pursuit.

To mount the III Corps mobile guerrilla force, Colonel Kelly named Captain James G. "Bo" Gritz, a veteran of Project Delta reconnaissance missions, whom he thought of as "the best Special Forces captain I ever saw." Gritz put out a call for volunteers, and he put a twelve-man team to work as soon as it had been assembled. Some of the men recruited soldiers from among the ethnic Cambodians, others began to construct a training camp, and others worked on developing logistical networks. The soldiers scavenged for many of their needs: The team medic, Sergeant James C. Donahue, managed to procure tents, cots, boots, uniforms, and M79 grenade rounds from the 1st Infantry Division. When the team members greeted the Cambodian recruits two weeks later, they had a camp fully outfitted with a combination of authorized and scrounged gear and weapons.

After two months of intensive training, in early January 1967 Gritz led 100 guerrillas into the jungles of War Zone D. Operation Blackjack 31 continued for thirty-one days. Carrying packs that weighed 80 to 100 pounds, the guerrillas roamed War Zone D, conducting what Gritz termed "a running gun battle." They engaged enemy soldiers fifty-four times and suffered only one Cambodian CIDG killed. They also raided fifteen enemy company or battalion headquarters, attacking through the latrine area where the Vietnamese usually posted no guards.

The guerrillas rose and moved out before dawn. With reconnaissance teams far ahead and a rear guard behind, the force moved up to ten or fifteen kilometers per day through dense jungle. Constant movement prevented enemy units from finding their location. They mined and booby trapped the bodies of enemy soldiers by attaching the pull cord of a hidden claymore mine to the body or by leaving beneath the body a grenade with the pin removed and rigged for instant detonation. An explosion in the distance told them not only that they were being tracked, but also how far back the enemy was located.

The guerrillas received supplies from propeller-driven A-1E Skyraiders, which dropped 500-pound napalm canisters containing food, ammunition, and sometimes uniforms to replace those beginning to rot in the jungle climate. While other planes dropped high explosives at a distance in order to deceive any nearby enemy, the napalm canisters floated down beneath small reserve parachutes. The resupply of food, however welcome, presented no break from monotony. "Since we have to travel light, we are eating indigenous rations," Sergeant Donahue noted in a diary he kept during Blackjack 31. "Different meals we have invented: Rice, plain; rice with instant cream and sugar; rice with cocoa; rice with carrots; rice with hot peppers; rice with instant soup; rice with fish (dried); rice with shrimp (dried); rice with spinach; rice with Tabasco sauce."

Blackjack 31 proved to be a success, as had Blackjacks 21 and 22 before it. Invited to interview the Fenlon, Orms, and Gritz teams, General Westmoreland became an enthusiastic supporter of guerrilla forces and authorized more of them.

Between 1965 and 1967, the number of Special Forces soldiers assigned to the 5th Group in Vietnam never exceeded 2,700. Yet the Green Berets exerted an impact on the war disproportionate to their numbers. With CIDG troops, Mike Forces, and Regional and Popular Force units, the Special Forces commanded or advised more than 60,000 Vietnamese and ethnic minorities, many of whom brought the tactics of unconventional warfare to the guerrilla base camps and sanctuaries. "The enemy is beginning to realize," Colonel Kelly reported upon turning over the 5th Special Forces Group command to Colonel Jonathan F. Ladd in June 1967, "that he no longer has exclusive dominion over his safe areas."

selves and their pursuers. They hurriedly radioed that they were in contact with the enemy but couldn't wait for any acknowledgment. They didn't know if they had gotten through.

As they had been taught, the Americans moved to the high ground, from which they could withstand an assault. The Vietcong occasionally sprayed the jungle with their automatic weapons to draw return fire. But the SOG team did not shoot back; in the thick jungle neither side could see the other, and to shoot would only disclose their location. The men ascended a broad plain of elephant grass—they were nearing the mountain peak—and then formed a perimeter, lay down in the grass, and waited. The enemy soon set fire to the elephant grass, sending smoke and flames drifting up toward the team's position. Even with the enemy closing, Kauhaahaa felt confident. "I didn't think I was going to die," he said, "or that it was my last day on earth."

A beating of helicopter blades gradually grew louder, and soon two CH-34 helicopters came into view. The flames were a beacon. The men jumped to their feet and stomped around in the grass to clear a rudimentary landing zone. Taking heavy fire, the Vietnamese pilot named Cowboy brought his bird down right on the team. The Vietnamese climbed aboard. The door gunner sprayed the enemy positions as Cowboy lifted the chopper out. The second helicopter then settled into the elephant grass, and Warren, Kauhaahaa, and Donaldson clambered in. The team escaped without a scratch.

Back at Kham Duc, Kauhaahaa and Donaldson immediately boarded a plane for Saigon to be debriefed, while Warren climbed into a Cessna Bird Dog with a forward air controller to return to Laos and search for the way station. From the air Warren spotted three thatched-roof buildings hidden in the jungle, and the FAC called in air strikes. When several F-4 Phantom jets bombed the buildings, they also hit a nearby ammunition dump, setting off tremendous explosions. "The fast movers [jets] got in there," said Warren, watching from in the FAC plane, "and it looked like half the world blew up behind them."

SOG ran five more cross-border missions in 1965. One team, led by Master Sergeant Richard Meadows, discovered a battery

Operation Market Time. *The crew of a Vietnamese mechanized junk prepares to search a boat for enemy soldiers and supplies.*

of Russian-made howitzers still coated with rust preventive. Meadows removed the firing mechanisms and brought them back to Vietnam where he hand-delivered them to General Westmoreland. They provided the Americans with the first tangible evidence of North Vietnamese infiltration of heavy war materiel through Laos. Such intelligence coups led to the expansion of Op 35: An increasing number of Shining Brass patrols "hopped the fence" to reconnoiter and harass movement of men and supplies along the Ho Chi Minh Trail.

War of interdiction

SOG was not the only outfit concerned with infiltration. In 1964 Washington began to permit limited campaigns of aerial reconnaissance and interdiction. In May of that year air force and navy aircraft initiated reconnaissance flights over the Laotian panhandle in a program known as Yankee Team. Missions were limited to about five per week, and the aircraft could fire only if fired upon. By December another program called Barrel Roll began sending planes to attack planned targets and "targets of opportunity," such as North Vietnamese transport and troop concentrations in northern Laos. Barrel Roll initially launched only two missions per week of four aircraft each, and a dissatisfied General Westmoreland, who sought more stringent measures, wrote, "It was hardly surprising that the North Vietnamese failed to discern that a new program was underway." In April 1965 the air force began Operation Steel Tiger: bombing of targets visible on the trails from the seventeenth parallel north to the Mu Gia Pass, a major crossover point from North Vietnam into Laos. Attack on targets such as a truck park located more than 200 meters off the trail, however, had to be cleared with the U.S. Embassy in Vientiane, Laos.

Aided by the intelligence gathered by SOG's Shining Brass teams, MACV won permission in late 1965 to expand the bombing into the southern Laos panhandle—the area adjacent to South Vietnam—from the seventeenth parallel south to the Cambodian border. In December 1965, the bombing campaign called Tiger Hound began in Laos. The combination of Tiger Hound bombing and Shining Brass patrols began to impede what had been the enemy's untrammeled use of infiltration trails directly into South Vietnam.

While the programs directed at Laos were clandestine, other less secret campaigns to stop infiltration were used to combat the problem that existed along Vietnam's extensive irregular coastline. Although based on little tangible evidence, MACV intelligence in 1965 posited that as much as two-thirds of the enemy's externally delivered supplies entered South Vietnam not from Laos but from seaborne infiltration. To counter this, a

SFC David Kauhaahaa *and a Vietnamese teammate embark on the second Shining Brass infiltration into Laos in October 1965.*

joint U.S. and South Vietnamese naval operation was created for coastal surveillance.

In the most visible of all anti-infiltration programs, Operation Market Time, inaugurated in March 1965, established a picket line of ships along the 1,000-mile coastline to spot enemy infiltrators among some 50,000 white-sailed junks and sampans engaged daily in fishing and commerce. A massive undertaking, Market Time dispatched U.S. Navy and Coast Guard vessels to observe coastal shipping, board suspicious boats, and seize VC suspects and materiel. Navy destroyers and destroyer escorts, Coast Guard cutters, and Vietnamese mechanized junks covered territorial waters up to the twelve-mile limit, while Swift PT boats darted among the bays and inlets. Twin-engine seaplanes patrolled farther out to sea in a search for mother ships that might be supplying coastal smugglers. To declare one of the thousands of nearly identical fishing boats "suspicious" was at best a random decision.

The destroyer escort U.S.S. *Vance* joined Market Time at its inception and according to W. T. Generous, Jr., then twenty-six years old and a lieutenant (junior grade) and operations officer:

> We were all frightened to death. We thought everyone of those people was going to be a VC gun runner. We had two .50-caliber machine-gun mounts, forward and aft, six or seven sailors on the main deck with Thompson submachine guns. Everybody was in flak vests, with helmets and sidearms. We were armed to the teeth. We'd board these junks as they rolled and pitched. They were about twenty feet long. Three or four Vietnamese seamen were on board, all smiling and bowing and trying to be polite because they were frightened to death. We'd go through their fish lockers and ice tubs. A Vietnamese officer did the interrogating. He was nasty to them, and they'd bow and scrape. You'd get your hands cut from handling the fish.

Another Market Time officer pointed out that the navy gunners often had jittery nerves as they pulled alongside a junk or sampan, and as a result, some boats were fired upon by mistake. (Reports of such incidents might read "One VC junk evaded stop and search operations and was destroyed.") The Vietnamese were equally nervous and, often, angry behind their subservient demeanors since the huge navy and Coast Guard ships sometimes inadvertently cut through fishing nets trailing in the water and damaged the junks and sampans when they were lashed to the great steel hulls. The search parties infrequently found VC suspects or evidence of smuggling and usually left the hapless fishermen with gift packets put together by the psyops people, containing items such as rice, T-shirts, a bar of soap, and a wash cloth.

Failing to capture any suspects, the servicemen and their officers soon lapsed into a state of boredom, and vigilance deteriorated. The number of searches fell off dramatically. Yet with command headquarters demanding daily progress reports, many in the field sent inflated figures. "The commanding officer was always embarrassed by the number of boats we had truly seen and truly inspected and truly boarded," Lieutenant Generous recalled. "What they wanted was to beef up the numbers. We used to report at night that we had seen 500 and inspected 150 and boarded 25. We would actually inspect maybe 10 or 15, and go aboard possibly 2."

Whatever the true figures, Market Time show-of-force patrols evidently had a dampening effect on the enemy; U.S. intelligence detected a distinct drop in maritime infiltration. Although relying on sparse evidence, General Westmoreland estimated that prior to 1965 the enemy "had received about 70 percent of his supplies by sea; by the end of 1966, our best guess was that not more than 10 percent of his requirements arrived by that route."

The Cambodian connection

With coastal infiltration blocked, North Vietnam diverted shipment of arms and other supplies through international waters to the Cambodian port of Sihanoukville. War materiel and supplies, including rice purchased on the Cambodian market, were moving into South Vietnam along a complex of dirt roads called the Sihanouk Trail that linked up with the Ho Chi Minh Trail in the area where Laos, Cambodia, and South Vietnam meet.

MACV developed contingency plans to blockade Sihanoukville and attack seven major enemy sanctuaries just across the Cambodian border, not only to damage the enemy but also to demonstrate he did in fact have rear areas. MACV also sought permission for "hot pursuit" of enemy units retreating across the border. The State Department opposed all such plans, however. One 1965 State Department memorandum on the question of "hot pursuit" stated, "It would seem at least necessary to show Cambodian government connivance in the use of its territory as a base for armed attack before the GVN (and the U.S.) would be justified in using armed force against Cambodian territory." Cambodia's leader, Prince Norodom Sihanouk, took an official posture of neutrality, which preserved Cambodia from ground attack, although conventional units continued to flirt with the border.

MACV also had contingency plans to invade Laos. Under a plan produced in 1966 the 1st Cavalry Division would have been lifted into the Bolovens Plateau in the southern Laos panhandle to strike north toward Saravane and then toward Savannakhet on the Thailand border. The 3d Marine Division, launching from Khe Sanh, was to capture Tchepone, the vital communications spur on the Ho Chi Minh Trail. The U.S. 4th Infantry Division, joined by a South Vietnamese division, was slated to move northwest from Pleiku to seal the center of the Laos panhandle.

A later operational plan called El Paso I conceived of three divisions driving west out of South Vietnam toward Tchepone to link up with a fourth division moving east from Thailand. The rear areas in the panhandle would have been secured by Thai and Laotian troops. All such plans to thrust into the enemy sanctuaries, lamented General Westmoreland, "gathered considerable dust."

The constant wrangling between U.S. military and civilian strategists over the means to impede infiltration reached its peak in Project Dyemarker/Muscle Shoals, also known as the McNamara Line (see *America Takes Over,* another volume in The Vietnam Experience). Over strong military objections, construction began in September 1967, with the clearing of a 600-meter-wide strip east of Con Thien on the demilitarized zone. A short section was announced to be in operation in December, but resources were soon diverted elsewhere and the McNamara Line never became reality. Scientists nonetheless used the research to produce electronic sensors and detection devices that were put into use on the Ho Chi Minh Trail beginning in 1968. Throughout the war the United States continued to stab at the critical problem of infiltration. But MACV-SOG's covert Operation 35 was the only one to enter the enemy's sanctuaries and attack his infiltration routes and LOCs on the ground.

SOG's unconventional warfare

In 1966 and 1967, SOG expanded rapidly, sending nearly 300 American-led reconnaissance patrols into Laos in addition to 83 platoon-sized forces to "exploit" targets discovered by the recon teams. Colonel John K. Singlaub, who succeeded Colonel Blackburn as commander of SOG in April 1966, oversaw this expansion. Singlaub's acquaintance with Vietnam dated back to World War II when he had operated along the Sino-Vietnamese border with Chinese guerrillas. SOG commander for more than two years, Singlaub brought overall force levels up to 2,500 Americans and 7,000 Vietnamese and indigenous mercenaries, primarily Nungs, a tribe of Chinese origin. He also reorganized the forward operating bases for Operation 35 and changed their names to Command and Control North, Central, and South, located, respectively, at Da Nang, Kontum, and Ban Me Thuot. The code name Shining Brass changed to Prairie Fire, and the recon teams picked up an official nickname of "Spike" teams while exploitation forces became known as "Hatchet" teams. Spike teams from the different bases took the names of states, poisonous snakes, and tools. In 1966 the average Spike team expanded to 12 men—3 Americans and 9 indigenous soldiers.

In May 1967, MACV's need for intelligence from Cambodia finally prevailed over Washington's policy of not violating that country's neutrality, and SOG went into Cambodia in an operation called Daniel Boone (later Salem House). Approval for Daniel Boone, like that for Shining Brass, came with several restrictions. Because it was conceived strictly as an intelligence operation, only recon teams and no exploitation forces could be committed; because combat was to be avoided, helicopter gunships only—without tac air—were allowed. No more than ten missions per month were authorized. Some restrictions were later relaxed. In the seven remaining months of 1967, for example, ninety-nine recon missions were launched into Cambodia. But most of the limitations remained in force.

SOG obtained its own small air force of unmarked C-123s and C-130s, called "blackbirds" because of their lack of insignia. UH-1F helicopters, some of them converted to gunships, joined the versatile CH-34s piloted by Vietnamese. Unmarked air force A-1E Skyraiders provided tactical air support for SOG ground operations in Laos. The 7th and 13th air forces had planned to replace the propeller-driven A-1Es with jets, but Singlaub argued for the slower plane's maneuverability and its capacity to support troops in very close contact with the enemy.

In addition to the radio programming it beamed into North Vietnam, SOG's psyops group collaborated with the recon teams in a unique psychological warfare project called Eldest Son, which began in September 1967. Having discovered numerous caches of enemy ammunition in Laos, the Spike teams brought some 82MM mortar shells and Chinese-made AK47 ammunition back to Vietnam. Flown in a SOG blackbird to Okinawa, the ammunition was dismantled by CIA technicians and filled with a more powerful explosive that would detonate with great force in the mortar tube or rifle chamber, killing the user, and, it was hoped, instilling a mistrust of their equipment in other soldiers. Spike teams then replaced the ammunition, or, in some cases involving AK47 cartridges, simply dropped them on a trail near a way station where NVA soldiers, so protective of their ammunition, were likely to pick them up. Although results of this ploy were difficult to measure, the psyops group had at least one aerial photograph showing an enemy mortar site that had exploded outward from doctored ammunition.

The most lucrative potential source of intelligence from the enemy's sanctuaries was an enemy soldier, and a prisoner "snatch" was often an alternative objective for a SOG Spike team, which carried special equipment such as handcuffs, concussion grenades, and a .22-caliber pistol with silencer. The best targets were soldiers traveling in small groups or straggling behind a larger unit. A favored tactic was to spring an ambush, killing forward and rear soldiers and sparing one or two in the center. One ambusher shot the intended prisoner with a small caliber pistol which, unlike the high velocity M16 and AK47 bullets, could incapacitate rather than kill.

SOG made snatching prisoners a priority by offering American team leaders a reward of five days of R&R and awarding the indigenous soldiers a total team bounty of $700 for each POW. "It was an incentive not to kill a guy," remarked one veteran. Yet capturing prisoners proved difficult. Only fifty POWs were taken in Cambodia and Laos during the war, thirteen of them by the teams of Master Sergeant, and later Captain, Dick Meadows.

SOG's logisticians labored, often with help from the CIA, to supply the teams with the tools of unconventional warfare. According to one NCO, "Whatever someone thought would help do the job, he got." SOG maintained a huge arsenal of weapons, including those used by the enemy. VC and NVA uniforms were also used.

Two particularly useful innovations were the Stabo rig, a chest harness, and the McGuire rig, a "saddle" made of nylon webbing, both of which allowed men to be plucked out of the jungle by a hovering helicopter. If no landing zone could be found in an emergency, a helicopter lowered a cable that fastened to the Stabo harness or lowered a McGuire rig. Two or three men, their arms free for firing or carrying, could be extracted on one McGuire rig. They dangled 30 meters beneath the helicopter until the pilot found a secure landing zone where he could set down to allow the men to climb inside. Sometimes the chopper returned all the way to the launch site with the rescued soldiers dangling below. When leaving on a mission most men donned Stabo rigs in place of combat suspenders.

Reconnaissance tactics

The first SOG teams entering Laos held the advantage of surprise, and they met the least organized resistance. During the first fifty-three cross-border operations, casualties from hostile action were acceptably light: eight Americans wounded, two Vietnamese killed, and two others missing. But as operations escalated, North Vietnamese countertactics evolved rapidly. SOG teams found themselves confronting an enemy gaining experience in a deadly game of manhunt.

Shortly after the first cross-border missions were launched, many potential landing zones bristled with antihelicopter stakes and booby traps. Fortunately the helicopter's down draft usually flattened the elephant grass to make the punji-stakes visible. Montagnard tribesmen working for the enemy along the border presented another problem. Armed with obsolete weapons, they did not pursue the recon teams but simply fired their rifles in the air—the first signals of the "jungle telegraph."

SOG avoided the border sentinels by going deeper into Laos. In that jungle region, however, the number of potential landing zones was sufficiently limited that the enemy could watch over most of them. Observers posted at an LZ fired a prearranged number of shots when a helicopter landed. The pattern of shots signified in what sector the helicopter had landed and in what direction the recon team was traveling (if, in fact, the team could be seen). The best defense against this technique was a series of false landings, with helicopters touching down in several landing zones over a wide area, but with only one depositing a recon team. Since infiltration occurred at last light, the team had the opportunity to hide in the jungle before a search could be mounted.

Fully equipped, a recon man going across the border carried from 60 to 100 pounds, depending on the type of mission and its duration. The men dressed in gray, green, or black fatigues like those of the enemy. (Camouflage "tiger" suits had been eliminated as too recognizable.) A Stabo rig fitted over the shirt. An "indigenous" Vietnamese rucksack contained a poncho, food, extra socks and foot powder, possibly a sweater, a length of rope, tape, perhaps two or three claymore mines (each weighing three and a half pounds). Two canteens rested in pockets on the back, and two others hung from the pistol belt. Those on the rucksack were used first, to insure a supply of water if the pack had to be abandoned. Grenades were likewise separated between rucksack and belt—smoke grenades on the pack and fragmentation and tear gas (CS) on the belt. A sheathed bayonet and first aid kit were attached to one shoulder strap, and a container of serum albumin (blood expander) or battle dressing was fastened to the other.

In addition to grenades, at least two ammunition pouches holding four magazines each—or canteen covers, which each held six magazines—hung from the pistol belt. If heavy combat was a possibility, a man might pack thirty to forty magazines. Some men wore a sidearm, often a 9MM automatic, and at least one man on the team usually carried a .22-caliber pistol with silencer. Pockets were stuffed with insect repellents, maps and signal mirrors, a pencil flare gun, and possibly a rifle silencer. By prearrangement, Americans kept maps and notebooks in a single pocket for hasty removal in the event of casualties. They tied compasses to their shirts and wore extra bandages as neckerchiefs and sweatbands and threaded others through trouser belt loops.

Most teams carried a variety of weapons, including the Swedish K submachine gun, the AK47, the M16, and the similar but shorter-barreled CAR15. Vietnamese normally carried the AK47 in order to pass for an enemy soldier if spotted from a distance. Some men chose a weapon based on weight. With its 5.56MM round, M16 ammunition weighed half as much as the AK47's 7.62MM cartridge (one twenty-round M16 magazine weighs twelve ounces) and thus more could be packed on a mission. Every potential noisemaker—snaps, buckles, even the rings of grenades—was taped. Tape also secured the sling swivels of rifles, and a patch of tape over the muzzle kept out dirt and water.

Training booklets included warnings against smoking, cooking, or using soap, because the enemy possessed a keen sense of smell. Other tips were more subtle: "Many Americans when moving off a landing zone or out of a RON (remain overnight site) tend to pull at leaves or pick grass to put in their mouths. This is a nervous habit"—and a clear sign of the presence of Americans. Team members were taught to remain mobile by

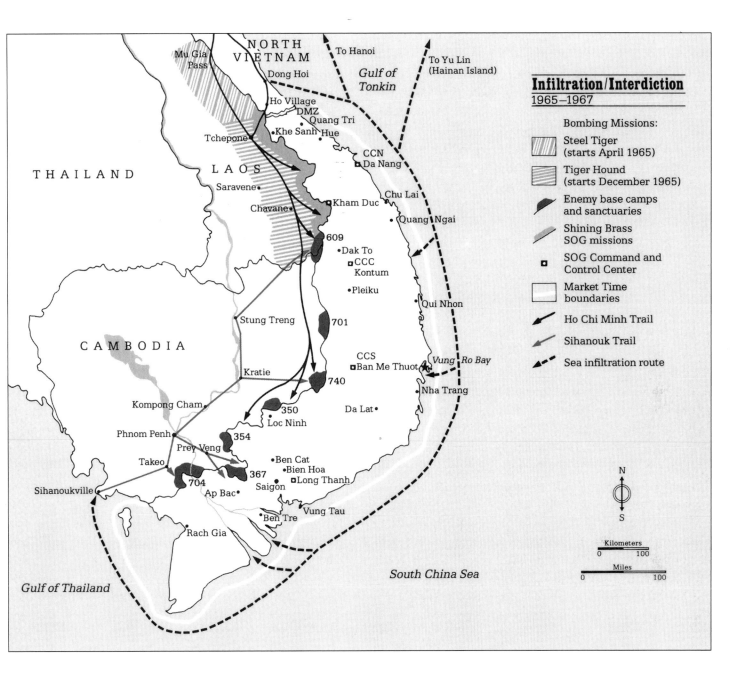

Infiltration/Interdiction
1965–1967

Bombing Missions:

Steel Tiger
(starts April 1965)

Tiger Hound
(starts December 1965)

Enemy base camps
and sanctuaries

Shining Brass
SOG missions

SOG Command and
Control Center

Market Time
boundaries

Ho Chi Minh Trail

Sihanouk Trail

Sea infiltration route

not taking off rucksacks for more than a moment, even when sleeping, and no more than two team members could remove packs at once. But so great was the relief of taking off the heavy packs that the men regularly broke this rule. They took off only one boot at a time, even when changing socks, and tried never to put down their rifles. They listened for encroaching or following enemy by taking frequent "listen halts"; one manual suggested a listen halt of twenty minutes for every advance of ten minutes. Americans used a black grease pencil like lipstick to camouflage the backs of their hands and their faces.

Teams had to remain alert for likely ambushes even in areas that appeared most secure. The enemy ambushed, as it also defended or attacked, in three-man cells or in multiples of three-man cells. Each cell was usually equipped with a B40 rocket launcher, an AK47 automatic rifle, and an SKS semiautomatic carbine, thus providing the capability of destroying a point target, directing a great volume of fire, or sniping.

The men were most vulnerable at night in their bivouac, which they called a RON. They slept within arm's reach of each other so that anyone who coughed or snored could be awakened immediately. If the enemy discovered a SOG team during the day, he might follow on the flank. After tracking the team to its bivouac, the enemy would throw a platoon-sized cordon around the team and patiently and silently tighten the noose throughout the night. By first light the RON would be completely surrounded. Unable to fire for fear of hitting his own men and unwilling to engage in a firefight with the heavily armed team, the enemy simply threw grenades.

A countertactic used by some SOG recon teams was to establish a false RON at nightfall and then move to another preselected site after dark. Special Forces NCO Tim Kephart, who ran the remarkable number of eighty-five cross-border missions in a five-year period without being wounded, used that tactic every night. A soft-spoken Californian who grew up camping and hunting, Kephart possessed a looseness and sangfroid perfect for operating behind enemy lines. Toward the end of every day on patrol, Kephart decided on a RON as he passed it but always led his team 200 meters farther. They set up guard positions and ate as night fell. To anyone following, that site appeared to be the team's bivouac. After dark, however, the team crept back to the designated RON.

One night in thick Laotian jungle, that precaution saved their lives. The team was sleeping on the side of a hill. Kephart was awake, pulling guard. "The sound of movement started coming in around 2:00 A.M.," he recalled. "The people who'd followed us were good because we didn't know we'd been followed. They were above us on the ridge line. They made a huge perimeter, and they kept tightening it and tightening it around that area where we ate. But we were outside their perimeter. They kept creeping, away from us, maybe five of them at a time. They whispered. It sounds like a little buzz.

"I alerted everybody. You wake up pretty damn fast when you can hear that movement so close. They're moving and you're quiet and so you have the advantage. Everybody sat there listening. It took a couple of hours.

"Nobody on my team runs. Anybody who runs gets left, and they know that. Running, you break bush and you make noise. One noise and they find out where you are and the chase is on.

"We didn't move until first light. As soon as I could see where I was going, we started moving. I move extremely slow. We did about ten meters every ten minutes. Only one man moves at a time. He stops and the next guy comes up close. We practice that. It's still a little dark out and all you can see are shadows. If you break a twig, you freeze a long time, a few minutes. We slowly worked our way out that morning. Once we're past fifty meters in that jungle, we're gone. There's no way they're going to catch me."

Such life or death situations called for a team unity and trust between the American and indigenous members. To instill that trust, the Americans worked to build the belief that if anyone got hit—including a Vietnamese soldier or Nung mercenary—every effort would be made to administer first aid or recover the body.

Kephart lost a Nung during a bungled POW snatch when two North Vietnamese wandered into their ambush and the Nung on point fired prematurely. The pair was in fact the point element of a company, and a large firefight broke out. The Nung was shot in the head and fell far from the rest of the team. Crawling forward under fire, Kephart saw that the Nung was dying. He administered serum albumin, hanging the bag on a tree to let it flow while he fired at the enemy. He eventually dragged the Nung back to the team. After calling for air support, they retreated. With Kephart carrying the Nung over his shoulder, they conducted a running firefight through the jungle until helicopter gunships arrived to suppress the fire.

Following directions given by evacuation helicopters, the men hiked some six kilometers toward a hole in the jungle canopy. The Nung died in the first kilometer, but Kephart carried him nonetheless. When they reached the opening, the helicopters lowered cables and the team was evacuated by McGuire rigs. Kephart, the slain Nung, and the rest of the team were pulled through the air for perhaps twenty kilometers before the choppers found a landing zone. "I only did it for one reason," Kephart said. "I wanted to be carried out someday when my turn came. I wanted to show the Nungs, I'll do it for you, you do it for me."

The legacy of SOG

Throughout the war, SOG's Operation 35 ran some 3,000 missions into Laos and Cambodia. Other Special Forces detachments, such as Omega and B-36, which sometimes operated in conjunction with SOG, also performed cross-border missions. As unconventional warfare teams operating behind enemy lines, the SOG units inflicted numerous casualties on troop formations and base areas through ambushes and tactical air strikes. They also destroyed significant stores of enemy ammunition and supplies. In one raid, a SOG team called in napalm strikes on a cache containing ninety tons of rice. SOG operations obliged the enemy to protect its entire logistical network with armed guards, effectively tying up infantry that might have been employed elsewhere. Tactically, the SOG teams made an impact simply by forcing the North Vietnamese to react to them. "In areas where we operated, they had to move," says former SOG commander Major General Singlaub. "If they tried to protect their area after being observed, they became targets for air strikes."

Yet the potential of SOG was never fully realized because of the inhibitions imposed by the United States' observance of the 1962 Geneva accords for Laos and of Cambodia's neutrality.

Prisoner snatch in Laos. *Master Sergeant Jerry Wareing and a team member hustle two captured North Vietnamese soldiers—two of fifty plucked from their sanctuaries during the war—toward a waiting CH-34 helicopter in 1966. Wareing later received one of the Vietnam War's rare commissions to captain for his courage in SOG missions.*

In addition, the United States harbored continuing fears that widening the war into those countries might elicit greater involvement from the North Vietnamese or, worse, direct intervention by Communist China. SOG men chafed under the necessity of carrying on a secret war that was officially at odds with stated U.S. policy, a war whose missions always remained "deniable."

In a practical sense, SOG was also limited by its needs to coordinate with the air force and to win cooperation from the MACV staff. Although General Westmoreland was personally enthusiastic about the intelligence gathered by SOG, especially since it added justification to his own proposals to move against Laos and Cambodia, the MACV staff tended to give SOG less than full backing. Nor was coordination with the air force always what it might have been. Sometimes SOG failed to get timely air strikes when speed was critical.

A great deal of intelligence on enemy movement and locations that was gathered by SOG and passed on to MACV was never acted on. Beyond the tactical intelligence collected and the unconventional warfare waged, SOG commanders viewed their organization in a sense as the advance guard of a conventional ground attempt at interdiction which, as it turned out, never came to pass. "I don't think the United States ever really understood what was at stake with infiltration," says former SOG commander Brigadier General Blackburn, reflecting the military view. "We knew the North Vietnamese were coming down the Ho Chi Minh Trail, and we didn't introduce conventional units. As a result, they built a highway and drove tanks down it. This was a bigger problem than SOG alone could have handled."

During the war, SOG suffered the deaths of more than 300 American soldiers in Laos and Cambodia. Numerous other Vietnamese and indigenous soldiers also died, and not all the bodies were recovered. Because official policy kept the clandestine activities secret (though they were known to the enemy), the Americans' next of kin were notified that they had died in "Southeast Asia" or "along the border" or on a classified mission. The true locations of their deaths were not disclosed until after the U.S. had left Vietnam. Medal citations likewise named such locations as "Republic of Vietnam" or "west of Dak To."

Despite the hazards and lack of public recognition, SOG never lacked volunteers. In praising the "incredibly brave deeds" of the men who served with SOG, General Westmoreland wrote, "It said something for the intrepidity of the American soldier that SOG always had a waiting list of applicants." No United States soldiers in Vietnam, he later added, did more or better.

Arty

One of the closest relationships among American combat units in Vietnam existed between the infantry and the artillery—the grunts and the gunners. In this war without fronts, helicopters set down infantry units as bait somewhere in the bush. Ordered to "find, fix, and destroy" enemy troops, sometimes infantry units found nothing but deserted tunnels and abandoned supplies. Other times they found aggressive, dedicated enemy fighters who possessed the tactical advantages of surprise, superior numbers, greater firepower, and familiarity with terrain. If infantry units embarked on a "fishing expedition" suffered a sudden attack, they needed artillery fire support and they needed it fast, or they wouldn't get out alive.

In order to provide the infantry with immediate and reliable artillery fire support, the American military deployed artillery pieces in two ways. One was the unprepared, or "hasty," artillery position. It consisted of one or more 105MM howitzers, each airlifted to a location by a CH-47 "Chinook" helicopter, or towed by a two-and-one-half-ton truck—"a deuce and a half." The more elaborate artillery position was the fire support base (FSB). A typical FSB was a semipermanent emplacement that contained an artillery battery of six 105MM howitzers and fortifications for self-defense. Constructed in the midst of an infantry unit's tactical area of responsibility (TAOR), a fire support base's guns delivered thirty-three-pound explosive shells with a "kill radius" of 30 meters at a range of 11,000 meters under all conditions of weather and visibility. Often, the fire was augmented by larger 155MM howitzers to provide support at longer ranges. When friendly infantry was operating at great distances from the FSB the artillery commander sometimes added eight-inch howitzers or 175MM guns. Usually several fire support bases were established in a TAOR, so that any part of it could be reached by fire. Positioned within range of each other, FSBs provided mutually supporting interlocking fires.

Whenever possible, sites for fire support bases were selected in open areas, away from tall trees. This served the dual purpose of making it difficult for enemy infiltrators to sneak up on the position and permitting the artillery pieces to be fired at lower angles of

Set on high ground *in the middle of the contested A Shau Valley, a firebase of 105mm howitzers provides support for U.S. infantry troops below.*

Marines put their backs *into maneuvering a 105. The older model weighed nearly 5,000 pounds while a version produced in 1966 with some aluminum parts weighed 3,300 pounds.*

elevation. Sometimes, however, the FSB had to be carved out of the deep jungle by huge bulldozers called Rome plows. To minimize the area that was to be cleared and to provide for a better all-around defense of the FSB, the combat engineers sometimes drove a stake in the center of the area and then inscribed a forty-meter circle, measuring with a rope tied to the stake. Within the circle the engineers built an observation tower, a command post, and supply and ammunition dumps. Working with artillerymen they set out six 105MM howitzers, collectively called a "battery," often in a "star" pattern. Emplacements for the batteries included sandbagged walls, ammunition racks, a tool room, and crew quarters. Among the six howitzers, soldiers set out four 81MM mortars and dug bunkers at five-meter intervals along the FSB perimeter for infantrymen armed with rifles, grenade launchers, and machine guns.

Next, combat engineers used another rope, often 75 meters long, and inscribed a second circular perimeter (usually misshapen as a result of terrain irregularities). Along the outer perimeter they set one or more coils of barbed wire, fixing claymore mines and trip flares to the wire. At one point on this perimeter a fortified and guarded point for exit and entry was built. From it, infantry patrols moved out to perform surveillance of the area around the FSB. The FSB also included a landing zone for helicopters.

Soldiers in artillery units performed three sorts of fire missions. One was harassment and interdiction (H&I) fire aimed at targets where military intelligence suspected enemy activity. Another was reconnaissance or preparation fire, fired in the hope of detonating booby traps and dispersing concentrations of enemy troops before an American or ARVN infantry unit entered the target area. The third sort of fire mission was direct support to assist infantry units engaged in battle with enemy forces.

Coordination of infantry operations and artillery fire missions was a complicated and exacting procedure. A field artillery forward observer (FO) traveled with each rifle company on operations. Serving as the eyes and ears of the artillery, the FO radioed a description of the target—troops, bunkers, or vehicles—to the fire direction center (FDC). At the FDC, a fire direction officer (FDO) evaluated the FO's request with the aid of his staff of five enlisted men. A radio telephone oper-

A 3d Marine Division gun crew *fires a 105mm howitzer and quickly reloads. The 105 was capable of firing three rounds per minute.*

ator (RTO) maintained communications between the FO in the field, the FDC, and the gun crews. Enlisted fire direction specialists plotted the target location on a chart or map and then established its distance and direction. Based on this information a fire direction specialist then plotted the distance to the target and the difference in elevation between the guns and the target on slide rule-like devices called graphical firing tables. These calculations allowed the specialist to determine the elevation at which the gun muzzles needed to be set to reach the target. Next, the fire direction officer determined the number and type of shells to be used and ordered the RTO to relay the

information to the gun crews. Each artillery piece was controlled by a chief who supervised aiming, loading, and firing. A gunner set direction, an assistant gunner set elevation, and two or three cannoneers attached fuses to shells, loaded them into the breech, and removed the spent casings.

Artillery in action

One morning in the middle of June 1966, army First Lieutenant John D. Lewis returned from a seven-day R&R leave in Bangkok to Tuy Hoa, the coastal II Corps district where his unit, C Battery, 5th Battalion,

27th Artillery, was based. But C Battery was gone. Ordered twenty-two kilometers due north to an area five kilometers west of Tuy An, all six guns of C Battery were in place at an unprepared, or "hasty," artillery position. Its fire direction center was located in a schoolhouse nearby. Lieutenant Lewis was flown by helicopter to the area. He walked through the door of the ramshackle plywood schoolhouse and asked what was going on. "We're supportin' the 2d of the 327th," someone answered, "and they're surrounded. Things are hot!"

Two companies of the 2d Battalion, 327th Infantry (Airborne), of the 1st Brigade, 101st Airborne Division, had been dropped by

Soldiers of the 1st Battalion, *28th Infantry, 1st Infantry Division, plot supporting fire coordinates to relay to a nearby artillery unit during Operation Battlecreek in Tay Ninh Province, November 6, 1966.*

helicopter on a hill six kilometers north of C Battery's position. Ordered to drive elements of the NVA 95th Regiment east to the sea, the two infantry companies were ambushed soon after landing. "They got their asses kicked," Lewis said. "That is, they were in a very untenable position." Fortunately for them, C Battery's guns had been registered, or sighted in, on the area. For the next two days Lieutenant Lewis acted as artillery fire direction officer for C Battery.

Inside the schoolhouse the fire direction center's personnel manned equipment. On one wall hung a large situation map plotted with the locations of friendly units and known enemy units. On a table with folding legs was the firing chart used by the FDC crew to compute the firing data for the howitzers.

"It was organized chaos," Lewis said. "You reacted to what was going on. When you fired missions you checked the calculations of the computers, listened to battle activity over the radio loud-speakers, decided whether to fire and if so what kind of shells and how many. If you weren't firing

missions, you kept up with the ammo count and stayed close to the situation map.

"I don't know how many thousands of rounds we fired," Lewis said. "Every call that came over the radio was 'Help! Help!' As soon as the FO's keyed their mikes, we could hear the rounds landing, we could hear the small-arms fire. We could hear guys screaming orders like 'Get the one over there, man!' 'Hurry up with that machine gun ammo!' or 'Somebody get a medevac, so and so's hit!'" When the FO evaluated the effect of the artillery fires, he might abandon standard radio procedure and say something like, "That landed right on top of them!" or "You got the sons of bitches! I see five bodies layin' there!"

Outside the FDC among the six 105MM howitzers there was a frenzy of activity. "It was like watching a war movie with the artillery in action," Lewis recalled. With their shirts off and their trousers out of their boots, the sweating six-man gun crews responded quickly to each fire mission. "They were working hard, but they were

happy because they were firing. They get real keyed up when they're firing." At the end of the second day the recoil mechanisms on each of the guns began to break down from constant use.

Despite lack of sleep and the stress of decision-making, Lewis found the experience exhilarating. "A situation like this, you know there are troops out there in contact, and you know somebody's ass depends on whether you hit the target." When the FO called in after a fire mission and reported enemy casualties Lewis felt satisfaction. "But it's more a sense of helping the friendlies than hurting the enemy. You're shooting because somebody's out there screaming for help, not to see how many guys you can waste." Some days later soldiers in the artillery of C Battery received patches bearing the "screaming eagle" insignia of the infantry companies' parent division, the 101st Airborne Division. Many of the 105 men of C Battery proudly wore them on their right shoulders, signifying they had served with units of the 101st in combat.

"About halfway through the village a nine-year-old girl came from behind a hooch with a grenade in each hand, heading straight for me. I did not have time to try to stop her. Through experience and my quick reaction, I shot this child."

Marine Corporal Andrew Garner

The kind of a war a soldier experienced depended on where in Vietnam he fought it. A marine rifleman's thirteen-month tour among the densely settled hamlets around Phu Bai, for example, bore few resemblances to that of an army reconnaissance scout's twelve-month tour in the sparsely populated central highlands around Pleiku. The kind of Vietnam War a soldier experienced also depended on what he did in it. A slightly built army combat engineer who, with flashlight in one hand and a .45 caliber pistol in the other, crawled into an enemy bunker complex to install explosives had a different view of Vietnam from the air force F-100 pilot flying out of Udorn, Thailand, in predawn darkness to drop 2,000-pound bombs on the Vinh rail yards in North Vietnam. A navy corpsman tying tourniquets around the stumps of limbs severed by booby traps north of Cam Lo experienced Vietnam in a different way from an army transportation specialist driving a truck in convoy through the mine-laden, ambush-ridden An Khe Pass on Highway 19. And yet a specialist who spent every day monitoring radio transmissions before retiring to dinner and secure quarters scarcely knew he was in a war zone. The kind of war a soldier saw also depended on the sort of person he was and often on his age. A nineteen-year-old infantryman hesitating at the helicopter door before jumping for the first time into a hot landing zone was a different man from the platoon sergeant who yanked him out and told him to keep down and keep moving. Like a maze of rice fields in the Mekong

The experience of Vietnam *was both simple and strange, a matter of fact and of mystery. ... A soldier of the 11th Armored Cavalry gazes pensively from the hatch opening of his tank in Quang Ngai Province, 1967.*

Delta, or triple-canopy jungle in the Ngoc Krinh Mountains, the experience of Vietnam was both simple and strange, a matter of fact and of mystery.

Here, in their own words, are a few Vietnam experiences of Americans from the early years of the war.

John Wayne would do better

Michael Jeffords
Sergeant, Company B, 1st Battalion, 3d Marines, 3d Marine Division, March–November 1965, Da Nang.

We spent that first month acclimatizing to the country, the people, and the situation. Watching the build-up of forces. Listening to Hanoi Hannah on the radio. Fighting the huge, choking clouds of dust, the mosquitoes, large bugs, centipedes, snakes, and the smell of the little village on the edge of the base, Dogpatch. And, of course, the ants. It was very sandy in the area around Da Nang. When you slept you could hear them moving under your poncho. Out of all those months, those damn ants stick in my mind.

A recon squad got ambushed one afternoon and we were ordered to saddle up. We were the reaction force. We were pretty cocky. We were proud and anxious to get into action. We ran to helicopters, made the first helicopter assault of the war by an American unit and stumbled around in the bush for hours. It was anticlimactic. We expected to be facing hordes of screaming enemy and facing death. All I remember is sneaking up in a small clearing in a jungle and watching a Vietnamese family eat lunch before I slipped away with my squad. John Wayne could have done much better. It was pretty boring—so we thought. One guy in the second platoon, after they entered a village, shot a farmer who had a pocket knife in his hand. That left an awful bad taste in our mouth. ...

Common knowledge was that [an] officer over captain and [a] non-commissioned officer over staff sergeant was useless baggage in this war. Small unit action was where it was at. The problem was everyone over those ranks wanted in on the action. Majors and colonels were telling platoon commanders how to maneuver over the radio. "Move over to this position," they would radio, and the young lieutenant would try to explain to an officer used to the flat terrain of Korea that one-half mile on a map was hours away when you only moved yards through a jungle in a half an hour. I personally had a captain come down in a Huey gunship when I had a couple—two people, understand—cornered on a hill under a huge boulder across a ravine we were crossing. He wanted me to pull the other squad back so he could unload his rockets and ordnance so he wouldn't have to go back with his ammo. So, I pulled them back. He came in like the cavalry, shot up all his ammo, and of course the two people surrendered. Couple of farmers burning charcoal in the hills. They just hid until the captain in the sky had shot his wad. ... We learned to stay off the radios unless we absolutely needed help. I used to think 90 percent of the men on the other end of the radio were really killing themselves to be in our shoes or trying to kill their boredom by outdoing each other.

A boy named Dong

Robert V. Smith, Jr.
Private First Class, Company A, 1st Battalion, 26th Infantry, 1st Infantry Division, December 1966–December 1967, Binh Duong Province.

While waiting for assignment to a combat unit at Long Binh, I was stuck on a guard detail, guarding the trash dump. We had to guard trash and garbage because the Vietnamese would use almost anything to build a hut to live in or eat almost anything we thought was nonedible, and almost everything else could be used to make weapons of one sort or another.

There were about six guards and each had a post that he stayed at during the day. Each guard was adopted by some young Vietnamese kid as soon as he was posted. The kid would be your gofor—sodas, women, whatever was in demand. I had a young boy, about fourteen, named Dong, take up with me. The little guy was always getting me Cokes and fruit, talking to me about America and how much he had heard about it and how bad he wanted to go so that he could make a lot of money to send home to his parents. To him America was IT. Over a period of two weeks I came to like the kid. Heck, I was only nineteen myself.

Each day before we left the dump we had to pour gas on the day's garbage to be sure that the VC did not get into it and use it against us the next day. We, the guards, had a way of getting out of the messy job of pouring gas, we let the kids and old men and women who picked through the trash each day pour for us from three fifty-five-gallon drums. On this day there was a problem, a hot spot in the dump, a fire burning down inside the trash that kept smoldering. The kids and old folks went about gassing the dump down. Dong was down in the dump and had just filled his half-gallon can up when the whole dump blew up. The gas had gotten down to the hot spot and ignited. Dong's can went up in his face, the others caught fire or were killed outright. By the time we got down to the dump site there was little we could do. I found Dong about fifty feet from where he had been. He was calling for me, otherwise I doubt I would have stopped. I did not recognize him as he was burned so bad that it was impossible to even tell if he were young or old, male or female. I was sick to my stomach. I talked to him, telling him to be calm and I would get help. A truck that had just been to the dump came back and the other guards and myself loaded about ten very burned people. When I picked Dong up parts of him came off in my hands. He never complained of pain or anything. All he ever said was that I would take him to America and make him well. This he said over and over all the way to the base hospital. The doctor told me there was nothing they could do as he was burned too bad. I stayed with him for over six hours till he died.

Environmental management

Walter Dunlap
Specialist 4, 509th Army Security Agency Group, Tan Son Nhut, August 1967–1968, Saigon.

My first plane ride within Vietnam was aboard a C-130, and my flight took me from Saigon's Tan Son Nhut air base to Nha Trang. From my seat I didn't have much of a view, but I saw a shimmering chain of perfectly round lakes bathed in late afternoon sun when we banked. It took several moments of musing over round lakes before it dawned on me that B-52 sorties had taken up on lake planning where mother nature had left off.

An irritable war

Michael Boston
Corporal, Company B, 1st Battalion, 4th Marines, 3d Marine Division, October 1966–November 1967, Thua Thien and Quang Tri Provinces.

People get very irritable over long stretches of hot humid weather here in this country. You get roughly five or six hours sleep a night because you can't sleep through the night (you're always in a perimeter or out on an ambush some place). You're not under a tent away from the climate, the rain. You're always just out there in the elements, and on top of that, there's this fear that you can be killed at any second, during any minute, at any point in time during your whole tour of Vietnam. There's no such thing as a rear, so half a night's sleep in good weather is pretty rough. Sometimes there was almost no sleep when we got reports of an NVA unit progressing towards our line, or a lot of activity in the early or middle part of the night up north further away. It caused us to be on 50 percent alert all night, and so while it's dark,

only getting a half hour sleep, one hour on, one hour off, or two on, two off, it seems like those two hours go by in a minute and you got to get up again. It doesn't even feel like you're sleeping.

You're always kept busy for morale purposes, 'cause idleness is just something that the Marine Corps wouldn't tolerate. You're filling sandbags, building your bunkers up, digging new positions, cleaning your rifle, going to chow. There's always something to do, and if there wasn't, they'd make something up, like putting an extra strand of wire around the whole perimeter, making your fortified position an extra sandbag deep in case of a rocket attack.

"Each guard was adopted by some Vietnamese kid. ... " A streetwise, crippled thirteen-year-old boy who calls everyone "sweatheart" and goes by the nickname "Louie" hangs around with marines stationed in Hoa Hiep in 1967.

U.S. firepower

Mark M. Smith
Private, Company A, 1st Battalion, 5th Cavalry, 1st Cavalry Division (Airmobile), February 1967–February 1968, Binh Dinh Province.

On a patrol in August, my platoon found a dud butterfly bomb and determined to blow it up in place. We spent twenty frustrating minutes without managing to set it off, using hand grenades—pull the pin and run like hell for cover—and well-aimed shots with the M79s. Finally one of the grenadiers, who had fired at it five or six times, was fed up and snapped, "Fuck the motherfucker—call a B-52 strike in on it!" That was always the solution—wipe things out. Run into an enemy scout, call in the gunships; meet an enemy patrol, send for the fighter-bombers; take a burst of sniper fire, radio the howitzers.

When I achieved a position of real responsibility in Nam, platoon sergeant and platoon leader, I always told the new guys as they came to the field: "Forget everything they taught you except how to use your weapons, and follow your squad leaders." What this indicated, of course, is not that the training was that awful but that in actual combat nothing goes according to the book. Everything is hellishly confused, you can't remember hand and arm signals, you haven't the time to yell out formations, so you just yell, "Let's go, let's go! This way, let's go!" and hope your people come along.

Something for the wife

L. Erick Kanter
Ensign, Navy Public Affairs Officer, Detachment Charlie, 7th Fleet, June 1967–1968, Saigon.

Some of my official duties also had bizarre aspects. Whenever an American navy fighter plane crew shot down an enemy MIG, we had them flown down to Saigon to stand up in front of the press at the Five O'Clock Follies and describe their adventure. I was in charge of arranging their lodging—usually in a downtown hotel or bachelor officers quarters—and their entertainment. I usually took them to a good French restaurant, which was mind boggling to them after months of cramped and weary existence on an aircraft carrier and never setting foot on the Vietnamese soil that they were bombing every day. After dinner, many would be very tired and go to bed. But some craved female companionship, which I steered them toward, generally stopping short of actually making arrangements.

I was also in charge of buying ceramic elephants for visiting admirals, whose wives back in the States needed them as status symbols (I think). As a very junior officer, it was a privilege for me to have such an important job, because whenever I went to the elephant factory to select a fresh pair of elephants, I would observe air force and army bird colonels on the scene, performing the same chore.

Making friends

PFC Robert V. Smith, Jr.

My squad leader, Lopez, was a pretty good guy who took me under his wing and tried to show me the ropes and tried to help me stay alive long enough to open my eyes and see what to do and more important, what *not* to do! I had been in the squad for about a month and had really gotten to like my squad leader, we sat around at night and talked about home and he shared his packages from home and I shared mine with him. One day on a patrol we came to a clearing about 100 yards wide and in order to get across it we had to send a team across to secure the other side so that there was some type of cover. ... My team was chosen to be the cover team and as we were lining up to go across I was having trouble with my web gear, it was twisted and bunched up so Lopez told me to move to the rear and he took my place. We each had a particular spot to enter the jungle and as Lopez entered the jungle there was a large explosion that was followed by several smaller ones, and then there was a lot of small arms fire and the remaining men in the squad broke cover to run across and give help to the guys pinned down. I ran to where Lopez was and all I found was a body that had no face. Lopez had caught a claymore mine in the face and when I got there he was not dead but was choking on his blood and there was no way to stop it. He died and I don't know if he even knew I was there. After that I made myself a promise not to have any more close friends, but being young that was a lesson I had to learn again.

Beware the children

Andrew Garner
Corporal, Company K, 3d Battalion, 7th Marines, 1st Marine Division, November 1966–August 1967, Chu Lai, Da Nang.

My strongest memory was the morning that 2d Platoon was just about wiped out. We were patrolling through a village that we patrolled just about every day. I was walking point, and this was one time that I let my guard down. Upon entering the

"You're always just out there in the elements. ..." *Following a battle near Bu Dop on the Cambodian border, a soldier of the U.S. 1st Infantry Division tries to keep warm, December 15, 1967.*

"I made myself a promise *not to have any more close friends, but being young that was a lesson I had to learn again. ..." A soldier from Company A, 2d Battalion, 7th Cavalry, 1st Cavalry Division, breaks down and is consoled after his platoon took heavy casualties in Operation Byrd, August 26, 1966.*

village, I saw some soldiers, but I thought that they were ARVNs. The village did not show any signs of the enemy. About halfway through the village a nine-year-old girl came from behind a hooch with a grenade in each hand, heading straight for me. I did not have time to try to stop her. Through experience and my quick reaction, I shot this child. The two grenades went off and wounded two of my men. At this point, all hell broke loose. We were surrounded in the village, and the VC were letting us have everything they had. They didn't care who they killed—they were after us. We knew that we had only one chance for some of us to make it, and that was for us to try and break through their lines. That was a mistake because on our way out we tripped two booby traps, killing six marines and wounding fourteen. That stopped our assault, and we took cover where we could fire. The firefight lasted for three hours before help came. Even today I think that if I just followed my instinct then, some of these men would still be alive. ... I think

a lot of the child I had to kill. There's not a day that goes by that I do not think about this experience, especially since I have a little girl of my own.

The family doctor

Mike Clark
Specialist 5, Medic, Company A, 4th Battalion, 39th Infantry, 9th Division, January–September 1967, Bear Cat, Long Binh.

Five months after our arrival, many of the originals in our unit were gone, and those of us left tended to cluster together for survival. We had a special bond that we could never share with the replacements. As time went on, those of us who survived became seasoned veterans. We also learned to hide our feelings and appeared to be quite detached from it all. One day a fellow stumbled across a trip wire and pretty much blew himself up. I was working on him, trying to staunch the flow of blood. A new medic, fresh from the States, ran up to help me. Our fatigues were soon drenched with blood. After the man had been medevacked, the medic complained about his clothes being covered with blood. I saw clouds forming in the sky and knew we'd soon be rained upon. I told him not to worry, the rain would soon wash a lot of the blood away.

Line medics did not wear the Red Cross armband, nor did they wear the emblem on their helmets as World War II medics did. To do this would only have made a more inviting target for the VC. We did carry weapons, either M16s or .45s, and did fire them when possible.

You were in effect the family doctor. A smiling and cheerful Dr. Marcus Welby. Each infantry company (about ninety men) consisted of four platoons. Each platoon had a medic (I was medic for 1st Platoon). You wanted to gain the confidence of your platoon. This was done if you were good at what you did and if they believed that you would go out and get them when they were wounded, no matter what the circumstances—or at least make a decent attempt. Once this was accomplished, you

found that you'd receive preferential treatment from the enlisted men and officers alike. At night in the jungle when everyone would have to stand watch, I wasn't required to. Back at base camp, everyone would be required to arise early and stand inspection or work at various duties. I'd get to sleep in. Also at base camp, going through the chow line, I'd get an extra scoop of food, or on rare occasions when we'd have ice cream, an extra scoop of that luxury. I would accept this treatment without guilt feelings because often during a firefight my chances of getting hit were very good because of the moving around I did going from wounded to wounded. I was always called "Doc." Most guys never knew my last name.

We carried morphine, of course, and it was vital to know when to give it and when not to. Generally if a person had a chest, stomach, or head wound, you did not administer morphine because it retards the functions of the nervous system. Sometimes there were exceptions. It was a judgmental thing. All you could do was pray you had made the right decision. It wasn't easy to listen to someone crying in pain and try to

"I always told them yes, *they were going to make it. ..." Waving the blood-soaked bandages of his wounded comrade, an army medic calls for assistance during a 1966 battle in the hills southwest of Pleiku.*

explain why you couldn't give him morphine. Sometimes you might give him a harmless sugar type pill and tell him it's for the pain. Other times—stomach wounds—you couldn't give them anything by mouth. You might inject a syringe of water and tell them it's morphine for pain.

Most guys, if they were conscious, wanted to know how bad it was. Were they going to make it? I always told them, yes, they were going to make it. No matter how bad their wounds, or what I really thought, I told them they were going to make it. The human body is capable of surviving some horrendous damage, and even when I thought there was no way this fellow was going to survive, I'd tell him I thought he was going to make it. Who was I to take that last chance of making it away from someone?

A typical firefight was sudden, short, and violent. Loud noises, screams, and confusion. People calling "medic," some down and not calling. Me running around, trying to work as quickly as possible, stop the bleeding, sometimes put on a tourniquet, use pressure bandages, give morphine, a few times perform a tracheotomy, sometimes try to find an artery and tie it off. Try to ignore the whine and buzz of bullets, try not to think that at any time you could be hit. Don't think of the other medics you knew who were killed. Think, if you must, that you won't be hit because you are the doctor and have immunity to being hit. Most of all, just try to concentrate on what you are doing. After a while, you notice the silence as the battle has died out, but still you keep on working.

When it's really all over, when the WIAs and the KIAs have been evacked, then you go into a kind of shock and struggle to control the shakes. You are covered with blood, and it smells of a fish odor that makes you sick. You think about the guys who were badly wounded and wish them luck. You think about the KIAs and silently mourn for them, for their families who do not yet know of the tragedy. You think about all the rich, red blood that has drained into the soil of Vietnam. If blood enriches soil, then Vietnam soil must be very fertile indeed.

My most pleasant and enjoyable experiences as a medic were the MEDCAPs. With the platoon as guards, we would go to a village and give people medical treatment. Sometimes, the battalion doctor would accompany us, other times he would not, and I'd be the doctor. The most common ailment we treated the Vietnamese for was infection. Many times they had open sores that were infected. We'd give them soap with instructions on how to use it, clean the sore, put ointment on it, then bandage it. Sometimes, we'd give them penicillin injections with tablets to take afterwards. We'd hand out candy to the kids and food to the adults. It wasn't much, what we did, but it was a positive thing, and I enjoyed it immensely. The opportunity to listen to the children laugh and the adults smile made me realize that the Orientals weren't as inscrutable as I had been led to believe but that they had the same emotions and feelings as people everywhere. To this day, I remember the Vietnamese with fondness.

Night ambush

Fredrick D. Jones
1st Lieutenant, 5th Special Forces Group,
August 1967–November 1968, Ho Ngoc Thao.

We launched out of Ho Ngoc Thao, directly north of Saigon, into an area north of Xuan Loc. We had intel that the area was well utilized, and we felt they might be using the road. Aircraft had identified what looked like fresh tire tracks on portions of that road.

We inserted late that afternoon, about 4:30. Three helicopters in trail landed right on this road in an area that had been defoliated. There were twenty-one of us, six Americans and fifteen indigenous, seven to a helicopter. We jumped off the helicopters right at the edge of a logging trail and moved off into this defoliated wood line. This was more woods than jungle, single canopy. We intended to move about two miles to set up. As we moved east and north we got out of the defoliated area and into heavier woods.

We moved very quickly. I became increasingly concerned that we were not going to get back to the road before dark and that I had underestimated how long it would take. We needed to get there before it got pitch dark or we'd be trying to get set up with absolutely no light. We knew it was going to be a very dark night. That was one of the reasons we went that night. There was no moon.

We made it at dusk and started to set up. I remember being extremely conscious of the noise. At dusk, every twig snaps, you feel like someone's hearing your every move. The road itself was four meters wide and the road surface was dirt, single lane, rutted, and partially overgrown. There were no large trees within another four meters of the road, so from wood line to wood line was about twelve meters. But in front of the tree line were some small bushes and scrub trees. My troops set up just inside the tree line so they had good cover and concealment as well as good firing lanes. We spread out over about seventy-five meters, all on one side. This was a hasty ambush and so we did not set mines or booby traps on the opposite side of the road. On our side we did set two claymore mines at each end of the ambush, protecting our flanks. We had M16s with forty magazines of ammunition each, some M79 grenade launchers, and a minimum of four hand grenades per man.

I inspected them as they were setting up, moving from the far right flank, making a few minor adjustments as to where an individual was or what his field of fire was. It was very quickly getting dark. I moved down to the left flank and then returned to my position, which was in the center about five meters behind my troops. I felt that in that position I could still see the road clearly and could initiate and control the ambush. Behind me there was a large bomb crater, about fifteen feet across at the top and probably ten feet deep. That was the rally point. It was planned that when I indicated cease-fire, everybody would move back to the bomb crater.

Just at the instant it became dark I heard some faint talking, and I said to my Cambodian interpreter and radio operator that the indigenous troops just can't keep quiet, they've got to keep quiet. I heard more talking and saw just a glimmer of light on the ground. It caught my eye. Could it be that my men closest to the road maybe had a light with them? I didn't know. It didn't take more than another second to see more light and hear more talking. At that point I could detect movement, although it was so dark I couldn't distinguish figures. It was not my troops but someone else. They came out of the woods directly across from my position at the center of the ambush and moved single file two meters apart to the right flank of the ambush and suddenly stopped. They talked in louder voices and the point man started moving towards a large tree in front of which we had placed a claymore mine. I was trying hard to determine at what instant I was going to initiate the ambush. I was trying to figure out if these guys were alone, if there was more movement coming through the woods. Do I have the point element of a platoon, a battalion, what do we have here?

"To this day, I remember the Vietnamese with fondness. ... " *Major Garold Tippen, a civil affairs officer in the 25th Infantry Division, lets a montagnard child listen to his own heartbeat, near Pleiku, 1966.*

"Ordinary patrolling in the countryside *was very much like being out in the fields at home. ... " During Operation Virginia, a marine of Charlie Company, 2d Battalion, 1st Marines, moves through elephant grass near the Laotian border, April 20, 1966.*

The NCO at the right flank who had control of the claymore blew it, and everybody opened fire. It was intense, everyone firing two or three magazines on automatic. Then I yelled cease-fire several times.

Everybody immediately pulled back to the rally point in the bomb crater without going forward to check the bodies. They all came back quickly, and we did a head count. I was missing one man, an American NCO, and I was really concerned. At that point we heard a lot of noise in the woods. It could have been animals, it could have been just twigs and small brush hit by gunfire that were breaking and falling and snapping off in a delayed reaction. But we heard noise and it was intensified in our minds. I got on the radio and asked for a light helicopter fire team. We heard another noise. It was the American sergeant low crawling up to the bomb crater. He was furious. He hadn't heard me yell cease-fire. The guy he was with on the buddy system just pulled back and left him. He was very angry. "You left

me," he said. But then he realized that nobody had intentionally left him. All twenty-one of us were now there.

The light fire team came up on station pretty quickly, I would say within ten minutes. We identified ourselves by putting a strobe light in the bottom of the crater so it couldn't be seen from ground level but it could be seen from the air. The fire teams ran up and down north-south along the road, three passes each, just firing their mini-guns which make a tremendous racket in the woods. It was random fire on either side of us to keep anybody down who was there. But time was passing and we hadn't seen anybody else. Helicopters were on the way to get us.

One of the pilots kicked out a flare and we went back to the road and searched the area, searched the bodies, and counted seven people. Actually there were six bodies on the road, pretty well riddled, and an indication that there was a seventh body. There was a seventh weapon. That was the guy in front of the claymore when it blew. There was not a complete body, just a weapon.

We picked up the AK47s, the gear, and the map case. They continued to drop flares above us, and we quickly moved to an open area up the road. We had strobe lights with us and there was enough room to spread people out. Three helicopters came down in trail, one, two, three, each landing to a strobe light, and at that point we ran to the three choppers and took off. We went back to Ho Ngoc Thao, and the debriefing was pretty short. What happened? What was your route? Then a run-through of the ambush. I imagine that we were finished by four in the morning.

Vietnam the beautiful

John Yeager, Jr.
Sergeant, Company C, 2d Battalion, 502d Infantry, 1st Brigade,
101st Airborne Division, November 1966–September 1967,
Kontum and Quang Ngai Provinces.

Ordinary patrolling in the countryside was very much like being out in the fields at home. It was not like hunting, and I don't want to cheapen the experience by saying that. It was more like just being out for a pleasant walk most of the time. My experience was that we only came into contact with the enemy once or twice a week and these encounters were usually brief. In the absence of fighting, it was an extremely interesting country to walk around in. We saw montagnards still living in thatched longhouses on poles. We saw all manner of snakes and animals. The country is incredibly beautiful. ...

There were wood ticks to contend with, and there were numerous leeches. When a leech senses your presence, he raises his head off the ground and "sniffs" around. I do not know if he finds you by heat-seeking or by smell, but he will come your way as soon as he locates you. It is upsetting to be smoothing your poncho on the ground in the evening and to see them in the grass trying to get a fix on you. You're sure that as soon as you're asleep they'll be all over you. They also live in the water, and when you're filling your canteen, you can see them swimming around, probably looking for you. When they are on you, you can't feel them bite, and you're often so sweaty in the jungle that you can reach inside your shirt and rub your hand across them and never feel them. They're as slimy as you are sweaty.

On the day I was shot through the leg, an air force jet dropped a bomb so close to my company that a huge rock was thrown into the air and came down on the legs of another soldier. He lost them both. Unless you've seen it, nothing prepares you for what a bomb blast is like. The power released is awe-some. A white shock wave flashes out and fragments spray the ground around the explosion. Large fragments sometimes fly as far as the positions of friendly troops, and you can hear the shards whirring through the air like huge boomerangs.

What to say to God

Rick Eilert
Lance Corporal, Companies L & M, 3d Battalion, 26th Marines,
3d Marine Division, July 1967–December 1967, Quang Tri and Thua
Thien Provinces.

I was on this narrow path when I got hit with a grenade. An NVA soldier came out to shoot me, I went to pick up my rifle, but realized my arms were broken. One arm was dangling. My rifle barrel was bent from the blast. Then I went for my knife. I looked at the knife and I looked at the NVA and it was like, what am I going to do with this? Throw it at him? Even when my arms weren't broken I couldn't get a knife to stick in a board at two feet.

The corpsman running up to help me shot the NVA in the throat with his .45. His head fell off and I said, "Gee, that was a great shot." The corpsman said, "I was shooting at his nuts." I thought, "Maybe you better let me bandage myself because if you bandage as good as you aim, I'm in a lot of trouble."

The grenade ripped my left leg—the corpsman got a tourni-quet on it. I didn't feel too bad laying there. I didn't hurt. It wasn't as bad as what you'd envision being wounded is like. It was pins and needles all over and I was watching everybody else. They were singing to me so I wouldn't go into shock—so I would stay awake. That was the first time I had somebody sing to me since I was a little boy when my mom sang to me. They sang "I'm in pieces, bits and pieces," from the Dave Clark Five song of the sixties. They were encouraging as hell. The corps-man came up. My leg was up laying on my shoulder and he said, "Well, I think you lost one leg." And then he looked down at the other leg and he said, "They might have to cut off both of them, but what counts is still there." I said, "Big deal." Shortly thereafter I saw a helicopter. They got me out of there after about thirty minutes.

I had also been wounded in the neck. The jugular vein was pierced and it ruptured when they were taking me out to Phu Bai. I passed out in the helicopter. The crew chief was slap-ping me and trying to get me to talk. You know, you just feel yourself going under, but you're aware of what's happening around you.

They had to revive me with these paddles. I had singe marks on my chest. I look down and my chest hair is smoldering. My leg—my pants and flesh—is still smoldering from the blast and

I got a chaplain over me saying, "Are there any last words you want to say to your God?" Crap! Oh God! Until him, I didn't even think I was going to die. I didn't know what the hell to say to him. I couldn't talk 'cause all my teeth were blown out on the left side of my mouth. I tried to talk. I was gurgling blood and spitting out my teeth, all I could think of was—Get this guy out of here!

They had all the wounded laying around on tables. They took people who were the worst off first. They cut and ripped your clothes off while you're laying there. There was a woman in there, this old mamasan with betel-nut teeth standing at the other end of the room, selling things and trying to get my boots! I wanted to tell her, "Could you just wait until they get my boots off?" Then they expose me. I'm dying, but I'm embarrassed because this woman is standing there.

People were falling all over because the blood was covering the floor. You know, it's kind of sticky and slippery. Oh my God, I looked down at the floor and I said to myself, is that all my blood? 'Cause it was everywhere. It wasn't blood coming out of me any more. It was plasma, so I figured I'd had it anyway. But that chaplain, he scared the hell out of me. It wasn't my smoking chest or my smoking leg or even all the blood … when that chaplain started coming at me, I got mad. I wasn't feeling like giving up. I looked around and I had a lot of strange things going through my head. But I wasn't frightened.

The Marine Corps thought I was dying so they sent someone out to the house. My mom opens the door and there is a marine standing there in his dress blues and, Holy Jesus, can you imagine my folks?

Before I went to Vietnam I prayed to God that if I lost an arm or leg, he would let me die. When I got in country, I made all kinds of promises to God. "You get me out of here and I'll be a priest." Two weeks after that it was, "You get me out of here and I'll be a virgin forever." I prayed that I'd lose an arm or leg so I could go home. Now that I was going home, I felt I was getting out cheap—they were able to save the leg although I would never have use of it.

I have a picture of the general who gave me the Purple Heart. I asked him how much it was worth and he said eighty-four dollars as the standard is now because there is some gold in it.

Sometimes it seems like a million miles away, like it never happened, and other times, gee … eating the air, the sun, and the dirt. That's what I remember.

The grim task

Allen Perkins
Corporal, Casualty clerk, Special Landing Force Alpha, 9th Marine Amphibious Brigade, April–October 1968.

My job in Nam was casualty clerk. The duties were helping the navy corpsmen with the wounded, taking personal effects from the dead, checking bodies for booby traps, identifying the dead, and typing up radio messages and condolence letters. I did these things mostly on the U.S.S. *Princeton* and sometimes at Delta Med—a MASH-type unit—at Dong Ha. I must've helped process at least 200 to 250 bodies. After I saw my first batch, which included one with his feet on his chest, I went out on a catwalk and dry-heaved for ten minutes. That was my adjustment to Nam. … A few months later a chopper brought in a bag of remains with one name on it. I took it to Graves—the refrigerated morgue—and opened it. It had three feet in it. I never did figure that one out.

Just do the job

Suzanne McPhee
1st Lieutenant, medical-surgical nurse, 67th Evacuation Hospital, May 1967–May 1968, Qui Nhon.

In my first experience with triage [medical sorting for treatment], over fifty patients arrived at once in the emergency room. There were five prisoners and I made an error in judgment. Even though two of them had severe head wounds, I put all the prisoners in the lowest category when they should have received priority for immediate care. I was angry because our prisoners were not given equal treatment by the VC or NVA. The two with head wounds died. I was called before the hospital commanding officer and informed not to make judgments, just do my job. … I worked long hours, a minimum of fourteen to sixteen hours a day. We had time off when "business" was slow. On a day off, I'd volunteer for MEDCAP activities at the provincial prison dispensary. I found it easier to be doing something all the time. The time passed by faster. …

America's welcome

John A. Whitfield
Corporal, Company K, 3d Battalion, 26th Marines, 3d Marine Division, October 1966–July 1967, Phu Bai, Dong Ha.

Upon returning to the States following our tour's end, four of us marines were sitting in a lounge at the Los Angeles International Airport waiting for our flights home. We were toasting our lives, having passed the test of war. A young lady, about

"You think about the KIAs ... *and their families who do not yet know. ... " After a battle in Long Khanh Province, northeast of Saigon, SP4 Ruediger Richter (left) and Sergeant Daniel W. Spencer of the 4th Battalion, 503d Infantry, 173d Airborne Brigade, wait for a helicopter to carry away a fallen comrade, 1966.*

twenty-one or twenty-two years old, approached us at our table and asked if we were just back from Vietnam to which I answered, "Yes." Without another word she threw a shot glass of whiskey in my face and said, "Baby-killer, raper; are you proud?" We had heard of public opinion of veterans in the States, we didn't believe it. Now we did.

That loss

Corporal Allen Perkins

Because Dong Ha was relatively secure, we could really party hearty. Given the brutal realities just beyond the perimeter, we had every reason necessary to enjoy each day fully. Each moment fully. When you're bullshitting with a guy who just might never be around you again, you can very easily sort out what's important and what's not. Tags like "Baptist," "Mexican," "black," and "Polish" didn't mean shit in Nam. That purity, that simplicity is the one thing I miss about it. And that loss is the most difficult one to convey to those who weren't there.

Dispatch from Hill 875

Pulitzer Prize-winning correspondent Peter Arnett spent thirty hours with 173d Airborne paratroopers during their bloody struggle for Hill 875—climax of the month-long Battle of Dak To. Here is his Thanksgiving eve, 1967, report.

By Peter Arnett

Hill 875, Wednesday, November 22, 1967 (AP)—War painted the living and the dead the same gray pallor on Hill 875.

For fifty hours [starting Sunday] the most brutal fighting of the Vietnam War ebbed and flowed across this jungle hilltop and by Wednesday was still not over.

Death picked its victims at random and broke and twisted their bodies.

At times the only way to tell who was alive and who was dead amongst the exhausted men was to watch when the enemy mortars crashed in. The living rushed unashamedly to the tiny bunkers dug into the red clay of the hilltop. The wounded squirmed toward the shelter of trees that had been blasted to the ground.

Only the dead, propped up in bunkers,

As an officer gives orders (far left), *the men of Company B, 4th Battalion, 503d Infantry—reinforcements for the decimated 2d Battalion—peer beyond the U.S. perimeter on Hill 875 to sight enemy positions.*

With the North Vietnamese deeply entrenched, *tactical air support such as this napalm run proved immensely important.*

where they had died in direct mortar hits, or face down in the dust, where they had fallen to bullets, didn't move.

The 2d Battalion [503d Infantry] of the 173d Airborne Brigade that first ascended this remote hill in the western sector of the Dak To battleground, nearly died.

Of the sixteen officers who led their men across the ridge line of Hill 875 on Sunday, eight were killed and the other eight wounded.

Of the thirteen battalion medics, eleven died.

The days and nights of fighting, the waits for a reinforcing column that inched across the ridges, the stench of the dead and moans of the wounded etched deep lines in the young faces of the paratroopers who clung to the hill.

Some of the wounded cracked under the strain.

"It's a goddamn shame that they haven't got us out of here," gasped one paratroop sergeant with tears in his eyes early afternoon Tuesday. He had been lying on the hill for fifty hours with a painful groin wound. All around him lay scores of other wounded. You could see who had lain there the longest.

Blood had clotted their bandages, they had ceased moaning, their eyes were glazed.

The bandages of those hit in the recent mortar barrages were still wet with blood.

These wounded still squirmed with pain.

The most seriously hurt were stretched on a carpet of leaves next to a helicopter landing zone that lay between towering trees. These casualties were wrapped in bloody poncho liners to protect against the night chill. The North Vietnamese forward positions began just forty-five meters along the ridge. Each helicopter that came in drew heavy mortar and automatic weapons fire.

One helicopter made it and carried out five seriously wounded Sunday and ten other ships were disabled in trying.

"The wounded can see the choppers trying to get in. They know they are not being left to die," a young officer, himself wounded, said.

Yet some did die as their blood seeped away into the clay of Hill 875. Some of these were the men blasted by a 500-pound bomb dropped by mistake from an American plane late Sunday during an air strike in the nearby enemy bunkers. [Forty-two] men were killed in that explosion, "a foul play of war" one survivor said bitterly.

When another landing zone was being cut below the crest of the hill late Tuesday and evacuations of the wounded began, it was found that others had died in the last hours of waiting. Whether this was from shock, thirst, or just plain giving up, none of the medics knew.

The battalion took its first wounded midday Sunday as it crested Hill 875, one of the hundreds of knolls that dot the ridges in the Dak To fighting region on the Cambodian-Laos border. All weekend as the paratroopers moved along the jungle hills enemy base camps were uncovered.

The biggest was on 875 and Company D lost several men in the first encounter with the bunkers.

Company A moved back down the hill to cut a landing zone and was chopped to pieces by a North Vietnamese flanking attack. The remnants managed to flee back to the crest of the hill while a paratrooper propped his [machine] gun on the trail and kept firing at the advancing enemy troops, ignoring orders that he retreat with the others.

"You can keep gunning them down, but sooner or later when there is enough of them they'll get to you," commented Specialist 4 James Kelley, from Fort Myers, Florida, who saw the machine gunner go down after killing an estimated seventeen Communist troops.

Company D, hearing the roar of battle below them, returned to the crest of the hill and established a fifty-meter perimeter "because we figured we were surrounded by a regiment," one officer said.

On November 21, 1967, the third day of fighting on Hill 875, wounded from the 173d Airborne Brigade wait for evacuation helicopters.

At one end of the U.S. line, *where bombs had not ravaged the foliage, one soldier passes a loaded M16 to another guarding the perimeter.*

Flanked by extra M60 belts, *Staff Sergeant Clarence Neitxel, a squad leader in D Company, 2d Battalion—the lead company on the assault of Hill 875—aims his machine gun from the U.S. perimeter, November 22.*

As the battalion was regrouping late in the afternoon for another crack at the bunker system, the [American] bomb came in at tree-top level, the burst smashing shrapnel into those below.

The bomb crippled the battalion, killing many of the wounded who were strung along the ground under the trees.

From then on until the reinforcing battalion arrived the following night, the paratroopers on the hill desperately dug in. Only one medic was able to work on the numerous wounded, and the enemy kept fighting off the rescue helicopters.

The relief battalion, the 4th of the 503d, linked into the tiny perimeter on 875 Monday night. The moonlit scene was macabre. Bodies of the dead lay spread-eagled across the ground, the wounded whimpered.

The survivors of the battalion, hungry and thirsty, rushed up eagerly to get food and water only to learn that the relief battalion had brought enough supplies for one day and had already consumed them.

Monday night was sleepless but unevent-

Toward the end of the struggle for Hill 875, *a paratrooper surveys the wrapped bodies of his fallen comrades. No dead could be evacuated until a landing zone was secured on the battle's fourth day.*

ful. On Tuesday the North Vietnamese struck with fury.

From positions just 100 meters away, they began pounding the American perimeter with 82MM mortars. The first rounds slapped in at daybreak, killing three paratroopers in a foxhole and wounding seventeen others on the line.

Then, for the rest of the day, the Communists methodically worked over the hill, pumping rounds in five or six at a time, rewounding those who lay bleeding in the open and tearing through bunkers. The plop of the rounds as they left the enemy tubes gave the paratroopers a second to dash for cover.

The foxholes got deeper as the day wore on. Foxhole after foxhole took hits. A dog handler and his German shepherd died together: Men who were joking with you and offering cigarettes would be writhing on the ground wounded and pleading for water minutes later. There was no water for them or anyone else.

Crouched in one bunker, Private First Class Angel Flores, twenty, of New York City,

said, "If we were dead like those out there we wouldn't have to worry about this stuff coming in."

He fingered the plastic rosary around his neck and kissed it reverently as the rounds blasted on the ground outside. Does that do you any good?" a buddy asked him. "Well, I'm still alive," Flores said.

His buddy replied, "Don't you know that the chaplain that gave you that was killed on Sunday?"

The day's pounding steadily reduced the platoon commanded by First Lieutenant Bryan MacDonough, twenty-five, from Fort Lee, Virginia. He started out Sunday with twenty-seven men. He had nine left midday Tuesday. "If the Viets keep this up, there'll be none left by evening," he said. The enemy positions seemed impervious to constant American air strikes. Napalm fireballs exploded on the bunkers twenty-five meters away. The earth shook with heavy bombs.

"We've tried 750-pounders, napalm, and everything else, but air can't do it. It's going to take man power to get those positions," MacDonough said.

By late afternoon Wednesday a new landing zone was cut below the hill. The enemy mortars searched for it but the helicopters came in anyway. A line of wounded trudged down the hill and by evening 140 of them had been evacuated.

The arrival of the helicopters, and food, water, and ammunition, seemed to put new life into the paratroopers. They talked eagerly of a final assault on the enemy bunkers.

As darkness was falling flame throwers were brought up. The first stubborn bunker yielded and the final rout was beginning.

The paratroopers were at last started on the way to gain the ridge line which they had set out to take three days earlier. They deserved every inch of it.

The "final" attack with which Arnett closed his report was not, as it turned out, the end. Thrown back that afternoon, the 4th Battalion, 503d Infantry, succeeded only the following morning, Thanksgiving Day, in taking Hill 875.

8 | The Border Battles

"*[We] will entice the Americans close to the North Vietnamese border and bleed them without mercy. In South Vietnam, the pacification program will be destroyed.*"
Ho Chi Minh

One of the linchpins in General Westmoreland's strong point obstacle system along the DMZ, Con Thien (the "Hill of Angels"), a barren plateau of brick-colored soil, was in every way a hardship post, forsaken by the angels and occupied by U.S. Marines. One hundred fifty meters high, the three hills of Con Thien and the surrounding terrain had been bulldozed by marine engineers. To the east, like a runway to nowhere, lay the 600-meter-wide strip of land that had been cleared for the ill-starred McNamara Line. At Con Thien itself, trenches and bunkers dug into the red earth had replaced the vegetation. The August 1967 garrison, the 1st Battalion, 9th Regiment, 3d Marine Division, lived and worked in those bunkers, ringed by sandbags piled three meters high. Trained as rapidly moving assault troops, the marines were here fixed into static defensive positions. They seemed to be reenacting a variation on the trench warfare of World War I, except that instead of exchanging rifle fire and attacking frontally across a no man's land, they dueled long-distance with artillery and patrolled out from their garrison in search of enemy units maneuvering to attack.

Con Thien daily received a punishing hail of artillery from enemy batteries tucked away in the northern hills of the demilitarized zone, some ten kilometers wide, and above the zone in North Vietnam itself. In August, the barrage ranged from 30 or 40 shells per day to a peak of 550. The enemy artillery included new Soviet 130MM and 152MM long-range guns, which they had

obtained since the first foxholes were dug out of Con Thien in late 1966. The North Vietnamese also fired 122MM stabilized Soviet barrage rockets, a somewhat inaccurate but particularly destructive long-range heavy field weapon. The enemy rolled his guns out of well-camouflaged and protected positions—especially caves—to fire and rolled them back again. They were also shifted about to prevent spotters from fixing their locations for air force bombers and offshore navy guns. Marine artillery retaliated from Con Thien and other nearby bases at Gio Linh and Cam Lo. The heaviest fighting, however, and the greatest number of casualties, occurred outside Con Thien where other U.S. Marines grappled with enemy units. The NVA also launched harassing ground attacks against Con Thien itself.

The marines were absorbing the first blows induced by a new North Vietnamese strategy. The Hanoi Politburo had decided to replace the tactical defensive component of its protracted war strategy with a bold offensive aimed at the populated areas of South Vietnam. The plan was an inversion of orthodox revolutionary warfare, which held that control of the countryside would result in strangulation of the cities. It was dictated in part by the flight of up to one million people per year from rural areas to GVN relocation camps and cities and by modest allied pacification gains—in short, by the erosion of the Communists' population base.

The preliminary phase of the 1967–1968 winter-spring campaign was a series of probes that North Vietnamese General Vo Nguyen Giap instigated along South Vietnam's frontiers. These clashes, destined to become known as the "border battles," ranged from the DMZ and the jungle-covered central highlands in the tri-border area to the flat terrain of rubber plantations near the Cambodian border in III Corps. Over a period of three

In the climactic struggle *for the scorched summit of Hill 875 in late November 1967, U.S. paratroopers of the 173d Airborne Brigade move against entrenched—and virtually invisible—NVA regulars.*

months, as one battle wound down, another seemed to heat up.

In each case, the North Vietnamese, operating from their sanctuaries, grouped Main Force units so that their actions appeared to be continuations of their normal Main Force tactics. But the massing of forces served other purposes as well—to disguise Hanoi's real intentions, to draw American attention and resources from the populated areas, and to screen infiltration of NVA troops into South Vietnam.

Giap sent his first large-scale probe against Con Thien. He had been increasing pressure against the northern provinces, and despite heavy losses in battles with the marines, two full NVA divisions were still believed to be located in the vicinity of the DMZ and just above it in the southern areas of North Vietnam. By moving against Con Thien, Giap kept alive the threat of an invasion from the North. His forces appeared ready to fulfill the words of another North Vietnamese strategist: "[We] will entice the Americans close to the North Vietnamese border and bleed them without mercy. In South Vietnam, the pacification program will be destroyed."

The siege of Con Thien

Early in September, the North Vietnamese intensified both artillery fire and ground attacks, and the 3d Battalion, 9th Marines, understrength at perhaps 1,000 men, relieved its beleaguered colleagues of the 1/9 on the hill. At best a dismal outpost, Con Thien soon became a very public hell, and the isolation of the base and the combination of infantry and artillery tactics evoked the specter of Dien Bien Phu. Through the lenses of television cameras, and in print, the world followed the marines' predicament. "I hated every day, and every hour, and every moment of breath," said one marine.

Monsoon rains arrived in September, a month ahead of schedule, and the laterite soil of Con Thien turned into a red bog that was at least ankle- and sometimes knee-deep. The gray skies opened daily, and the rain fell with frustrating regularity. The mud was both friend and foe: It absorbed the shrapnel from high explosive artillery rounds, but it also pulled at the feet of men caught in the open running for cover at the cry of "Incoming!" In addition, the mud concealed dud rounds, and the marines' own base was a mine field of unexploded shells. The men suffered from trench foot, which caused feet to ache and to turn a shade of pale green, with the skin sloughing off. Armpits and crotches were rubbed raw from constant dampness, and most marines suffered skin rashes. They shared their bunkers with rats, drank rainwater collected in five-gallon cans, and ate but one or two C-rations per day, since priority went to shipments of ammunition and troop replacements. Fog some-

times closed in at night, obscuring any view beyond the barbed wire perimeter, and transforming every muffled sound into an enemy sapper for the anxious defenders.

Mortars, artillery, shells, and rockets fell randomly but incessantly on the base. Rockets came in fast, providing but a second's warning. The high whine of artillery shells could be heard about three seconds before impact. Mortars were much preferred: On hearing the hollow steel "whump," a man had five to ten seconds to get under cover. The September bombardment ranged from 100 to 150 rounds per day to a maximum on September 25 of 1,190. When combined with outgoing artillery (the U.S. fired an estimated 6,000 rounds daily), occasional "mad minutes" (in which every U.S. weapon, including M16s, was fired), and bombing strikes on the enemy, the cacophony of war left the marines temporarily hard of hearing. Even in moments of calm, they often had to shout in each other's ears to be heard.

The marines called themselves "the walking dead." Hollow-eyed and shell-shocked, they hurried through the mud, bent over, carrying stretchers, dodging sniper fire, taking up posts, waiting for incoming rounds. It eroded the nerves. And the aimless pattern of explosions and casualties elicited superstitious responses. "Don't follow me when you see me running down the side of the hill," one officer lectured a visitor. "I like to be off by myself when the shells come in. I have this feeling that the round that has your number on it shouldn't kill anyone else—and I certainly don't want to get someone else's round." Another feeling running through the minds of the 3/9 Marines was pure befuddlement at the reason for holding Con Thien. That frustration was often expressed irrationally. "President Johnson must like to see marines get killed," said one.

"We all lost a friend there," David P. Martin, an artillery forward observer from New Jersey, later wrote of his days at Con Thien. "I lost a few boot camp buddies, due to rotate on the big silver bird home soon. Red, a forward observer with a silver star, from Georgia, died there. An artillery shell blew him in half. He already had two Purple Hearts. He had single-handedly wiped out a machine-gun nest in early July and earned his medal. He was a bull of a man, strong, loud-mouthed, brave and he died. He died. And alone after the news, in my bunker twelve feet underground, I cried. He was blown in half for a shit-hole place that had no strategic value, no military value, no sense to it, save to prove to Russia or China or North Vietnam or God or somebody that nineteen-year-old low-and middle-class Americans would die for their country."

General Westmoreland belittled the media's portrayal of Con Thien as a repeat of Dien Bien Phu, and he surely had no intention of allowing the outpost to fall. His means of breaking

During a lull in the artillery bombardment on September 23, flak-jacketed marines slog through the red mud of Con Thien to bring one of their wounded to an evacuation point.

the enemy's attack was Operation Neutralize, a forty-nine-day campaign that introduced SLAM (seek, locate, annihilate, monitor), a concept devised by 7th Air Force commander General William M. Momyer. SLAM involved a coordination of the entire spectrum of heavy fire support—B-52s, tactical air support, and naval gunfire—with artillery and other ground fire. To relieve Con Thien, this devastating concentration of firepower was directed into an area about the size of Manhattan.

For seven weeks, Operation Neutralize pummeled known and suspected enemy positions, with B-52 Stratofortresses striking first, followed by tactical air, then naval guns, and artillery. Carrying nearly 60,000 pounds of bombs, B-52 bombers were the most awesome weapon used in Vietnam. In a so-called Arc Light strike, three planes bombed an area one kilometer wide and three kilometers long, causing a thunderous earthquake and throwing up a fountain of earth and trees in its wake. Of 820 B-52 sorties over Vietnam during September, 790 dropped their bombs in Con Thien's front yard, tearing the surrounding area into a terrain of water-filled craters ringed with collars of earth.

Operation Neutralize delivered from 35,000 to 40,000 tons of bombs in nearly 4,000 air sorties, and by early October, it had broken the enemy's siege. The SLAM strikes persuaded General Westmoreland that massed firepower could force a besieging enemy to desist. It was, he later noted, "a demonstration that

was destined to contribute to my confidence on a later occasion," that of the siege of Khe Sanh four months later in January 1968. With Con Thien relieved, Westmoreland could not resist poking a barb at pessimistic reporters as well as at his counterpart, Vo Nguyen Giap, whose concentration of heavy weapons and troops had provided SLAM such vulnerable targets. "If comparable in any way to Dien Bien Phu," he wrote, "it was a Dien Bien Phu in reverse. The North Vietnamese lost well over 2,000 men killed, while Con Thien and Gio Linh continued to stand as barriers to enemy movement."

Loc Ninh

As Operation Neutralize pried loose the enemy's grip around Con Thien, the North Vietnamese and Vietcong provoked two other border battles far to the south of the demilitarized zone. On October 27, men of a North Vietnamese regiment attacked the command post of a badly outnumbered ARVN battalion in Song Be, capital of Phuoc Long Province, but were thrown back from strong ARVN defensive positions and lost 134 killed. Two days later, in the Cambodian border town of Loc Ninh, an area of rubber plantations 120 kilometers north of Saigon, in Binh Long Province, the Vietcong 273d Regiment provoked a fight that resulted in perhaps the most lopsided—and clearly

"Hill of Angels." *Marines huddle in a muddy trench reinforced with sandbags as North Vietnamese mortar shells fall on Con Thien, September 22, 1967.*

definable—American victory of the war.

On October 29, the Vietcong launched a two-pronged nighttime attack against the Loc Ninh Special Forces camp and the district headquarters. In a striking demonstration of the tactical mobility of U.S. forces, Major General John H. Hay, Jr., 1st Infantry Division commander, had two combat battalions and two artillery batteries on the ground by midmorning, with two other battalions poised at a nearby base camp for deployment once the enemy committed himself. Two more battalions entered the fray several days later.

In the six major engagements of the ten-day battle at Loc Ninh, the Vietcong and North Vietnamese lost at least 852 soldiers killed against 50 U.S. and South Vietnamese dead. Most American officers believed the true number of enemy casualties was well over 1,000. In one battle, an almost suicidal assault against a fortified night defensive position by troops armed with heavy machine guns, mortars, and Soviet-made flame throwers, the VC 273d Regiment lost 263 killed against one dead American soldier. Although the battle of Loc Ninh may have been provoked in part to allow NVA and VC Main Force units to practice maneuvering together for the coming winter-spring offensive, the major defeat knocked at least two regiments out of the field for the campaign's next phase.

Kontum Province, in the 4th Infantry Division's TAOR, had been so quiet that the "Ivy" Division had but one mechanized battalion stationed there. Little of military value existed in the area of Dak To except a Special Forces camp and a base for 175MM guns (with a range of thirty kilometers) being constructed at Ben Het in case General Westmoreland won permission from Washington to fire on enemy sanctuaries across the border.

In a country notorious for difficult terrain, the Dak To region presented some of the worst. Mountain peaks and ridges rose to 1,800 meters, and three layers of vegetation—the so-called triple-canopy jungle of hundred-foot trees, vines, and bamboo—covered the slopes, leaving the ground in a permanent twilight. Some bamboo stalks grew eight inches thick. The dense foliage provided natural cover and concealment, enough to permit undetected movement. Numerous mountain caves also offered the enemy excellent cover. Temperatures reached muggy nineties during the day and dropped into the fifties at night. Among the malarial valleys, widely scattered montagnard villages contained the only population.

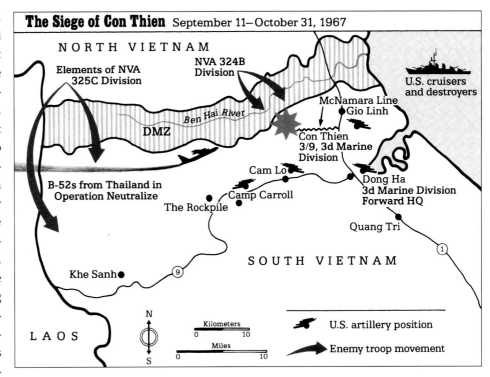

The Siege of Con Thien September 11–October 31, 1967

NORTH VIETNAM

Elements of NVA 325C Division

NVA 324B Division

U.S. cruisers and destroyers

Ben Hai River

McNamara Line
Gio Linh

DMZ

Con Thien
3/9, 3d Marine Division

B-52s from Thailand in Operation Neutralize

Cam Lo

Camp Carroll

The Rockpile

Dong Ha
3d Marine Division
Forward HQ

Quang Tri

SOUTH VIETNAM

Khe Sanh

9

N

S

Kilometers
0   10

Miles
0   10

LAOS

U.S. artillery position

Enemy troop movement

Preparing the battlefield

The enemy's plans for a campaign in the Dak To region came into focus on November 3 when a North Vietnamese soldier defected. Sergeant Vu Hong, an artillery specialist with the NVA 66th Regiment, surrendered to a Popular Forces soldier in the remote Sedang hamlet of Dak Ri Peng.

One of the fifty men of a reconnaissance team of forward artillery observers and gunnery experts, Vu Hong had been in the Dak To area for three weeks scouting firing positions for 122MM rockets, 82MM mortars, howitzers, and antiaircraft guns. His regiment was one of four infantry regiments—and one artillery regiment—forming the NVA 1st Division, which was assigned to attack Dak To with a hammer-and-anvil tactic. The 66th was to attack from the southwest, along the valley toward Dak To, while the 32d Regiment, south of Dak To, screened any U.S. counterattacks against the 66th. The 24th Regiment took up a position in the northeast to leap on allied reinforcements, and the 174th Regiment, northwest of Dak To, was to act as a reserve or offensive force as the need arose. The 40th Artillery Regiment, consisting of a 120MM mortar battalion and two 122MM rocket battalions, supported each regiment. The 1st Division's mission: to destroy an American brigade.

Vu Hong seemed to know entirely too much for a mere sergeant in the decentralized North Vietnamese Army; in fact, he was at first thought to be a "plant." But his tale confirmed and expanded on what intelligence already suspected. In addition to

Tac Air

Tactical air support, commonly called tac air, frequently made the difference between disaster and success for American ground units that engaged enemy troops in Vietnam. When a marine or army unit came under sudden fierce attack, particularly out in the "bush"—the unsettled jungle areas beyond the perimeters of U.S. bases—the unit commander motioned to the radio telephone operator (RTO) who shadowed him, reached for the quickly proffered radio handset, and placed a request to his headquarters for tactical air support. Usually within ten to thirty minutes tactical fixed-wing aircraft arrived above the battlefield ready to deliver a hail of deadly ordnance. Besieged "grunts" on the ground usually cheered the arrival overhead of gray or camouflaged-mottled aircraft and admired their speed and power as they orbited and prepared to dive toward enemy targets. After the aircraft rolled in and began its dive, the grunts talked at them, sometimes murmuring, "Come on baby, come on, lower … lower … now—yeah, lay it in tight!" Stealing glimpses as they flattened to avoid bomb fragments, deafened by the noise of screeching engines, the infantrymen encouraged the aircraft with expressions like "Zap 'em, man!" or "*Git* some!" and shouted curses at the enemy as explosions shook the ground.

Coordination of tactical air strikes was a carefully practiced procedure performed by highly trained army, navy, air force, and marine personnel. Tactical air controllers flying high performance jets and airborne forward air controllers (FACs) in light spotter planes or helicopters talked with other FACs who accompanied engaged units on the ground, pinpointing their location and the position of the enemy. The FACs' extensive training and experience enabled them to communicate effectively with pilots. After receiving a request for a tactical air strike, the controllers alerted the headquarters that commanded air power over the area to "scramble" aircraft from airfields, or more commonly, to divert aircraft already airborne on a less urgent mission and direct them to the target location. While they waited for aircraft to arrive the FACs conferred among

themselves and with the engaged unit's commander to plan a route of attack. When the bomb- or rocket-laden attack aircraft arrived at the scene, the FACs talked them toward the target area, marked the target's location with white phosphorous rockets or colored smoke grenades, and then helped direct the bombing run. Usually these aircraft worked in pairs, each called a section, one flown by the lead pilot with a wingman following. Once the lead aircraft made its run and dropped its ordnance, the FAC called any necessary corrections to the wingman, such as "drop your bombs at six o'clock twenty-five meters from lead's hit." On most close air support missions the grunts taking fire on the ground required fast action by the fighter-attack aircraft pilots, who frequently operated under the stress caused by adverse conditions such as darkness, "marginal" or inclement weather, difficult terrain, and heavy enemy ground fire, all of which made target identification difficult.

Marine tac air

U.S. Navy pilots catapulted off the decks of carriers in the South China Sea and U.S. Air Force pilots roared off air bases throughout South Vietnam to aid friendly troops. U.S. Marine Corps pilots operated from runways at Da Nang and Chu Lai in I Corps. Part of a marine aviation tradition that began during the island campaigns in the South Pacific during World War II, all marine pilots were trained in infantry tactics to give them a feel for ground unit maneuvers. The ground-based FACs who served with marine units and communicated with marine tactical aircraft pilots were almost always marine pilots, which made coordination of marine tac air very efficient. As a result of their tradition and training, marine pilots were highly skilled at delivering ordnance close to friendly troops. At very close quarters marine forward air controller Peter Erenfeld, who directed tactical air strikes from an 0–1 Bird Dog, preferred aircraft with marine pilots at the controls. "Within 100 meters of the friendlies," Erenfeld said, "we asked for marine air."

During 1967 First Lieutenant Jay C. Lillie flew an A-4E Skyhawk with the "Tomcats," Marine Attack Squadron 311, based at Chu Lai. Lieutenant Lillie's Skyhawk could carry up to 8,200 pounds of ordnance, including some combination of 500-pound napalm

canisters, 250-pound high explosive bombs, 2.75-inch rockets, and 20MM cannon ammunition. A typical ordnance load included 100 rounds for the two 20MM cannons mounted in the Skyhawk's wing roots and either ten 250-pound bombs, four 500-pound napalm canisters, or two pods of 2.75-inch rockets (each pod containing nineteen rockets) mounted on pylons under the wings. The type of ordnance used depended on "how close you were to the good guys," according to Lillie, on the nature of the target, and on the type of terrain in the target area.

A marine tactical air strike began with a call to the duty officer in the squadron ready room where pilots waited on alert, dressed in full flight gear. When Lillie was on duty a call to the ready room sent him scrambling for the cockpit of his Skyhawk to start its Pratt and Whitney J52–6 two-shaft turbojet engine. After individual takeoffs Lillie joined up with his wingman for the day and tuned his radio to the Chu Lai Direct Air Support Center, which assigned his section to work with a FAC orbiting the target area. Switching to the FAC's radio frequency, Lillie made contact and received navigation instructions. "The FAC called you up and told you what direction to fly and how far, such as 'Fly the 270 radical west from Da Nang thirty miles.'" When Lillie arrived over the target area, he checked in with the FAC, telling him how many other sections accompanied him, what ordnance they carried, and how much time they could remain "on station" before having to return for fuel. Then the FAC briefed him on the mission.

Punctuated by occasional static, with voices electronically enhanced, radio traffic during this part of a typical mission sounded something like this:

"Chain 41 this is Smokey 19. The target today is enemy troops on a ridge line that runs east-west. They're firing on a friendly unit located in a valley 500 meters to the south. There's a cloud cover at 2,000 feet, broken to overcast. Visibility is good underneath at five miles. Make your run from the east on a heading of two-seven-zero and make a left hand pull. You can anticipate small arms fire. … Do you brief?"

Lillie answered the controller's question by repeating his description of the target, conditions in the target area, and flight instructions. When Lillie understood the target's location, he said "I have a tally on the target."

"OK Chain, I'd like you to drop two Delta-2 Alphas [500-pound bombs] on your first pass, make two passes, and salvo your remaining ordnance on your second pass. If you're in position I'm ready to roll in and mark the target." After Lillie confirmed he was near the target area the FAC fired a white phosphorous rocket where he wanted ordnance dropped.

"OK, have you got my mark?" the FAC asked.

"I have your mark," Lillie replied.

"OK Chain lead, you're cleared in. Come wings level when you're set." This transmission authorized the pilot to roll into a final dive pattern. When Lieutenant Lillie entered a dive pattern, he headed in the direction ordered by the FAC, adjusting his air speed and altitude according to the FAC's instructions. "You'd roll in from a 2,500-foot altitude at 450 knots—equal to better than 500 miles per hour—establish yourself in a ten-degree dive, line up your sight with the target, and come wings level." If his approach looked good when he "came wings level," the FAC authorized him to drop his ordnance at will.

"OK, you're cleared in hot," the FAC said.

"Roger, I'm tally-ho the target," Lillie replied to the FAC, meaning he had the target in sight.

At this point the pilot was under a great deal of pressure. Target identification was often difficult because of scattered clouds, ground fog, or ridge lines that obscured the pilot's view. And often the enemy began popping misleading smoke grenades, making it difficult for the pilot to determine which smoke marked the target and which the position of the friendlies. Smoke and dust coming up from ground explosions caused by mortar fire further obscured terrain features.

The pilot usually rolled in at 450 knots and maintained that speed throughout the run. If he flew too slow he would drop his bombs short. If he was too low his bombs might not have time to arm: The bomb-nose arming device generally required four to six seconds of free flight to arm. If the pilot released the bombs too low they might travel for only three seconds before impact. If this happened either they would not explode and the VC could use them for land mines, or they would explode and the pilot might

be caught in the "fragmentation envelope" and blow himself out of the sky.

As he approached the target the pilot knew if he dropped left or right of the line-up he would not only miss the enemy position but might hit friendlies. He also knew he must carefully monitor his air speed and altitude in order to insure that the bombs did not fall long or short. While he was doing all of this he had to identify the target and pick his way through any clouds over the target area. Additionally, as he approached the target—if it was "hot"—he might see white, green, or red tracers drifting up toward him as the enemy directed fire at his

> "Pilots who flew close air support forgot about politics. When there are eighteen-year-old kids on the ground screaming for help, you do whatever you have to do to help them."
>
> Marine aviator

aircraft. The pilot had to disregard all this and concentrate on the target.

The A-4E Skyhawk's bombsight was a point of light called a "pipper" projected on a plate of glass mounted on top of the instrument panel in front of the wind screen. Lillie looked through the sight and out the wind screen simultaneously to "put the pipper on the target." While crosschecking instruments the ground rushed up at him. "At first it's just a blur, but in the last ten seconds of the run you pick up ground features like ditches, water buffalo, people. But you don't see the detail until the last few seconds," Lillie said.

A button called the "pickle," located on the side of the top of the control stick,

released the Skyhawk's bombs. When Lillie was set to drop his ordnance he "pushed the pickle." Half a second later when the bombs had released he hit full throttle, wrested the aircraft out of its dive, and pulled off the target left or right as previously instructed, gaining altitude to avoid enemy fire. Approximately four seconds later the bombs struck the earth and exploded. To those on the ground the Skyhawk's bombing run sounded like a freight train roaring overhead, and infantrymen "pancaked" to escape flying shards of hot metal. But to Lillie, traveling downrange of the target, the explosions were distant and muffled. "If you came in high, you might hear nothing at all." His run completed, the pilot then called the airborne FAC, reported that he had released his bombs, and waited for an evaluation report. He hoped the FAC came on the radio net to make a brief report such as "Nice run lead. All bombs on target."

Tactical air strike missions were subject to all kinds of problems. Bad weather hindered or prohibited close air support. If aircraft carried ordnance unsuitable for a target—such as 750-pound bombs when 2.75-inch rockets were needed—they couldn't attack. Sometimes the bombs failed to release from the aircraft's wings or they failed to explode on impact. Once Lillie made four passes over a target, taking fire on each pass, but each time his ordnance hung fast. "I tried all the switches but nothing worked. I was furious," Lillie said. "I landed back at Chu Lai with all my bombs still on the aircraft after being in the air one hour and forty-five minutes." At other times inadequate or confused communication between airborne FACs and ground-based FAC units made emergency attacks inadvisable. On one occasion, after orbiting a target ten miles west of Hue for half an hour, Lillie's section returned to base without dropping any bombs because the ground FAC could not verify that all friendly troops were clear of the target area. But when tac air missions proceeded normally the feeling of pilots was one of satisfaction. "Pilots who flew close air support forgot about politics," one marine aviator recalls. "When there are eighteen-year-old kids on the ground screaming for help, you do whatever you have to do to help them."

information gathered by LRRP patrols, modern tools such as airborne personnel detectors—the "people sniffers"—had turned up evidence of enemy movement. The NVA 174th Regiment, recently infiltrated from Laos, was known to be a good unit. The 24th Regiment, battered in Operation Hawthorne, an action mounted in 1966 by the U.S. 1st Brigade, 101st Airborne Division, had been pulled back to secure enemy infiltration routes that led east from the Ho Chi Minh Trail. Meanwhile, it had been built up with fresh troops from the North. Both the 32d Regiment and Sergeant Hong's unit, the 66th, had participated in the Ia Drang Valley campaign two years earlier and were manned by seasoned troops led by experienced officers. Both also had replacement troops as a result of losses suffered in U.S. Operations Paul Revere II, Sam Houston, and Francis Marion.

What puzzled American strategists was the enemy's purpose. At least a partial answer was suggested with the capture early in November of a document from the North Vietnamese B-3 Front Command, which controlled the central highlands. It listed the following objectives for the 1967–1968 winter-spring campaign:

- to annihilate a major U.S. element in order to force the enemy to deploy as many additional troops to the western highlands as possible. ...
- to encourage units to improve, in combat, the technique of concentrated attacks in order to annihilate relatively large enemy units. ...
- to effect close coordination with various battle areas throughout South Vietnam in order to achieve timely unity and stratagems.

The Americans intended to cooperate fully with the enemy's desire to lure U.S. deployments to the highlands, where U.S. firepower could be used to best advantage. Sixteen battalions, totaling some 16,000 men—the 4th Infantry Division, a brigade from the 1st Cavalry Division, the 173d Airborne Brigade, and six ARVN battalions—were soon attempting to fix and destroy the enemy who could be anywhere in the bewildering expanse of look-alike hills. Almost overnight, the sleepy Dak To Special Forces camp swelled into a virtual corps headquarters crammed with tents, communications shacks, and artillery batteries. Dak To was buzzed daily by an immense swarm of C-130 supply flights and helicopter medevacs, gunships, and troop transports landing, unloading, refueling, departing. The days and nights were disturbed by incessant sounds, from artillery and tactical air strikes during the day, and harassment and interdiction fires and the distant, eerie, low-pitched whine of AC-47 gunships after dark.

While the 4th Division under Major General William R. Peers built up its base at Dak To, and Brigadier General Leo H. Schweiter's 173d Airborne Brigade enlarged the fire support base at Ben Het, North Vietnamese troops slipped into positions preselected for purposes of ambush or defensive tactics. Dak To was to become the focal point of a struggle for several of the hundreds of similar, nondescript hills in the region that the enemy had chosen for tactical reasons to occupy and fortify. As the Americans and South Vietnamese began to comb through the hills, they discovered unmistakable signs of enemy preparation. Jungle roads and trails had been heavily traveled. Trees had been felled and dragged away, and buffalo dung near the work sites indicated the use of draft animals. In provoking a battle at Dak To, the North Vietnamese were picking a fight at a time and place of their own choosing. "The enemy had prepared the battlefield well," General Peers later wrote. "Nearly every key terrain feature was heavily fortified with elaborate bunker and trench complexes. He had moved quantities of supplies and ammunition into the area. He was prepared to stay."

The battle is joined

The first clashes with the enemy came on November 3 and 4. Patrolling a ridge line south of Dak To, two companies of the 3d Battalion, 12th Infantry (4th Infantry Division), came under mortar attack when they approached within thirty meters of an enemy position. Air strikes and artillery suppressed the North Vietnamese fire, and the Americans found thirteen bodies when they took the ridge, at a cost of four of their own soldiers. The following day, two companies of the 3d Battalion, 8th Infantry, cleared out an enemy post on a hill southwest of Dak To and set about constructing a firebase. They lost four men killed while claiming eleven enemy dead.

Two days later, the 173d Airborne saw its first action at Dak To. Two companies from the 4th Battalion, 503d Infantry, met elements of the NVA 66th Regiment on November 6 on the Ngok Kom Leat chain of hills south of Ben Het. Climbing one hill, Company D was attacked, and heavy artillery fire could not dislodge the enemy. Reinforced in the morning, Company D renewed its assault, only to find that the enemy had surreptitiously abandoned the hill.

The 4th Battalion was also ordered to construct a firebase somewhere south of Ben Het, and battalion commander Lieutenant Colonel James H. Johnson chose a hill covered with dense jungle numbered 823, where two large trails intersected. Tactically, control of 823 was important, and intelligence had indicated it was unoccupied. Lt. Col. Johnson chose to go in from above. A series of air strikes on November 6 succeeded only in blasting in the dense bamboo an LZ large enough for one Huey helicopter to hover, allowing the soldiers of Company B to jump into a tangle of shattered bamboo.

The hill was not unoccupied. Spreading out into a perimeter,

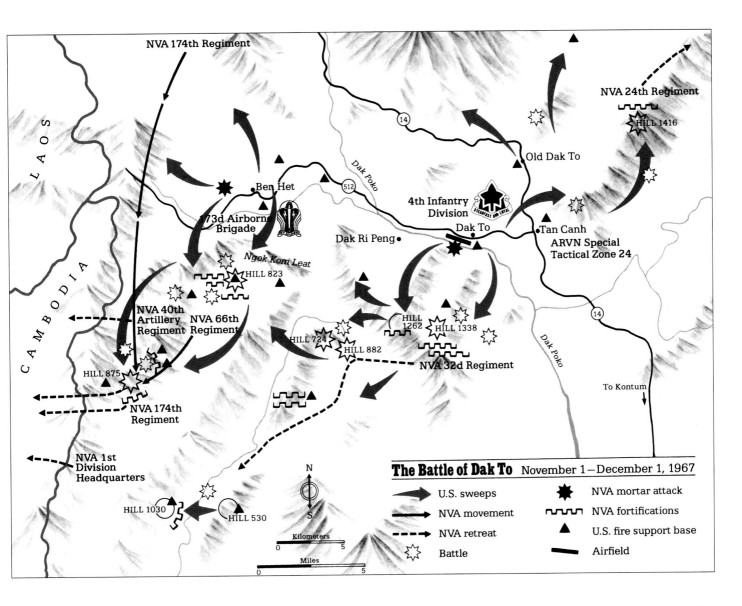

The Battle of Dak To November 1–December 1, 1967

→	U.S. sweeps	✦	NVA mortar attack
→	NVA movement	⌐⌐⌐	NVA fortifications
⇢	NVA retreat	▲	U.S. fire support base
✧	Battle	▬	Airfield

the third platoon quickly became embroiled with a group of North Vietnamese. Fifteen minutes later, seven Americans lay dead and another thirteen were wounded, but the company had pushed back the enemy attack.

The North Vietnamese were not through, however, and they continued to probe and fire throughout the night. When daylight arrived, tactical air support pounded enemy positions. Company B finally secured the hill, and the men discovered bunkers and camouflaged foxholes.

Slain North Vietnamese soldiers were laid in 500-pound bomb craters and covered with dirt. They were the bodies of robust men—fresh troops—not at all emaciated from living in the jungle. In fact, their khaki uniforms, although recently tattered from battle, had been crisp and new, as if folded away in boxes and taken out like dress uniforms for this campaign. Many of the enemy soldiers were bandaged, some in two or three places, a fact the Americans found remarkable.

On November 8, Company C of the 1st Battalion, 503d Infantry, relieved Company B/4/503. After a night, Company C, reinforced by two platoons from Company D/1/503, began patrolling down the ridge line. The company and a half, 200 men under the command of Company C's Captain Thomas McElwain, took the name Task Force Black. (A temporary group with components from different units—in this case one company with part of another—was often called a "task force.") As protection against ambushes, Captain McElwain sent out cloverleaf patrols in which soldiers from each platoon circled to the sides in a continual search of the flanks, and he also positioned a scout dog and its handler on point. Though the dog spent the day in a froth of snarling and barking, the unit never made contact with the enemy.

On the second night, the force cut a landing zone to allow helicopters to bring in supplies, and the men of Task Force Black dug deep foxholes and constructed overhead cover. They could "feel" the enemy and hear movement all around, and beneath them in the valley they saw the tiny red and green lights the NVA used to move troops. "Everybody knew there were large numbers of NVA regulars in the area, and sooner or later, we would find them," recalled First Lieutenant Ray Flynn,

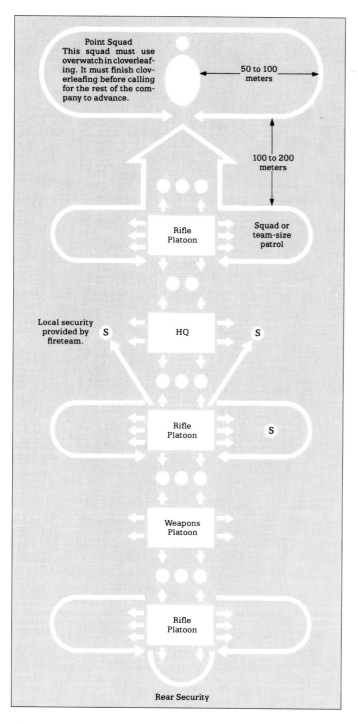

Point Squad
This squad must use overwatch in cloverleafing. It must finish cloverleafing before calling for the rest of the company to advance.

50 to 100 meters

100 to 200 meters

Rifle Platoon

Squad or team-size patrol

Local security provided by fireteam.

S   HQ   S

S

Rifle Platoon

S

Weapons Platoon

Rifle Platoon

Rear Security

The cloverleaf tactic, *or formation, was often used by American units when contact with the enemy seemed imminent. It was hoped that part of the cloverleaf would discover the enemy before the entire U.S. unit was engaged.*

the mortar platoon leader. "But we certainly didn't want to find them at midnight in this bamboo grove."

Veterans Day, 1967

Before 8:00 A.M., on November 11, Veterans Day, Task Force Black set out on day patrol, leaving Lieutenant Flynn and twenty-five men to hold the camp. The men left their packs and bedding and just took "load-bearing equipment"—web gear with weapons and ammunition, C-rations, and water.

As C Company's only Ranger-qualified platoon leader, First Lieutenant Gerald T. Cecil and his platoon often drew point responsibility. This morning, he sent five-man squads on either flank to patrol in cloverleaf patterns, as the bulk of his platoon, followed by the remainder of the reinforced company, set off down the trail. They had traveled 200 meters when PFC John Rolfe spotted a North Vietnamese soldier squatting on the trail. The soldier rose slowly from his haunches, turned, and moved away deliberately, perhaps believing he had not been seen. Rolfe fired one round and hit him in the back, killing him instantly.

Lieutenant Cecil moved up cautiously, and from his position far back in the center of the column, Captain McElwain also came forward to inspect the body. The slain soldier wore a fresh green uniform, and the barrel of his AK47 rifle still carried traces of preservative. Lieutenant Cecil guessed that the soldier had been a "trail watcher" whose function was to alert ambushers farther down the trail to the Americans' approach.

Captain McElwain returned to his position, and Lieutenant Cecil started the patrol moving again, following the narrow but well-used trail down into a depression. Beneath the enveloping trees forming the high jungle canopy, the dim landscape was one of tree trunks, bamboo groves, and small shrubs. Cecil and his men in the point platoon scoured the jungle for signs of movement and listened for any unusual noises. There was neither motion nor noise, only "an eerie absence of sound," Cecil recalled. He began to fear he might be walking the company into an ambush. After advancing a few more meters, he beckoned to his flank squads to return to the column and assemble in defensive positions. "I sensed that we were standing right on top of them," Cecil said. Breaking the silence, he ordered his men to commence firing near their feet and continue in sweeping arcs, spraying the surrounding bushes with bullets. The platoon began firing in short bursts.

The jungle erupted. NVA soldiers popped out of camouflaged holes. Bushes came to life, proving to be enemy soldiers firing automatic rifles. "We hit the deck, we were among 'em," Cecil said. He ordered his men to fire magazine after magazine. Machine gunners set up as quickly as possible. Men fell wounded and dead on both sides. One NVA soldier stepped out of a stand of bamboo and leaned over three wounded Americans, peppering them with fire. He was shot and killed. Enemy soldiers in trees dropped hand grenades, and one fell between Cecil and his radio operator. They spun away but not far enough to avoid shrapnel. Both fired into the tree above them and they saw a soldier crumple. Cecil gave his M16 to a soldier whose own was shattered by fire, and he began fighting with an AK47, picking up magazines from dead enemy soldiers.

The platoon kept up fire while some soldiers attempted to inch up the slope with the wounded to join the rest of the company. During a two- or three-minute lull in the shooting, the soldiers feverishly set claymore mines in front of their positions. As the firing recommenced, the men clicked off several of the mines. One bold enemy soldier grabbed at a claymore to turn it around, but an American saw him and detonated it. The explosion and disintegration of the soldier created another lull, which Americans took advantage of to move more wounded up the slope.

When the firing had begun 50 meters ahead of him, Captain McElwain ordered his men into a defense perimeter. Over the radio, Lieutenant Cecil reported contact with a platoon or company, he wasn't sure which, and McElwain was taking no chances. The rest of the patrol hustled up from the rear to establish an elliptical perimeter about 40 meters wide on the gradual hillside. No substantial cover existed but for bamboo, scrub bushes, and tree trunks. The soldiers could only flatten out. Cecil's platoon—the only one fighting for the first quarter hour—kept backing up the slope to form one extremity of the perimeter. When the strung-out patrol was finally deployed over the distance of more than 100 meters, the sides of the enemy's U-shaped ambush, manned by a battalion, snapped closed.

Medic Sp4 Ennis Elliott was moving across the perimeter, when, by instinct, he dove down. "They opened up on us, and the bamboo fell like it was cut by a giant scythe," said Elliott. "AK47 fire." Shells from preregistered mortars exploded inside the perimeter. Cries of "Medic!" came from every direction. The medics dragged casualties into the center of the perimeter. Men crawled flat on their bellies, pulling themselves by their elbows, as bullets whistled over their backs. They had no time to dig in. Some were hit in the head, others in the heels; they simply couldn't get low enough. Soon as many men lay wounded in the center as manned the perimeter firing M60 machine guns and M16s. Machine gunners presented raised targets, and the enemy concentrated fire against them. The NVA killed one machine-gun team and might have gained the lines, but PFC John Barnes dashed across the bullet-swept slope, slid in behind the machine gun and poured fire on a squad assaulting the perimeter. Barnes killed nine soldiers and that repulsed the attack.

Sp4 Elliott was shot early. Lying behind a wounded soldier and reaching over his back to apply a dressing, he saw an NVA regular pop up thirty meters away, sight down the barrel of his AK47, and fire. One bullet grazed the already wounded soldier. A second hit Elliott's left forearm, shattering the bone. The NVA soldier fortunately ducked away. Elliott wrapped his forearm and jabbed a morphine ampoule into his thigh, but the pain didn't ease for a long time. "When you see somebody else get hit, it doesn't bother you," said the experienced medic. "But when you look at your own arm and see the bone and blood, it's a shock." Elliott loosened the triangular bandage around his neck to fashion a sling and crawled to the center of the perimeter on his side, protecting his arm. Mortars and B40 rockets continued to pour in on the prostrate soldiers.

To Lieutenant Flynn at the camp just 250 meters back, the shooting down the trail was a muffled roar. When the heavy firing began, Captain McElwain called Flynn and told him to dump the mortars and get down the trail to help. The men wrapped the mortars and put them in the bunkers, covering them with dirt. As Flynn formed them for the march, setting out point men, flank, and rear security, the men noticed movement in the bushes. "That's when I knew we were going to get hit," Flynn recalled. "The attacks were coordinated and the worst thing I wanted was to be cut off from the company with just twenty-five men."

The enemy opened fire around the camp. Within moments, NVA soldiers filtered into the campsite, darting from bunker to bunker, firing at Flynn's platoon on the way out. An M60 machine gun rapidly set up by the Americans slowed them. Flynn pulled the machine gun back and started the men down into the maelstrom, in effect surrendering to the enemy the camp with its mortars, ammo, and U.S. gear. The heavy and constant firing forced them to crawl, and they covered the distance on their bellies. They arrived at the ragged end of the perimeter, crawled through a disheveled Company D, and pushed out into the defenses. Men lay everywhere, and Flynn sent his men to fill gaps left by wounded defenders. Task Force Black was now completely surrounded.

The tempo of the fighting rose and fell for hours. Captain McElwain worked artillery as close as possible to the site, bringing it to within twenty-five or thirty meters of his men. For the most part, however, the enemy was "bear hugging" the American perimeter, moving too close to allow effective artillery or tactical air support. The jungle canopy, in any case, all but prevented air operations, since pilots could not see the Americans. When the men on the ground released yellow smoke to mark their location, the NVA threw yellow smoke of their own—previously stolen from the Americans—to confuse any rescuers.

Ammunition began to run out. McElwain encouraged the men to hold their fire, to pick a target, aim, and fire. In late morning, with the ammunition situation becoming critical, back at Dak To Warrant Officer Gary Bass, a helicopter pilot who had long worked with the 1st Battalion, volunteered to resupply the surrounded task force. The men on the ground heard the bullets hitting Bass's chopper as it approached with a sling load of ammunition and grenades. But in the tremendously heavy fire (the chopper took thirty-five hits), Bass had to release the sling before he was ready. It dropped above the perimeter, on the ridge line, and tumbled even farther away into the hands of the enemy. The men's hopes sank. Not only had they no new ammunition, but now the enemy possessed U.S. grenades, more deadly than the Chinese ones.

Nearly every American was wounded by the grazing fire, but many never saw an enemy soldier that day. "The only way you could see them was that the bushes were moving or somebody was firing and you could see the smoke coming out of their rifles," said one. "You just couldn't see the NVA." One American, however, caught full sight of an NVA soldier moving near the U.S. line. His job was to cover that approach with the twelve-gauge double-pump shotgun he'd carried on patrol for months without ever having fired. Now he shot twice, and the enemy soldier parted at the waist, the halves spinning away.

Like many of his companions, Ennis Elliott, his left arm already shattered, was hit again and again. A mortar shell dropped where he lay among the wounded in the center of the perimeter, and shrapnel tore through his right wrist, while the concussion crushed his cheekbone, knocking him unconscious. "I didn't even hear it go off," he said, "but everything got deadly silent and I said to myself, well, I must be dead. I remember thinking about my wife, she'll at least get my insurance money. Things like that flash through your head. And then I felt blood on my face, and I said, if I'm dead, why do I feel blood on my face? Then the firing came back a little, I could hear it again, and things came back into focus." Elliott later took grenade shrapnel in the left side. About half the enemy's Chicom grenades thrown that day failed to explode, as did some of the mortar rounds. A 60MM mortar round fell among one clump of wounded and bounced on the ground. The men tried to roll away, but few could even move. They just lay there helplessly, willing it to be a dud. It was.

One grenade thrown into the midst of the wounded wasn't a dud. PFC John Barnes, who had earlier taken over a machine gun and repelled an assault on the perimeter, had run out of ammunition. He backed away from the machine gun and got up to search for more M60 belts, when he saw a Chinese hand grenade drop among a half dozen severely wounded soldiers. To

shield them, Barnes threw himself on the grenade just as it exploded. His action cost him his life, but it saved others, and his sacrifice was recognized with a posthumous Medal of Honor.

Late in the morning, Charlie Company, 4th Battalion, 503d Infantry, got the job of relieving the embattled force. Packing extra ammunition to share with their beleaguered comrades, the 120-man C/4/503, under Captain William J. Connolly, dropped into an LZ about 800 meters north of the ambush site. To prevent a similar ambush, Charlie Company called in artillery fire in advance of its trail. The company arrived at the abandoned camp to find the enemy gone and the packs looted and contents strewn about. Incredibly, the mortars were still there.

Leaving a squad, C Company moved quickly down the trail,

Members of Company C, *4th Battalion, 503d Infantry, en route to reinforcing Task Force Black, drop into a landing zone less than a kilometer from the site of the Veterans Day, 1967, ambush.*

using reconnaissance by fire on all sides. The enemy responded with automatic weapons fire against the 2d Platoon, but an M60 machine gun silenced it, and the rest of the company double-timed past and ran the final 100 meters with a rebel whoop. "We yelled and screamed as we came in because we wanted to make sure they knew we were coming," said Staff Sergeant Donald J. Ibenthal, "and also so they wouldn't fire at us when we came in. We came running in there and immediately went up into the perimeter and took over positions up in the front lines. The machine gunners we replaced were both shot in the head several times." Added Sergeant Charles R. Cunningham, "There were many wounded laying around, many in serious condition, a lot of dead. Quite a few Charlies were laying there dead ... right inside the perimeter." The relief force linked up

with Task Force Black at 2:37 P.M., by which time the task force had already been fighting for six hours.

By 4:00 P.M. the firing tapered off into sniping, and the 1st Battalion companies began to bring their wounded back to the camp. There were few able-bodied men to carry poncho stretchers or to help others walk. Some of the rescuers aided the wounded, while others fired at snipers and watched the sides of the trail. There were not enough men to carry the dead, so some bodies were left for the night at the ambush site. Medevacs took the wounded from the camp before dark. As a defensive measure, and also to catch any NVA who might be policing the battlefield, artillery and tactical air strikes, including napalm, raked positions the enemy had occupied during the day.

U.S. losses from the ambush amounted to 20 killed, 154

wounded, and 2 missing. No more than two dozen men from Task Force Black had escaped unscathed, and two U.S. companies had effectively been put out of action. The fierce battle resulted in numerous medals for valor, beginning with PFC Barnes's Medal of Honor and a Distinguished Service Cross won by Lieutenant Cecil. Captain McElwain earned one of five Silver Stars distributed immediately after the battle.

The following morning three platoons returned to the ambush site to recover American bodies and count enemy bodies. After the air strikes and artillery, veterans of the previous day's fighting had difficulty recognizing the scene. Many enemy bodies left on the battlefield had been dismembered by the artillery fire and were therefore difficult to count. Captain McElwain reported a body count of about eighty North Vietnamese, only to be told that the number was too low, considering his own losses, and that he should go out and count again. Explained Lieutenant Flynn, "If you lost so many people killed and wounded, you had to have something to show for it."

The men searched the area for two more days and discovered some shallow graves, which they were ordered to excavate to verify the number of bodies. McElwain ultimately stretched the body count to 116 enemy soldiers, which was accepted. Years later McElwain reiterated the lower number. "I'd probably put it closer to 70 or 75 enemy actually killed that day," he said.

Despite the wrangle over enemy casualties, it remained for Lieutenant Cecil to emphasize the few positive results of the battle. The Americans had built a tremendous base of fire in a classic demonstration of ambush defense. Although both sides suffered high casualties, the fact that the battle lasted all day was taken by U.S. officers to dramatize the success of the Americans' self-defense tactics. Quite simply, said Lieutenant Cecil, "The North Vietnamese in eight hours were unable to accomplish what should have taken them thirty-five minutes."

"Hold at all costs"

From the surrounding hills, the sprawling Dak To base camp presented an inviting target, and enemy mortars and rockets fell sporadically, aimed at the fuel and ammo dumps or at the headquarters area. On the morning of November 15, the enemy "walked" a dozen mortar shells across the airstrip, and the fourth or fifth round scored a direct hit on an empty C-130

Packing extra ammunition for Task Force Black, *a Charlie Company soldier moves through bamboo forest toward the ambush. Bamboo and thick undergrowth formed the lowest level of triple-canopy jungle in the Dak To region.*

transport. A second C-130 next to it was also destroyed, and shrapnel ripped through the fuel tanks of a third, causing a leak of high-octane aviation fuel that caught fire and quickly spread to a pallet of 105MM howitzer shells.

The same evening seventy-eight enemy mortar shells dropped into the camp, one round scoring a direct hit on the ammunition dump. Explosions sent shock waves through the valley. Aviation fuel blew up almost simultaneously, shooting a fireball and mushroom cloud into the air. "I thought, Jesus!" said Lieutenant Fred Drysen, an engineer. "It looked like Charlie had gotten hold of some nuclear weapons." Shrapnel from the ammo dump set fire to the tents and buildings of the adjacent Special Forces camp, and the residents were evacuated in armored personnel carriers because of the continuing intermittent explosions. Tear gas stored near the dump had also exploded, sending a noxious cloud over the camp.

Although destructive, the shelling of the base resulted in few casualties. It was as close as the North Vietnamese came to realizing their goal of taking Dak To. The quick deployment of allied troops had thwarted the enemy's plans, in fact putting him on the defensive. The 173d Brigade's sweeps south of Ben Het, and the 4th Division's capture of ridge lines to the south and southwest of Dak To, had battered the NVA 66th and 32d regiments. In mid-November, as more American and ARVN troops poured into the area, the two North Vietnamese regiments began a general southwest retreat toward the Cambodian sanctuaries. Even in retreat, however, the North Vietnamese, taking advantage of their battlefield preparations, fought tenacious rearguard actions.

The 32d Regiment still held Hill 1338, six kilometers south of Dak To, which provided them with an excellent view of the base. Troops of the 3d Battalion, 12th Infantry, attacked and engaged in a two-day fight up the demanding jungle-covered incline. The NVA stoutly defended their positions, and as they advanced the Americans discovered why. The ridge contained the most elaborate complex of bunkers yet found, all linked by field telephones. "Starting at the top of the hill," wrote Italian journalist Oriana Fallaci, "[the trenches] descended in a spiral like orange skin peeled off in a single strip. The circles were joined to one another by subterranean passages, the oldest of them six months old." Since June the North Vietnamese soldiers had been digging quietly under the Americans' eyes. The 3/12 took the summit in furious infantry battles after the air force had dropped tons of napalm on the trenches.

At the same time on Hill 1416, two ARVN airborne battalions were then locked in combat with the NVA 24th Regiment. The 3d and 9th battalions, ARVN's elite volunteer units, captured the hill on November 20 following a four-day battle in

Reinforcement of Task Force Black

The survivors were in very bad shape. Then a fiece firefight started and we received some mortar rounds which caused more dead and wounded. Some soldiers started to dig the earth with knives, which was useless *(below)*. The men abandoned their M16s without ammo. I saw one of them take an AK47 *(right)* to continue fighting in utter confusion. Medics were being called from all over. Most of the men were wounded, many several times *(opposite, top)*. We got close air support and artillery and the pressure became lighter. Everybody moved slowly to a giant bomb crater where resupply choppers came and evacuated the most seriously wounded *(opposite, bottom)*.

–Photographer Ghislain Bellorget

"Medic! Medic! Buddy's been hit!" *The 1st Battalion, 503d Infantry, battles for Hill 882, one of many hills near Dak To.*

which 247 NVA were killed. ARVN soldiers found a letter from the NVA regimental commander exhorting his men to hold the hill at all costs.

The enemy's reserve regiment—the 174th—had meanwhile left its position in the northwest, slipping south through the mountains to cover the retreat of the depleted 66th. Passing to the west of the 173d Brigade's base at Ben Het, the North Vietnamese took up positions at the top of a hill 875 meters high. On November 19, 173d commander General Schweiter ordered a battalion—the 2d Battalion, 503d Infantry—to assault Hill 875.

The fortress of Hill 875

Covered with scrub brush and bamboo and widely separated trees, Hill 875 rose in a gradual slope that leveled off at two ridge lines into broad "saddles." Following artillery and tactical air preparation, Companies C and D started up the hill in parallel lines at 9:43 A.M., the men picking their way over vegetation and bamboo gnarled and mangled from the bombing. Company A secured the rear. At 10:30, Sp4 Kenneth Jacobs, lead man of the point squad, neared the first of two ridges, when automatic weapons fire from a hidden bunker five meters away cut him down. As other point men moved up, a medic was

killed. All the soldiers dropped their rucksacks, moved up, and spread out on line. As the Americans came forward, the NVA added recoilless rifle and rifle grenade fire to the automatic weapons fire.

When the enemy firing lulled, the infantry advanced, using fire and movement tactics—shooting and advancing, shooting and advancing. One squad discovered the concealed bunker from which the first shots had come and tossed four or five hand grenades through the port. Moments after the explosions, an NVA soldier threw hand grenades out of the same bunker at passing soldiers. The bunkers were all interconnected by tunnels, and the enemy could scramble away from hand grenades and come right back. Another squad with M16s killed several enemy soldiers in bunkers and only minutes later were fired at by replacements who had scurried to the same bunker.

As infantry companies moved up all over the hill, the enemy resumed fire, felling U.S. soldiers and halting the advance. "There is no sound in this world like a bullet tearing through a human body," said Private Joe Aldridge. "It sounded like slaps." Artillery and air strikes began to work above the U.S. positions, but the soldiers continued to be hit by small arms fire and shrapnel fragments from enemy grenades. "Jesus, they were all over the place," recalled one paratrooper. "The noncoms kept shouting, 'Get up the hill, get up the goddam hill.'

Firebase Flint under attack. *A CH-47 Chinook resupplies the 4th Division firebase atop Hill 1338 as smoke from incoming enemy fire drifts toward the valley south of Dak To.*

But we couldn't. We were surrounded and we were firing in all directions." Company A, rear security, 100 meters back, was also under attack. The assault had bogged down, and C Company commander Captain Harold J. Kaufman ordered the infantry to pull back and form a perimeter. The men jumped at the order and began such a ragged and hurried withdrawal that Kaufman drew his pistol and fired it into the air to regain control. Halting the retreat, he established a perimeter just 20 meters in front of the bunker where the battle had commenced. The men began digging in furiously with their steel pots, bayonets, and entrenching tools.

Minutes earlier, a four-man squad from A Company, led by Sp4 James Kelley, had been set up in the rear to prevent attack from the bottom of the hill. The men began to hear twigs breaking near them, when suddenly machine gunner PFC Carlos Lozada yelled, "Here they come Kelley," and started firing. The heavy fire killed some of the enemy and alerted the rest of A Company to the attack. But the NVA kept coming. Lozada, Kelley, and Sp4 John Steer poured fire down the hill, and Kelley called for them to fall back. Lozada moved his machine gun up the hill, set it down again behind a fallen tree, and fired at the onrushing enemy. Kelley aimed his M16 at one camouflaged NVA with a blackened face whose rifle was wrapped in burlap. He shot and hit him, then the M16 jammed, and he knelt to work on the weapon. To cover him, Lozada jumped into the trail, firing the machine gun from the hip as he backed up the trail. Steer fought alongside him.

Having fixed his weapon, Kelley resumed firing just as Lozada ran out of ammunition. Lozada took off up the trail, but an AK47 slug hit him in the head, knocking him into Steer. Kelley got them moving up the trail and dropped fragmentation grenades on the trail to slow the pursuit. A squad from the company arrived to help and cover the withdrawal. Several of the relievers were wounded, one killed.

The remainder of A Company came under heavy attack, and mortar shells began to fall. The company commander fell dead. The 2d Platoon moved to protect a flank and was overrun by NVA coming up a well-constructed trail with steps cut into the side of the hill. Within fifteen minutes what remained of A Company had straggled up the hill toward Companies C and D. Soldiers firing cover for the withdrawal were swamped by charging NVA soldiers. Company A gained the perimeter, and the NVA followed them right up the hill. By 3:00 P.M. the C Company commander reported they were surrounded by 200 to 300 NVA and under attack by mortars, automatic weapons, and B40 rockets.

The wounded were pulled to the center of the perimeter near the newly formed command post. All the men were in need of water and resupply, but heavy enemy fire drove off relief helicopters. One chopper dropped a sling load of ammunition fifteen meters outside the perimeter, and enemy snipers killed the leader of a party sent out to recover it, forcing a hasty withdrawal back to U.S. lines. Six other helicopters were shot down that day, several by enemy soldiers in trees with automatic weapons. Toward the end of the day, two pallets of ammunition landed within the perimeter, easing that crisis, but the battalion was left without water and food for fifty hours.

The enemy had prepared the battlefield extremely well. Hill 875 was no less than a fortress, with bunkers and trenches connected by tunnels. The underground bunkers had as much as two meters of overhead cover to protect their occupants from bombing and artillery, and slit gun ports opened onto excellent fields of fire. When the NVA infantry went on the attack, the soldiers were camouflaged and had prepared avenues of entry and withdrawal from the battlefield. A standard NVA tactic at Dak To was to attack the rear of a U.S. unit that was already engaged against a fortified position and attempt to isolate some of the soldiers—a squad, a platoon, a company—and defeat it in detail. The enemy had decimated Company A with this procedure, and now they closed in on the rest of the pinned-down soldiers.

Friendly fire

The paratroopers continued to undergo sporadic but effective sniper and mortar fire. Despite the enemy's "bear hug," artillery and tactical air support—air force F-100 jets, propeller-driven Skyraiders, and helicopter gunships—bombarded NVA positions to within 50 meters of U.S. lines. As dusk faded into darkness, word passed around the perimeter to prepare for an assault by the enemy. The soldiers laid out magazines and grenades on the ground beside them and fixed bayonets. But the attack came not from the front or even from the enemy. It came from the presumably friendly sky. A jet fighter diving toward the enemy at 300 miles per hour released a 500-pound bomb short of the target, and it fell squarely on the command post and aid station in the center of the perimeter. Forty-two Americans, many of them already wounded, died in the blast, including several of the officers and chaplain Charles Watters, who had been administering last rites. Forty-five more were wounded. "We were doing okay until they dropped the bombs on us," said PFC John W. Blessinger. "That's what really messed us up."

Most of the companies' leaders were now dead or wounded, but new leaders—junior officers and NCOs—emerged from the ranks. "They were hitting us with mortars and recoilless rifle fire all night, and everybody was trying to get underground," one survivor recalled. "Every time you tried to dig, you put your shovel in somebody." Soldiers burrowed out foxholes amid the incredible clutter of the battlefield—discarded ammo boxes, spent magazines, ruined weapons, splintered wood and bamboo, ravaged trees and vegetation, bloodied bandages, comrades dead and wounded. AC-47 gunships flew over the hill illuminating the scene with flares, as the new company leaders "walked" artillery toward enemy positions. The temperatures fell, but the soldiers' warmer clothes were in rucksacks strewn all over the battlefield, most of them outside the perimeter. "Heaps of dead after that bomb," another shaken defender related. "You didn't know where to go, you didn't know where to hide. You slept with the corpses. I slept under Joe. He was dead, but he kept me warm."

On the morning of the second day, the 4th Battalion, 503d Infantry, set out up the hill to reinforce the 2d Battalion. Its companies advancing separately, 4/503 spent the day moving cautiously up the hill. Tree snipers continued to drive helicopters away from the U.S. perimeter, and a party sent out to find the snipers was cut down. One medevac helicopter managed to land just before dark, carrying off five critically wounded soldiers. Bravo Company of the 4th Battalion reached the perimeter by early evening, to the tearful relief of the 2d Battalion. Their medics set to work on the wounded, and the soldiers gave their food and what water they had to their shell-shocked comrades. Two other companies from the 4th Battalion arrived at the U.S. perimeter after dark.

The following day, November 21, the paratroopers cut and protected a landing zone, and the 2d Battalion began to extract its wounded. The dead were not removed until the next day. Food and water came at last. During the day artillery and tactical air pounded the hill with high explosives and napalm to prepare for an assault by the 4th Battalion.

Armed with flame throwers, shoulder-fired LAWs (light anti-tank rockets), and 81MM mortars to use against the enemy fortifications, the men launched the attack at 1505 hours.

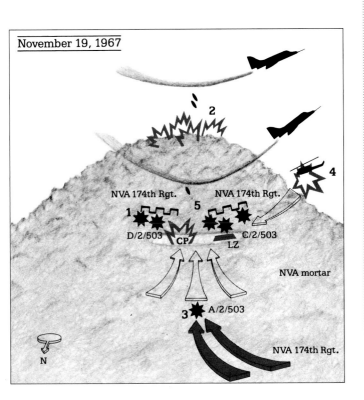

Hill 875

1. **From fortified positions** *NVA ambushes Companies C and D.*
2. **U.S. artillery** *and air strikes on the hill begin.*
3. **NVA ambushes Company A** *from the rear. A moves up to join C and D. 2/503 forms a perimeter.*
4. **Six helicopters shot down** *as fighting continues throughout the day. Battalion is without food or water for 50 hours.*
5. **After dark a U.S. jet fighter** *releases a 500-pound bomb on the command post, killing 42 soldiers and wounding 45.*

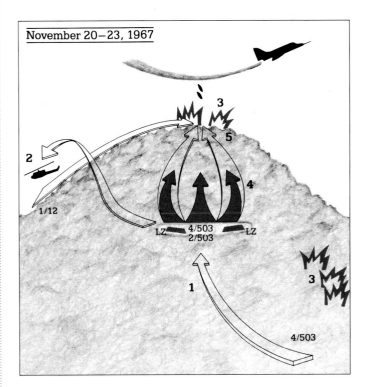

1. **November 20.** *4/503 sets out to relieve 2/503. Arrives that evening.*
2. **November 21.** *A new LZ is cut and 2/503 begins to extract the wounded. The dead are not removed until the next day.*
3. **November 20-23.** *U.S. artillery and tactical air continue to pound the hillside.*
4. **November 21.** *At 1505 hours 4/503 launches an assault on the hill. Unsuccessful, the men pull back after dark.*
5. **November 23,** *Thanksgiving Day. 4/503 assaults the hill. 1/12 advances from the south. Meeting little resistance 4/503 reaches the top of the hill at 1122.*

Under heavy fire, they crawled forward, but they could not see any enemy soldiers. When they finally located bunkers, from spotting the muzzle smoke, their weapons proved ineffective. The men had not been trained to use flame throwers, and they handled them badly. To be effective, LAWs required direct hits into the bunkers' slit portholes, a nearly impossible feat of marksmanship. Mortar shells exploded harmlessly atop bunkers with deep overhead cover. Many shells failed to explode at all in dirt that had been ground into soft powder by air strikes. The attack failed dismally. Bravo Company, which absorbed the worst casualties, pulled back to the perimeter at dark, more than half its numbers killed or wounded.

General Peers had vowed for two days that Hill 875 would soon be in the hands of the Americans, and by Thanksgiving morning, the fifth day after the 2d Battalion had started to clear Hill 875, a fresh battalion, the 1st Battalion, 12th Infantry, was poised to the south, ready to come up the mountain from the back side behind enemy positions. Within the defensive perimeter on the northern slope, the 4th Battalion readied a coordinated attack. Air force planes pounded the hilltop with bombs and napalm prior to the infantry assault.

Led by the vastly reduced Bravo Company, the 4th Battalion stormed out of the perimeter at 1100 hours, as its own mortar operators lobbed 81MM shells ahead. The soldiers suffered light sniper fire and some enemy mortar rounds, but enemy resistance had all but disappeared. To cries of "Airborne!" and "Geronimo!" the paratroopers overran the scorched hilltop in twenty-two minutes.

The North Vietnamese had decamped during the night, after removing most of their dead and their weapons. The harassing mortar fire was coming from a ridge to the west. On the desolate mountain top, the Americans found but a few blackened and dismembered bodies among the splintered trees and bomb craters. The top of the mountain was laced with trenches and bunkers.

The battalions' pent-up frustrations at being pinned down and pummeled found no release in a final victorious battle. At least few additional casualties were incurred, and that alone was a relief: The 173d Airborne Brigade had already spent a lot of men to take the fortress. "It was a happy day when we found that they had left the hill," said First Lieutenant Alfred Lindseth of Company B, 4th Battalion. Later that afternoon helicopters ferried in Thanksgiving dinners. The paratroopers sat in the dust eating hot sliced turkey, cranberry sauce, and potatoes. There was plenty for everybody to eat, and after days of C-rations, the soldiers ate their fill,

Paratroopers of the 173d Brigade *found themselves in an eerie twilight on Hill 875, where the jungle filtered the sun and concealed enemy bunkers. In five days of pitched fighting, many Americans never saw an enemy soldier.*

while around them, the process of assessing the battle began.

The enemy body count from the five-day Hill 875 battle was more than 300, but few survivors took the figure seriously. At week's end the 173d Airborne held a service, and the soldiers laid out the boots of their slain comrades, in the paratrooper tradition. The battalions had lost 158 men killed and 402 wounded. A Presidential Unit Citation and Medals of Honor for Carlos Lozada and Father Charles Watters would only begin to salve the brigade's wounds.

The "capture" of Hill 875 marked the climax of the battle of Dak To. In the final days of November, the American brigades encountered little resistance in their sweeps of the hills to the south and southwest of Dak To. The North Vietnamese regiments had left the field, withdrawing into sanctuaries where U.S. units could not pursue. A rearguard mortar attack on the Ben Het fire support base on December 1 was the enemy's concluding blow.

The ambiguity of victory

Trumpeting the "overwhelming success of U.S. arms," one army report later summarized the battle of Dak To as "a classic example of allied superiority in firepower and maneuver [in which] … U.S. and ARVN battalions beat the enemy to the punch and sent the survivors limping back to their sanctuaries." Indeed the U.S. mounted an astonishing logistical and fire support effort at Dak To—artillery batteries fired more than 170,000 rounds, the air force executed 2,100 tactical air and 300 B-52 sorties, and the aviation units delivered almost 900,000 gallons of fuel for helicopters and planes.

In evaluating the battle, General Westmoreland referred to the enemy objectives contained in the document captured from the North Vietnamese B-3 Front Command. The enemy had failed to annihilate a major U.S. unit, Westmoreland noted, and although the enemy had "lured" American units to the highlands, they had stayed there less than a month. Opinions on the enemy body count varied by as much as an NVA battalion. The army reported 1,644 killed, but in his memoirs General Westmoreland mentioned 1,400, and some staff officers suggested 1,200. Still, it was undeniable that the North Vietnamese had paid a substantial price. Three regiments—the 32d, 66th, and 174th—were sufficiently depleted that they were not able to participate in the next phase of the winter-spring offensive. Only the 24th Regiment took the field in January 1968. "In all three frontier battles," General Westmoreland wrote, "we had soundly defeated the enemy without unduly sacrificing operations in other areas. The enemy's return was nil."

Not everyone agreed with that assessment. While they had not been "annihilated" at Dak To, two U.S. battalions had been badly mauled, and the friendly death toll—289 Americans and 73 ARVN soldiers—was uncomfortably high. "It's been debated how great a victory it was," said marine Brigadier General John A. Chaisson. "I've even had guys in my office ask if it was a victory. They said, 'Is it a victory when you lose [362] friendlies in three weeks and by your own spurious body count you only get 1,200?'" And a U.S. correspondent, watching the wounded from Hill 875 disembark from helicopters, muttered to a colleague, "With victories like this, who needs defeats?"

Despite misgivings felt by some after the battle of Dak To, the allies were waxing confident, convinced that the enemy was losing the war on the battlefield. General Westmoreland, who had spent much of November in Washington conferring with political leaders, foresaw a continued strengthening of the South Vietnamese army, which, if successful, would allow the United States to "phase down" its role in the war. In one speech, however, Westmoreland sounded a warning: "The enemy may be operating from the delusion that political pressure [in the United States] combined with the tactical defeat of a major unit might force the U.S. to throw in the towel."

As 1967 came to a close, there were signs that the North Vietnamese might be contemplating just such a tactic. U.S. intelligence reported signs of a Communist build-up, which General Westmoreland relayed to President Johnson. Enemy truck traffic had doubled along the Ho Chi Minh Trail, infiltration had been stepped up, and the North Vietnamese were rushing supplies to the DMZ. Marines patrolling from their combat base at Khe Sanh—the westernmost anchor of the strong point obstacle system—began to detect major concentrations of NVA troops filtering into the area. U.S. intelligence soon estimated that between 20,000 and 40,000 NVA troops surrounded Khe Sanh.

President Johnson viewed such reports with alarm. As he digested intelligence about the enemy build-up, he worried particularly about the fight looming at Khe Sanh. "We must try very hard to be ready," he said. "We face dark days ahead."

General Westmoreland felt ready. He had meticulously planned for the defense of Khe Sanh, backing up a reinforced regiment of marines with the massed firepower of SLAM. When the battle came, if the battle came, Westmoreland intended to stand and fight.

Following page. *Weary paratroopers trudge through the rear area on Hill 875, located just 100 meters from enemy positions but out of the direct enemy fields of fire. After the hill was taken, the Americans gathered the debris of the battlefield and blew it up.*

Picture Credits

Cover Photograph
Sgt. Howard Breedlove, DASPO, U.S. Army.

Chapter One
p. **4**, Larry Burrows—LIFE Magazine, © 1965, Time Inc. p. **7**, Bob Gomel—LIFE Magazine, © 1965, Time Inc. p. **12**, Wide World. p. **13**, U.S. Army. p. **15**, card courtesy of William Beck. p. **16**, UPI. p. **19**, Don McCullin—Camera Press Ltd. p. **21**, Bill Strode—Black Star.

"You're All Mine Now!"
p. **22-23**, Dennis Brack—TIME Magazine. p. **24**, top left, Lawrence Fried—The Image Bank; top right, Mark Kauffman—LIFE Magazine, © 1965, Time Inc.; bottom, Bob Gomel—LIFE Magazine, © 1965, Time Inc. p. **25**, Mark Kauffman—LIFE Magazine, © 1965, Time Inc. p. **26**, top left and bottom, I.C. Rapoport; top right, U.S. Army. p. **27**, U.S. Army. p. **28**, U.S. News & World Report Inc. p. **29**, top, U.S. Army; bottom, Walter Bennett—TIME Magazine.

Chapter Two
pp. **30, 35, 38, 40-41**, Wide World. p. **34**, Hal Moore Collection. p. **39**, Henri Huet—Hal Moore Collection. pp. **43, 45**, UPI.

The War on Canvas
p. **47**, Pete Peterson—Bill Kurtis Collection. p. **48**, Leonard H. Dermott—U.S. Marine Corps Art Collection. p. **49**, Barry W. Johnston—U.S. Army Pictorial Branch. pp. **50-51**, Michael Kelley. pp. **52-53**, John Plunkett.

Chapter Three
p. **54**, Bill Eppridge—LIFE Magazine, © 1965, Time Inc. pp. **57, 59, 61-62**, Co Rentmeester, LIFE Magazine, © 1967, Time Inc. p. **64**, James H. Pickerell. p. **65**, Tim Page. pp. **68-69, 72, 73**, top, Wide World. pp. **70-71**, Wide World, courtesy Life Picture Service. p. **73**, bottom, UPI.

Chapter Four
p. **74**, UPI. p. **78-79**, Wide World. p. **81**, U.S. Army. pp. **82, 87**, Philip Jones Griffiths—Magnum. p. **85**, Don McCullin. p. **89**, table courtesy of the Department of the Army. p. **91**, Wide World.

Chapter Five
p. **92**, UPI. p. **95**, Alan Hutchinson Library. p. **99**, Eastfoto. p. **100-101**, Roger Pic. p. **102**, top, Ngo Vinh Long Collection, bottom, Camera Press Ltd. p. **103**, Camera Press Ltd. p. **105**, Collection of D.C. White. p. **107**, Nihon Denpa News, Ltd.

The North Under Siege
p. **108-109**, Marc Riboud. pp. **110-115**, Lee Lockwood.

Chapter Six
p. **116**, Special Operations Association. p. **124**, James C. Donahue Collection. p. **126**, Daniel Camus—Paris Match. p. **127**, David K. Kauhaahaa Collection. p. **133**, Special Operations Association.

Arty
p. **134**, Wide World. pp. **135-136**, U.S. Marine Corps. p. **137**, U.S. Army.

Chapter Seven
p. **138**, James Hesselgrave. p. **141**, Co Rentmeester—LIFE Magazine, © 1967, Time Inc. pp. **143, 145**, UPI. pp. **144, 147, 151**, U.S. Army. p. **148**, U.S. Marine Corps.

Dispatch from Hill 875
pp. **152-157**, UPI.

Chapter Eight
p. **158**, Gilles Caron—Gamma/Liaison. pp. **161-162**, UPI. p. **168**, diagram courtesy of the Department of the Army. pp. **170-171, 174, 175**, top, Ghislain Bellorget—Black Star. pp. **172, 175**, bottom, Ghislain Bellorget. p. **176**, U.S. Army. p. **177**, Donald R. Joyce. p. **179**, diagram courtesy of the Department of the Army. p. **180**, Gilles Caron—Gamma/Liaison. p. **182-183**, UPI.

Map Credits

All maps prepared by Diane McCaffery. Sources are as follows:
pp. **8-9**—Reprinted from *Vietnam Order of Battle*. Copyright 1981, U.S. News & World Report Books.
p. **36**—Department of the Army.
p. **77**—Department of the Army.
p. **131**—Office of Air Force History.
p. **163**—U.S. Marine Corps.
p. **167**—Department of the Army.

Acknowledgments

The editors wish to acknowledge the kind assistance of the following people: Chuck Allen, *National Vietnam Veterans Review;* Colonel Carl F. Bernard, U.S. Army, Retired, former province senior adviser, Hau Nghia Province; Jeffrey J. Clarke, U.S. Army Center of Military History; Major Edgar C. Doleman, Jr., U.S. Army, Retired; Charles W. Dunn, professor and chairman, Department of Celtic Languages and Literature, Harvard University; Barbara Flum; Raymond Flynn, former lieutenant, 173d Airborne Brigade; Jim Graves and Bob Poos, *Soldier of Fortune* magazine; Tom Hebert, *Vietnam War Newsletter;* Douglas Pike; the officers and members of the Special Operations Association; An Ton That, program coordinator, International Institute, Boston, MA; Melissa Totten; the staffs of the U.S. Army Center of Military History and U.S. Marine Corps History and Museums Division; and numerous veterans of the Vietnam War who wish to remain anonymous.

Index

U.S. Military Units

(see note below)

Air Force
7th Air Force, 20

Army
I Field Force, Vietnam (I FFV), *8, 9*
II Field Force, Vietnam (II FFV), *8, 9*
1st Aviation Brigade, *8, 9*
1st Cavalry Division (Airmobile), 6-9, *8, 9, 12, 13,*
    31, 32, 33, 46, 128, 166
  1st Brigade, 45
  2d Brigade, 44, 45-46
  3d Brigade, 15, 32-33, 34, 44
  5th Cavalry
    1st Battalion, *36,* 45-46
      Company A, 142
    2d Battalion, *36,* 45-46
  7th Cavalry
    1st Battalion, 31, 34, *36,* 39, 42
      Company A, 15, *40,* 42
      Company B, 34, 39, 42
      Company C, 39, 42
    2d Battalion, 32, 33, *36,* 37, 39, 42, 44
      Company A, *30,* 33, *36,* 37, *38, 39, 41,*
        42, *144*
      Company B, 37, 44
      Company C, *36,* 37, *41,* 42
  8th Cavalry
    1st Battalion, 7, 33, *36,* 46
  9th Cavalry (Aerial Reconnaissance)
    1st Squadron, 33, 37
  12th Cavalry
    1st Battalion, 31, *36,* 37
      Company A, 44
    2d Battalion, 31, 33, *36,* 37, 38, 39, 42, 44-46,
      45
  229th Aviation Battalion (Assault Helicopter)
    Company A, 42
1st Infantry Division, *8, 9,* 11, 14, 90, *143,* 163
  1st Brigade, *8*
  2d Brigade, *8*
  3d Brigade, *8*
  26th Infantry
    1st Battalion
      Company A, 140
4th Infantry Division, *8,* 20, 86, 90, 128, 166, *167,*
  173, *177*
  1st Brigade, *9*
  2d Brigade, *9*
  3d Brigade, *9*
  8th Infantry
    3d Battalion, 166
  12th Infantry
    1st Battalion, 180
    3d Battalion, 166, 173-176
9th Infantry Division, *8, 9,* 66
  2d Brigade, 16
  3d Brigade, *9*
  39th Infantry
    4th Battalion
      Company A, 144
11th Armored Cavalry Regiment, *8, 9, 138*
18th Engineer Brigade, *8, 9*
20th Engineer Brigade, *8, 9*
23d Infantry Division (American), *8, 9*
25th Infantry Division, *8, 9,* 15, 90, 98, *147*
  3d Brigade, *8*
39th Signal Battalion (Support), 17
50th Infantry (Mechanized Infantry), 90

67th Evacuation Hospital (Semi-Mobile), 150
101st Airborne Division (Airmobile), *8, 9,* 15
  1st Brigade, *8,* 10, 166
  2d Brigade, *9*
  3d Brigade, *9*
  502d Infantry
    2d Battalion, 19
      Company C, 149
173d Airborne Brigade, *8, 9,* 152, *155, 158,* 166,
  167, 173, 176, *180-181*
  503d Infantry
    1st Battalion, *176*
      Company C, 167, *172*
      Company D, 167
    2d Battalion, 154, 176, 179
      Company A, 155, 176, 178
      Company B, 10
      Company C, 176, 178
      Company D, 155, 176, 178
    4th Battalion, 166, 179-180
      Company B, *152,* 166-167, 180
      Company C, *170-173*
      Company D, 167
196th Infantry Brigade (Light), *8, 9,* 18
199th Infantry Brigade (Light), *8, 9,* 11, *91*
509th Army Security Agency Group, 20, 140
1st Special Forces Group (Airborne), 118
5th Special Forces Group (Airborne), *8, 9,* 146
  B-50 Detachment, Project Omega
    (Special Recon), 132
  B-52 Detachment, Project Delta (Special Recon),
    33, 37-41, 125

Marines
III Marine Amphibious Force (III MAF), *8, 9*
1st Marine Division
  1st Marines, *9*
    2d Battalion, *148*
  5th Marines, *9*
  7th Marines, *9*
    3d Battalion
      Company K, 142
3d Marine Division
  3d Marines, *8*
    1st Battalion
      Company B, 144
    1st Field Artillery Group, 17
    2d Battalion, 5
      Company H, 5
  4th Marines, *8,* 12
    1st Battalion
      Company B, 140
    3d Battalion, 60
  9th Marines, *8*
    1st Battalion, 60, 158, 160
      Company C, 6
    2d Battalion, 34
    3d Battalion, 5, 160
5th Marine Division
  26th Marines (detached to the 1st and 3d Marine
    Divisions), *9*
    3d Battalion
      Company K, 150
      Company L, 149
      Company M, 149

Navy
7th Fleet
  Detachment Charlie, 142
  Navy Task Group 76.6, 5

Note: Military units are listed according to the general organizational structure of the U.S. Armed Forces. The following chart summarizes that structure for the U.S. Army. The principal difference between the army and the Marine Corps structures in Vietnam lay at the regimental level. The army eliminated the regimental command structure after World War II (although battalions retained a regimental designation for purposes of historical continuity, *e.g.,* 1st Battalion, 7th Cavalry [Regiment]). Marine Corps battalions were organized into regiments instead of brigades except under a few unusual circumstances. The marines, however, do not use the word "regiment" to designate their units; *e.g.,* 1st Marines refers to the 1st Marine Regiment.

U.S. Army structure

(to company level)

Unit	Size	Commanding officer
Division	12,000–18,000 troops or 3 brigades	Major General
Brigade	3,000 troops or 2–4 battalions	Colonel
Battalion*	600–1,000 troops or 3–5 companies	Lieutenant Colonel
Company	150 troops** or 3–4 platoons	Captain

*Squadron equivalent to battalion.
** Size varies based on type of unit.

Time-Life Books is a division of Time Life Inc.

TIME LIFE INC.
PRESIDENT and CEO: George Artandi

TIME-LIFE BOOKS
PUBLISHER/MANAGING EDITOR: Neil Kagan
VICE PRESIDENT, NEW PRODUCT DEVELOPMENT: Amy Golden
SENIOR VICE PRESIDENT, MARKETING: Joseph A. Kuna

THE VIETNAM EXPERIENCE™
A Contagion of War

PROJECT EDITOR: Karen Sweet
ASSOCIATE EDITOR/RESEARCH-WRITING: Samantha Fields
PAGE MAKEUP COORDINATOR: Kimberly A. Grandcolas
PHOTO COORDINATOR: David M. Cheatham
Separations by the Time-Life Imaging Department

SERIES DESIGN DIRECTOR: Antonio Alcalá, Studio A,
Alexandria, Virginia

Special Contributors: Dale Andradé (consulting);
Martha Reichard George (research and writing); Cara A. Cox,
Marti Davila, Richard Friend (design).

*This volume is one of a series, conceived by Robert George and originally
produced by Boston Publishing Company, that chronicles events of the
Vietnam War.*

Authors:
Terrence Maitland has written for a number of publications, including *Newsweek* magazine and the *Boston Globe*, and has coauthored
other volumes in The Vietnam Experience. He graduated from Holy
Cross College and received an M.S. from Boston University.

Peter McInerney received his M.A. and Ph.D. at the Johns Hopkins
University and taught at the University of Pennsylvania. He has
published articles about literature and film of the Vietnam War.

Consultants:
Vincent H. Demma, a historian with the U.S. Army Center of
Military History, participated in compiling the center's history
of the Vietnam conflict.

Lee Ewing, former editor of *Army Times*, served two years in Vietnam
as a combat intelligence officer with the U.S. Military Assistance
Command, Vietnam (MACV) and the 101st Airborne Division.

Richard Hunt worked on the U.S. Army Center of Military History's
official history of U.S. pacification in Vietnam.

George MacGarrigle, who also worked on the U.S. Army Center
of Military History's Vietnam project, served in Vietnam with the
1st Cavalry Division (Airmobile) as a battalion commander.

Ernest May is Charles Warren Professor of History at Harvard
University.

The picture consultant, native Vietnamese *Ngo Vinh Long*, is a
social historian who specializes in China and Vietnam. His books
include *Before the Revolution: The Vietnamese Peasants under the
French* and *Report from a Vietnamese Village*.

OTHER TIME-LIFE HISTORY PUBLICATIONS
World War II Collectors Edition
Our American Century
What Life Was Like
The American Story
Voices of the Civil War
The American Indians
Lost Civilizations
Mysteries of the Unknown
Time Frame
The Civil War
Cultural Atlas

For information on and a full description of any of the Time-Life
Books series listed above, please call 1-800-621-7026 or write:

Reader Information
Time-Life Customer Service
P.O. Box C-32068
Richmond, Virginia 23261-2068